THE **strokesaver** GUIDE TO

The CLASSIC
COURSES *of*
GREAT BRITAIN
AND IRELAND

Nick Edmund · *Photographs by* Matthew Harris

Little, Brown and Company
BOSTON · NEW YORK · LONDON

For your love and patience Lynda, Ben and Damian
MATTHEW

And your patience and love Teresa and George
NICK

A Little, Brown Book

First published in hardback (large format edition) in 1997
by Little, Brown and Company
This paperback edition published in 2000

Text copyright © Nick Edmund 1997, 2000
Photographs copyright © Matthew Harris/The Golf Picture Library 2000
with the following exception: pages 28, 101 © Phil Inglis,
and pages 236, 239 © David Cannon.
Strokesaver graphics © DuCam Marketing (UK) Ltd 1997

Every effort has been made to ensure the accuracy of the information
contained within this book. Because golf scorecards are regularly revised and
tee positions altered, minor discrepancies may exist between
the hole measurements as indicated in the individual hole graphics and
the course scorecard. Please also note that the measurements for
Portmarnock and Lahinch are given in metres.
Tee distances are in red: green front distances are in black.

A CIP catalogue record for this book is available from the British Library.

ISBN 0 316 85389 5

Designed by Andrew Barron & Collis Clements Associates

Printed and bound in Italy

Little, Brown and Company (UK)
Brettenham House
Lancaster Place
London WC2E 7EN

Page 1: The sun sets over the Ailsa Course at Turnberry

Contents

FOREWORD

I WISH I HAD A POUND — OR A DOLLAR — FOR EVERY TIME I HAVE BEEN ASKED TO DESCRIBE THE MAIN DIFFERENCE BETWEEN PLAYING GOLF IN THE UNITED STATES AND PLAYING GOLF IN GREAT BRITAIN AND IRELAND. More often than not, I'm afraid, I've given a rather flippant response, such as, "About twenty degrees centigrade." The real answer is this: golf courses in America place an emphasis on *conditioning,* whereas golf in the British Isles is primarily about *conditions.* We seem to he obsessed with the weather in Britain; we talk about it all the time. This is probably because it changes so frequently. It is fascinating because it is so unpredictable. The weather invariably influences, and sometimes defines, a round of golf in Britain. Nowhere is it more relevant than on a links course. Here, on exposed land adjacent to the sea, the vagaries of the wind add an extra dimension to the challenge. In essence it determines a player's strategy – how a player approaches a hole and how he or she executes each shot. The wind forces you to think, and it encourages you to use your imagination. What is it the Scots say? … "Nae wind, nae golf."

Links golf is of course the original form of golf. In my view it also remains the finest form of golf. The conditions on a links, and I'm not referring to the elements but also the extraordinary terrain and the way the courses play 'firm and fast', is what makes links golf so endlessly interesting.

We are incredibly fortunate in Great Britain and Ireland because there are very few authentic links courses elsewhere in the world: the climatic conditions do not exist to make it possible. So while we may often curse our weather, it does have some plusses!

The other feature that I believe really distinguishes golf in Great Britain and Ireland is the enormous variety in our courses, by which I mean variety in the types of golf courses. In addition to links golf, there is heathland golf – which again is practically unique to Britain, indeed to England; there are parkland courses, moorland courses and downland courses. Where else in the world can you find such diversity and contrast? In Scotland, Gleneagles is less

5

The 15th at Portmarnock, County Dublin, Ireland.

than 40 miles from Carnoustie – 'beauty and the beast'; in Ireland,
The K Club is 30 miles from Portmarnock, and in England, my own design
at Chart Hills is a mere 20 miles from Royal St George's.

Attractively produced, with authoritative text, spectacular photography and
comprehensive hole graphics, '*The Strokesaver Guide to the Classic Courses of
Great Britain and Ireland*' is a celebration of golf in the 'Old World.' It may
not help you to master the game, but I am confident it will increase your
appreciation of golf in the land where it all began.

Nick Faldo
February 2000

PREFACE

PICTURE OLD TOM MORRIS IN A BASEBALL CAP. IMAGINE TIGER WOODS WITH A SNOWY WHITE BEARD. NOT EASY, IS IT? NOW CHOOSE TWENTY-FIVE OF THE BEST GOLF COURSES IN GREAT BRITAIN AND IRELAND.

It is obvious where you start, but where on earth do you finish? The game was invented in these islands. The world's oldest and most prestigious championship is staged here. Nowhere is there so rich a history or such a wealth and variety of outstanding golf courses.

The onus of selection fell to me, as author, and to Matthew Harris, the book's photographer. When we were informed that Strokesport would be providing the comprehensive Strokesaver graphics for each course we thought our task was going to be made much easier. Mixed blessings, as it turned out: Strokesport had fastidiously charted nigh on every major golf course in the British Isles.

So how did we decide which courses to include? In essence our choices were founded on considerations of history, geography and architecture. We felt certain courses must be included for reasons of historical significance; that is, those courses on which history has, and is being, made. The eight courses currently on the Open Championship rota: St Andrews, Muirfield, Royal St George's, Royal Troon, Royal Lytham, Carnoustie, Royal Birkdale and Turnberry therefore picked themselves. Historically, Ireland's three greatest championship venues are undoubtedly Portmarnock, Royal

County Down and Royal Portrush; they also had to be included. And what would Old Tom Morris have said if we had left out his beloved Prestwick? Major Championship golf started there, with Prestwick staging the first twelve Opens (Old Tom winning four of the first seven). Nor would he have been impressed if we had omitted Royal Dornoch, the third oldest links in the world, or Lahinch, once described as 'the St Andrews of Ireland'. Old Tom helped to fashion both and today they remain two of the most natural and charming golf courses in the world.

Open Championships aside, the great golfers of the modern era are very rarely given the opportunity to play the 'old classics'. As fascinating as it would be to see the likes of Seve Ballesteros, Greg Norman, Nick Faldo and Ernie Els battling head-to-head at Prestwick, Dornoch or Lahinch, it isn't ever likely to occur. It does happen each year, however, at Wentworth – the above four players shared thirteen of the seventeen World Matchplay Championships between 1980 and 1996. An even greater matchplay contest is, of course, the Ryder Cup. Traditionalists might question whether The Belfry warrants inclusion in a book entitled *Classic Courses of Great Britain and Ireland* but it has staged three

Opposite: A bridge with the past. Golf has been played at St Andrews since the Middle Ages.

genuinely classic Ryder Cup encounters, and since its Brabazon Course will host the first Ryder Cup of the 21st century, to exclude The Belfry would be to ignore the course (and much of the drama) of modern golfing history. Ireland stages two of the most important events on the European Tour, namely the Irish Open and the European Open; the spectacular Augusta-styled Druids Glen and the supremely challenging Arnold Palmer-designed K Club have been their most recent homes. Like Wentworth and The Belfry, we considered that Druids Glen and The K Club merited inclusion among our twenty-five.

King's Course at Gleneagles

We also wanted the book to have geographical balance; if 'history' were our sole judgment criterion, the contents might have been disproportionately Scottish. As it is, the book contains nine courses from Scotland, eight from England, seven from Ireland (two from the North and five from the Republic) and one from Wales. Royal Porthcawl is the lone Welsh inclusion, though it is hardly a 'token representative': the club has a distinguished history – past, present and future. In 1995 it staged a memorable (if decidedly wet and windy) Walker Cup encounter. The attempt to create a geographical balance was the sole reason for our leaving out Walton Heath in Surrey and Royal Liverpool, both more than worthy of inclusion.

As for 'architecture', we thought it important that the book demonstrated the diversity in the design of courses as well as illustrating their contrasting landscapes and types of terrain. Again, if we took the book's title literally, we could have restricted ourselves to exploring only links courses since, in the eyes of the purists, these are the only true 'classics'. The great links themselves present many striking contrasts. For example, compare the wildly tumbling terrain of Royal St George's and Lahinch with the elegantly sculpted architecture of Muirfield and Royal Portrush, or the stark ferocity of Carnoustie with the almost delicate beauty of Turnberry. But of course a much greater contrast exists between links and inland courses. How could we possibly pass over the glorious heather and pines of Sunningdale, the moorland splendour of Gleneagles, once heralded as 'Scotland in miniature' or golf amid the golden gorse of Ganton, the pride of Yorkshire and one of the finest inland courses in Europe?

We have also deliberately included a few examples of what we consider to be modern architectural classics, notably Chart Hills and Loch Lomond. To help atone for the absence of Ballybunion (not charted by Strokesport), we managed to include Ballyliffin, recently described by an eminent golf writer as 'the new Ballybunion' and 'maybe the best new links course to have been built this century'. All in all, we are confident that our twenty-five includes a fair representation of the old and the new, the best links, heathland, moorland and parkland courses.

None of the courses was selected on purely aesthetic grounds. It so happens that the twenty-five include several remarkably scenic layouts. Turnberry, Royal Portrush, Sunningdale, Gleneagles, Royal Dornoch and Ballyliffin could certainly be described as such, while Royal County Down and Loch Lomond might even be viewed as the most beautiful oceanside and most beautiful lakeside courses in the world. But each was selected for another, better reason. Besides, with a photographer of Matthew Harris' calibre providing the images, the book was never going to require beautifying. Matthew is undoubtedly one of the world's finest golf photographers; this book proves as much.

The book's graphics are also exceptional. It is barely possible to play a round of golf these days without overhearing someone on an adjoining fairway say, 'How far am I from the pin?', or 'Are there any bunkers to the left of the green?' And then, rather sheepishly, 'Can I borrow your Strokesaver?' It may not be overstating things to suggest that the Strokesaver guide has revolutionized golf. There are still one or two players who are happy walking the course in ignorance of where they are going or what they are trying to do. These are the people you hope to meet in the first round of the club knockout; you rarely come across

them in the second round. Produced with state-of-the-art technology, including infra-red measuring equipment, Strokesaver is the official distance guide to the Open Championship, the Masters and numerous international associations and federations.

I would like to take this opportunity to thank our publishers, Little Brown, and in particular, Viv Bowler, Arianne Burnette and Julia Charles for their enormous support, encouragement and patience. Midway through the book's editorial phase my son George decided to enter the world. Naturally I would like to dedicate this book to him and to my wife Teresa. Whether it was the excitement of the hour, or just too much coffee I'm not sure, but for a fleeting moment I seriously toyed with the name Royal St George. Surely as daft a notion as Old Tom Morris in a baseball cap.

Good golfing!

Nick Edmund

9

Photography Notes: The light is not always perfect, so I would like to thank Phil Inglis and Dave Cannon for their photographs. My thanks also to The Dupe Connection (process), Fuji (film) and Nikon (cameras) for their support and expertise.

Matthew Harris

St Andrews (Old)

ONE HUNDRED YEARS BEFORE COLUMBUS SAILED TO AMERICA AND TWO CENTURIES BEFORE SHAKESPEARE WROTE HAMLET AND MACBETH, GOLF WAS BEING PLAYED AT ST ANDREWS. IT IS THAT ANCIENT.

In the mid-1400s the game was sufficiently prevalent for the authorities to question whether it was contributing to the nation's poor performances on the battlefields. Apparently the youth of Scotland had taken to golf and football at the expense of practising archery. In 1457 King James II passed an Act decreeing that 'fute-ball and golf be utterly cryit down and nocht usit'. Records would suggest that his subjects did not take a great deal of notice, nor did his successors. It is known that in 1504 King James IV sneakily placed an order with his bowmaker in Perth for a new set of golfclubs and balls.

By the mid-1500s, golf was no longer outlawed, and the right to play on the links at St Andrews was confirmed in a licence issued in 1552. It permitted the public 'to play at golf, fute ball, schueting, at all gamis with all uther, as ever they pleis and in ony time.' The sport clearly flourished, for in 1691 St Andrews was described as 'a Metropolis of golfing'.

The first official golf club at St Andrews was established in 1754 when twenty-two 'Noblemen and Gentlemen' founded the St Andrews Society of Golfers. In 1834 this society became the Royal and Ancient Golf Club, courtesy of King William IV. Notwithstanding their interests, the rights of the public were protected and, at St Andrews at least, golf remained conspicuously democratic.

Today St Andrews is universally acknowledged as the home of golf. Historically, spiritually and architecturally every golf course in the world owes something – if not its very existence – to the Old Course at St Andrews. And yet, for all its significance, on first viewing it has the capacity to disappoint as well as to enthral. The Old Course invariably wins people over, but first there is a need to become acquainted. Bobby Jones's relationship with St Andrews provides the ultimate example. His first round on the Old Course in 1921 came to an abrupt end on the 11th green. Confounded and confused, he tore up his card and stormed off the links (an action he would bitterly regret). In 1927 he returned to win the Open by six strokes and, three years after this, captured the Amateur Championship at St Andrews in his Grand Slam year. 'The more I studied the Old Course,' Jones later said, 'the more I loved it, and the more I loved it, the more I studied it, so that I came to feel that it was for me the most favourable meeting ground possible for an important contest.'

So why the tendency for initial disappointment and the special need for familiarization? Aura aside, 'the Old

11

1	Championship	376 yards	Par 4
	Medal	370	Par 4
	Ladies'	339	Par 4

2	413 yards	Par 4
	411	Par 4
	375	Par 5

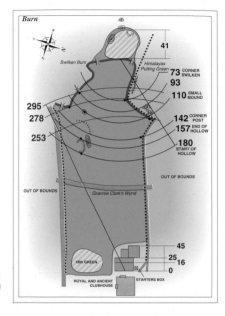

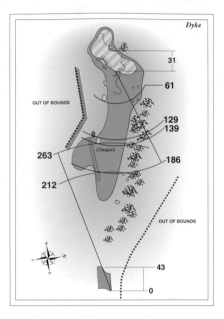

3	Championship	397 yards	Par 4
	Medal	352	Par 4
	Ladies'	321	Par 4

4	464 yards	Par 4
	419	Par 4
	401	Par 5

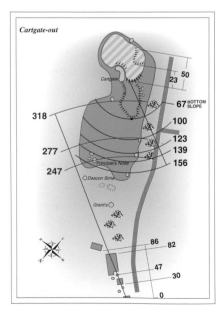

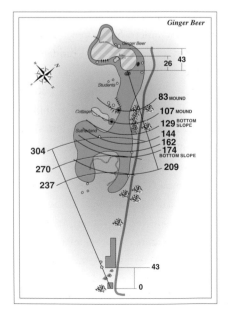

12

The notorious Road Hole. Ben Crenshaw once said of the 17th: 'The reason it is the toughest par four in the world is because it is a par five.'

Lady' is no ravishing beauty. The surroundings are attractive (and overwhelmingly historic), but the Old Course appears quite flat and squashed into a narrow strip of land. At first glance, there seems little definition to the holes, and the 'out and back' routing doesn't inspire or suggest variety. St Andrews is notorious for its plethora of hidden pot bunkers, many allowing just enough room, as Bernard Darwin put it, 'for an angry man and his niblick'. The rippling character of the fairways can both frustrate and perplex, while the sheer scale of the renowned double greens – there are seven in all and some are more than an acre in size – occasionally demoralizes. With shared fairways as well as greens, the Old Course doesn't resemble any other links. But it is different for the very best of reasons. Pat Ward-Thomas stated it perfectly: 'In the beginning [the Old Course] knew no architect but nature, it came into being by evolution rather than design and on no other course is the hand of man less evident.' St Andrews is timeless.

It is only on close examination that the Old Course's qualities are revealed. Far from lacking definition and interest, each hole presents the golfer (whatever his or her standard of play) with a range of alternative strategies and options. It is only when you have gained a greater appreciation of the hazards (especially the position of the bunkers), and when you are familiar with the subtle undulations and the natural contours that so brilliantly conspire to defend the greens, that you can make informed decisions and determine your strategy. The other essential ingredient is the wind. On a good day, with a moderately testing wind, the Old Course at St Andrews is probably the

5	Championship	568 yards	Par 5
	Medal	514	Par 5
	Ladies'	454	Par 5

6	412 yards	Par 4
	374	Par 4
	325	Par 4

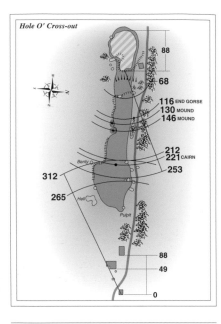

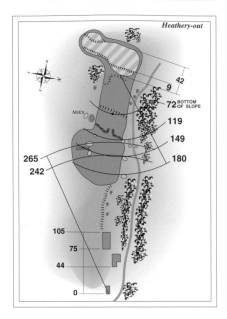

14

7	Championship	398 yards	Par 4
	Medal	359	Par 4
	Ladies'	335	Par 4

8	175 yards	Par 3
	166	Par 3
	145	Par 3

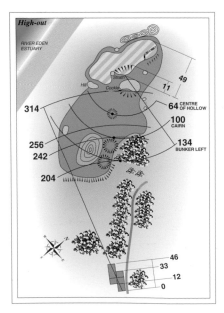

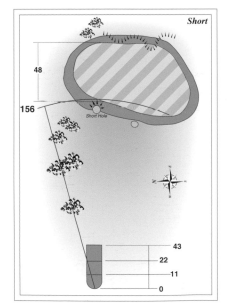

9

Championship	352 yards	Par 4
Medal	307	Par 4
Ladies'	261	Par 4

10

379 yards	Par 4
318	Par 4
296	Par 4

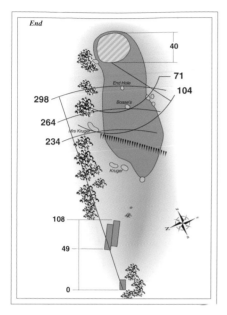

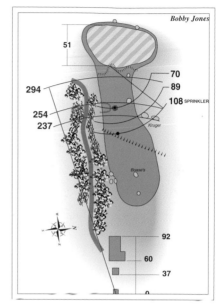

15

11

Championship	174 yards	Par 3
Medal	172	Par 3
Ladies'	150	Par 3

12

314 yards	Par 4
316	Par 4
304	Par 4

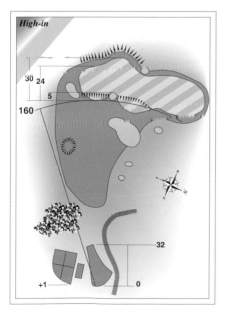

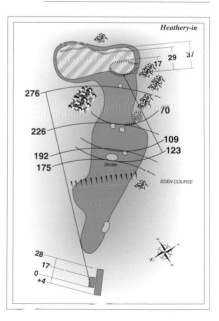

ST ANDREWS (OLD)

13	Championship	430 yards	Par 4
	Medal	398	Par 4
	Ladies'	377	Par 5

14	581 yards	Par 5
	523	Par 5
	487	Par 5

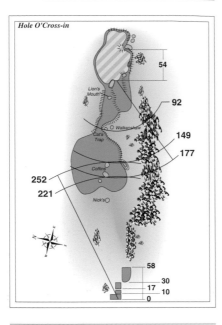

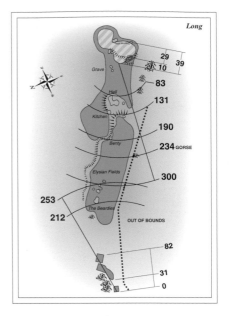

15	Championship	456 yards	Par 4
	Medal	401	Par 4
	Ladies'	369	Par 4

16	424 yards	Par 4
	351	Par 4
	325	Par 4

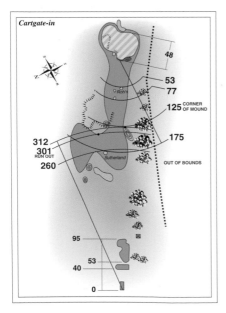

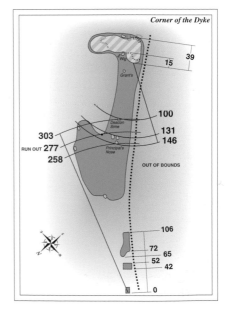

16

ST ANDREWS (OLD)

17	Championship	455 yards	Par 4
	Medal	461	Par 4
	Ladies'	426	Par 5

18	357 yards	Par 4
	354	Par 4
	342	Par 4

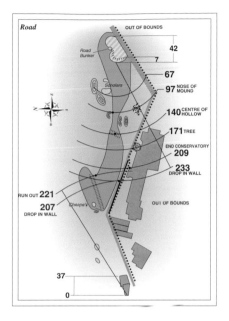

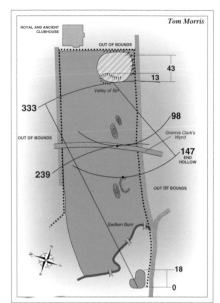

17

ST ANDREWS
THE OLD COURSE

Strathtyrum Course

Eden Course

New Course

Jubilee Course

Royal and Ancient Clubhouse

British Golf Museum

most strategic golf course in the world.

The round starts with a hole that it is extraordinary even by St Andrews' standards. The 1st has probably the flattest and widest fairway in golf (it is shared with the 18th). There is an out of bounds to the right, but a drive aimed 75 yards left of centre will not meet any trouble. The key shot is the approach, which is played over the Swilken Burn; the green slopes towards the burn. If the second is hit a little too firmly, an awkward downhill putt will result. The par four 2nd is much more typical of the Old Course. With thick gorse bordering the right edge of the fairway, there is an obvious temptation to play to the left again, where there is plenty of room. A brave drive to the right side, however, will be rewarded with a much easier second. The same applies at the 3rd, where an approach from the left must confront Cartgate bunker, which protects the front left entrance to the green.

The natural contours of the land play a prominent role at the following three holes. A large mound defends the putting surface at the two-shot 4th; the par five 5th features a high plateau green, which is 80 yards deep; and the par four 6th has a concealed depression immediately in front of the green. The fairways at these holes are effectively shared with those of the 15th, 14th and 13th; thus a particularly wayward shot at the 5th, for instance, may veer towards such unwelcome repositories as The Beardies or Hell bunker.

The Old Course routing is not strictly out and back. Often described as resembling the shape of a shepherd's crook, the layout includes a loop of holes between the 7th and 12th. The 7th is perhaps the closest St Andrews comes to a dog-legged hole. The fairway curves from left to right and the approach has to be deftly struck to find a high shallow green. Good scores at St Andrews are usually fashioned over the next five holes, which comprise two par threes and three short par fours. The par threes are the 8th and 11th; the latter is a much admired – and feared – hole. The green of the 11th, which is shared with the 7th, has very little depth and tilts from back to front; it is defended by two horrendously deep bunkers.

The Coffins and Hell now await! The Coffins, a series of pot bunkers, lurk in the centre of the 13th fairway. This is one of the strongest par fours, with another raised, large and well contoured

18

Classic contours: the Old Course was designed by Mother Nature.

green. In addition to the enormous Hell bunker, the par five 14th requires you to navigate the cavernous Beardies, Benty, Kitchen and Grave bunkers. An out of bounds also threatens the tee-shot. There is one safe place on this hole – the Elysian Fields, a haven of fairway midway between The Beardies and Hell.

The 15th and 16th tumble along classic links terrain; Sutherland bunker at the 15th and the centrally located Principal's Nose at the 16th are the major obstacles to avoid. Then comes the fabled Road Hole, the world of golf's most fascinating and most destructive par four. The drive at the 17th over the railway sheds is difficult enough – it must be steered close to the Old Course Hotel, risking the out of bounds on the right if the green is to be brought within range for the second shot – and the approach can be terrifying. The narrow plateaued green is guarded by the gaping, sheer-faced Road bunker at the front and by a road and stone wall at the back. Many of St Andrews' twenty-five Open Championships have been decided here. The classic Ballesteros versus Watson contest in 1984 was one memorable occasion. 'If I can par the 17th tomorrow I will win,' Ballesteros prophesied on the eve of the final round. The Spaniard did indeed make his four (for the first time that week). When Watson's second shot skipped through the green and came to rest against the wall, the Championship was effectively won and lost.

On any course other than St Andrews, the 18th might be considered a modest finishing hole. It is a short par four, potentially drivable with a strong helping wind, and the wide fairway resembles a town park. But framed by the famous St Andrews' buildings, the vast green is a wonderful stage. To land safely upon it, you must pass through – or pitch over – the Valley of Sin. For good measure, Ballesteros birdied the 18th: 'the happiest moment in my golfing life,' he called it. The two previous Opens at St Andrews had been won by Jack Nicklaus (in 1970 and 1978), and the one that followed in 1990 was won by Nick Faldo. Ancient and timeless she may be, but the Old Lady has always known how to pick her champions.

Hole	Championship	Medal	Par	Stroke Index	Ladies'	Par	Stroke Index
1	376	370	4	15	339	4	15
2	413	411	4	3	375	5	3
3	397	352	4	13	321	4	13
4	464	419	4	9	401	5	9
5	568	514	5	1	454	5	1
6	412	374	4	11	325	4	11
7	388	359	4	7	335	4	7
8	175	166	3	18	145	3	18
9	352	307	4	5	261	4	5
Out	3545	3272	36		2956	38	
10	379	318	4	10	296	4	10
11	174	172	3	17	150	3	17
12	314	316	4	6	304	4	6
13	430	398	4	12	337	5	12
14	581	523	5	2	487	5	2
15	450	401	4	8	369	4	8
16	424	351	4	14	325	4	14
17	455	461	4	4	426	5	4
18	357	354	4	16	342	4	16
In	3570	3294	36		3076	38	
Out	3545	3272	36		2956	38	
Total	7115	6566	72		6032	76	

ROYAL DORNOCH

W**HAT IS IT ABOUT** R**OYAL** D**ORNOCH**? I**S IT A MAGIC PLACE**? I**T DOES SEEM TO HAVE CAST A PECULIAR SPELL OVER SOME OF** THE GREATEST GOLFERS WHO EVER LIVED.

Dornoch is 600 miles from London. It is 50 miles beyond Inverness and, at 58 degrees North, it is on the same line of latitude as Hudson Bay in northern Canada. Dornoch is geographically challenged. Yet this fact didn't deter the Great Triumvirate, Messrs Vardon, Taylor and Braid, from visiting the links in the early years of this century. Nor did it discourage Joyce Wethered (according to Bobby Jones, the greatest-ever player, male or female), who made regular trips from the south of England. In more recent times, Tom Watson, Ben Crenshaw, Greg Norman and Nick Faldo have all embarked on what is a seemingly irresistible pilgrimage.

Tom Watson intended to play eighteen holes when he dropped in on Royal Dornoch, but eventually played three rounds in the space of twenty-four hours. He described the experience as the most fun I have had playing golf in my whole life'. Watson was clearly spellbound. So too, it seems, was his fellow countryman, Ben Crenshaw. He played the links in 1980 during a break in his preparation for the Open Championship. When asked on his return by the Secretary of the Royal & Ancient how he had enjoyed the course, Crenshaw replied, 'Let me put it this way. I nearly didn't come back.' So what is it that makes Dornoch so special?

First, there is the location and setting. Dornoch may be 'miles from anywhere', but this is part of the charm. Royal Dornoch can justifiably claim to be the world's most northern great course. It has been called 'The Star of the North'. This adds to the mystique. But the setting really is special. The links is bordered by the Dornoch Firth and, for its entire length, by a beautiful sweep of pristine white sand. All around, mountains and hills fill the horizon and create the illusion that you are somehow playing on a stage.

In spring and early summer, much of the links turns from green to gold. The gorse at Dornoch is as much a backcloth as a hazard, and when it is in full bloom, it is a glorious sight. If you see Dornoch at such a time and on a day when the weather is kind, you begin to appreciate the enormous attraction. Then there is Dornoch's extraordinary history ...

It is thought that golf has been played on the links since the 16th century; it is known that it has been played on the links since 1616. Officially, Dornoch is the third oldest golf course in the world after St Andrews and Leith. In 1630 Sir Robert Gordon wrote of Dornoch: 'About this toun ther are the fairest and largest linkes of any pairt of Scotland, fitt for archery, goffing, ryding and all other

Opposite: The penultimate challenge. Few greens are as elegantly sited or as beautifully backdropped as the 17th at Royal Dornoch.

1

Championship	332 yards	Par 4
Medal	275	Par 4
Ladies'	266	Par 4

2

182 yards	Par 3
167	Par 3
163	Par 3

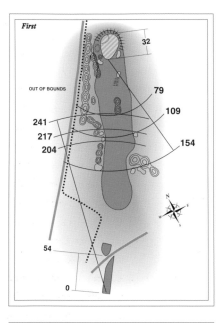

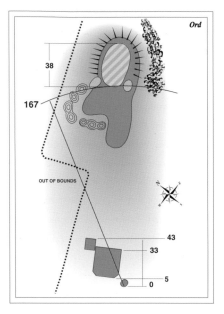

22

3

Championship	413 yards	Par 4
Medal	398	Par 4
Ladies'	389	Par 4

4

418 yards	Par 4
403	Par 4
391	Par 5

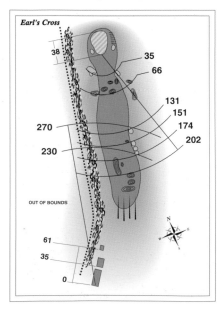

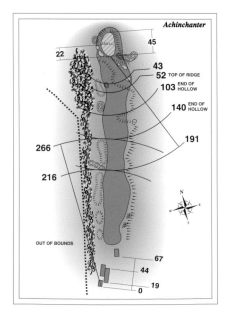

exercise; they do surpasse the fields of Montrose or St Andrews.' Precious little is known about the links during the next century, although records reveal that the last witch in Scotland, Janet Horne, was executed at Dornoch during the early 1700s. (Could it be her ghost who is somehow casting all these spells?)

A formal golf club was not established until 1877. A nine-hole course already existed, but the members must not have thought too highly of it, because in 1886 Old Tom Morris was invited to lay out 'nine proper golf holes'. Three years later he was asked to extend the course to a full eighteen. Old Tom was never paid a huge amount for his work – at Dornoch or elsewhere – and he never spent a great deal of time designing his courses, but one thing he knew better than most was when to leave well alone. Old Tom was the first architect to work at Royal County Down, Lahinch and Royal Dornoch. Is it merely a coincidence that these are three of the finest and most natural links courses in the world? At Dornoch Old Tom utilized the wealth of wonderful natural green sites. A number of people made subsequent alterations to the links, but he surely deserves the credit for highlighting and preserving the possibilities.

The man chiefly responsible for introducing Tom Morris to Dornoch was the club's young Secretary, John Sutherland. Appointed at the age of nineteen, Sutherland guided the club's affairs for nearly sixty years. It was he who encouraged the leading golfers of the day to play the course, and it was Sutherland, together with John H. Taylor, who made the first revisions to Old Tom's layout.

Another famous figure in Dornoch's history was Donald Ross. He was born in Dornoch in 1872 and, as a young man, moved to St Andrews to become one of Old Tom's assistants. In 1895 Ross returned to Dornoch and served as the club's professional and head green-keeper. In less than four years he was off again, this time to America. There Donald Ross became one of the greatest and most prolific of golf course architects. The influence of Dornoch, especially its renowned plateau greens, always shone through in Ross's creations, nowhere more so than at Pinehurst No. 2, a course that is consistently ranked (along with Royal Dornoch) among the world's top dozen courses.

23

In late spring and early summer the links is framed – and in parts enveloped – by golden gorse.

ROYAL DORNOCH

5	Championship	357 yards	Par 4
	Medal	318	Par 4
	Ladies'	311	Par 4

6	164 yards	Par 3
	150	Par 3
	135	Par 3

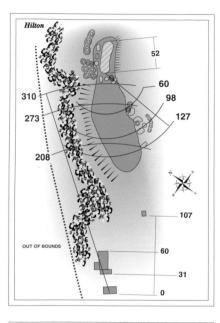

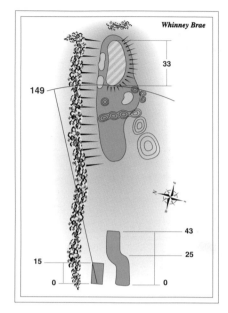

7	Championship	463 yards	Par 4
	Medal	416	Par 4
	Ladies'	412	Par 4

8	437 yards	Par 4
	385	Par 4
	380	Par 4

24

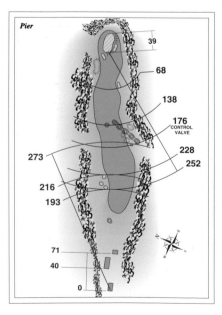

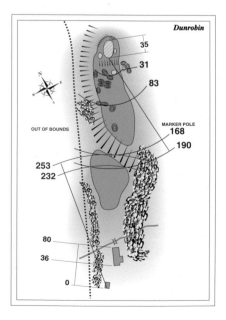

9	Championship	497 yards	Par 5
	Medal	442	Par 4
	Ladies'	435	Par 5

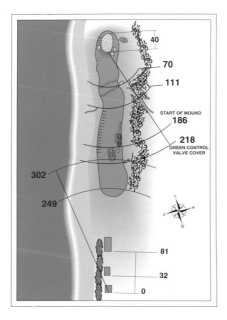

10	150 yards	Par 3
	140	Par 3
	137	Par 3

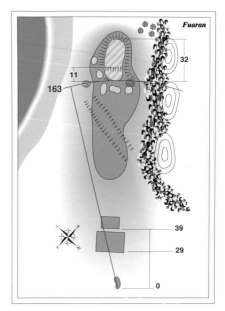

11	Championship	445 yards	Par 4
	Medal	434	Par 4
	Ladies'	426	Par 5

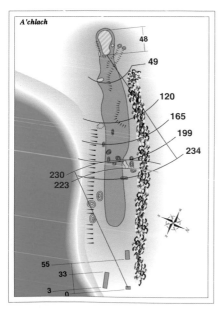

12	516 yards	Par 5
	483	Par 5
	472	Par 5

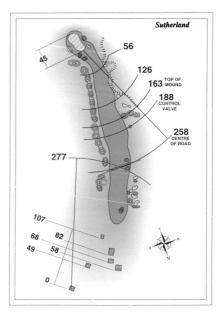

25

13	Championship	168 yards	Par 3
	Medal	143	Par 3
	Ladies'	137	Par 3

14	445 yards	Par 4
	435	Par 4
	401	Par 5

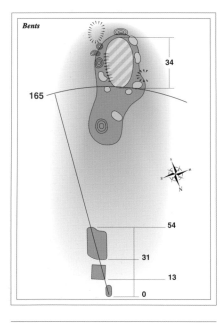

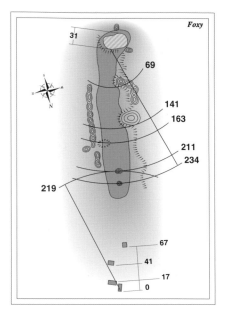

15	Championship	323 yards	Par 4
	Medal	298	Par 4
	Ladies'	288	Par 4

16	400 yards	Par 4
	387	Par 4
	387	Par 5

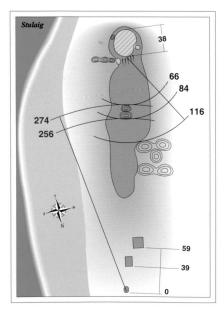

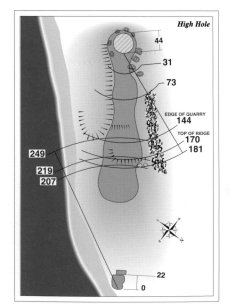

ROYAL DORNOCH

17	Championship	410 yards	Par 4
	Medal	389	Par 4
	Ladies'	384	Par 4

18	461 yards	Par 4
	449	Par 4
	442	Par 5

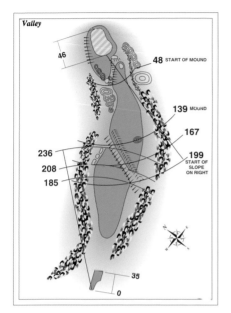

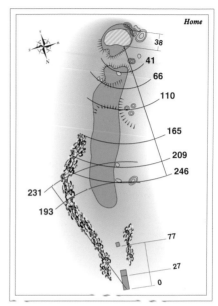

Valley

46
48 START OF MOUND
139 MOUND
167
236
208
185
199 START OF SLOPE ON RIGHT
35
0

Home

38
41
66
110
165
209
246
231
193
77
27
0

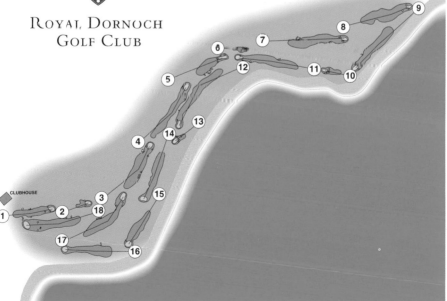

ROYAL DORNOCH
GOLF CLUB

CLUBHOUSE

The 'Star of the North' has beauty, charm and a wealth of history. The links is also acknowledged as one of golf's great natural wonders.

28

The third and most compelling reason for visiting Dornoch is the quality of the golf course itself. Royal Dornoch is widely regarded as the most natural golf links in the world. The course blends perfectly into its landscape: every feature and every hazard is either natural or appears completely so. It is golf in its original and purest form, and this explains why every budding golf course designer (including Watson, Crenshaw and Faldo) is drawn to the links.

On first impression the course appears to have a typical 'out and back' layout; in fact, the routing is more S-shaped and is unusual in that the course occupies two distinct levels. In broad terms, you head out along and occasionally in the lee of an upper level (for a hole and a half you are actually playing on top of a giant sandbank) and return along a lower level, adjacent to the shore.

The first two holes are on the upper level. The 1st is a short par four and is a fairly gentle opening hole. The 2nd, however, is deceptively tricky. It is a par three, again of no particular length, but if you miss the green, your next shot will be either an awkward chip or a tough bunker shot played from one of the two cavernous traps guarding the entrance to the green. Then the real fun starts.

The run of holes from the 3rd to the 6th is one of the finest sequences in golf. The 3rd plunges downhill from the tee. It dog-legs slightly to the left and is a strong, handsome two-shotter, but the 4th and 5th are even greater par fours. The 4th, which is entirely on the lower level, has a hog's back fairway and gorse all along its left side. The green is plateaued and surrounded by humps and hollows as well as a series of bunkers. The 5th, Tom Watson's favourite, measures

little more than 350 yards. Starting from a very elevated tee situated amidst a sea of gorse, you drive spectacularly downhill to a fairway that tilts sharply from left to right; this is followed by a delicate pitch over three bunkers to another raised green, one of the largest at Dornoch. Often heavily contoured as well as plateaued, the greens are, of course, Dornoch's most distinctive feature.

While it is important to find the green with your tee-shot at the 2nd, it is nigh on vital at the par three 6th. Played to a table green, the alternative punishments for failing to find the putting surface are thick gorse and sand to the left, sand to the front and a very steep fall-away to the right. The 6th provides one of those rare occasions when to be bunkered is a pleasant option.

The 7th is the hole that runs across the top of the vast sandbank. Gorse bushes (or whins as they are known in Scotland) frame both sides of the fairway. They begin to do the same at the 8th, until the fairway suddenly tumbles over the top of the ridge and cascades down to the lower level. A good tee shot can propel you over the edge, although the green remains some way distant and nestles in a dell close to the shore.

You are now beside Embo Bay and that beautiful sweep of pristine white sand. For the next seven holes you rarely move away from the shore. Between the 9th and 15th, you weave in and out of the dunes, the wind, as much as anything, determining your strategy. Each of the holes is a seaside classic, although the two

best known are probably the par three 10th, with its trio of bunkers barring entry to a two-tiered green, and 'Foxy', the bunkerless, double dog-legging 14th – a hole described by Harry Vardon as 'the finest natural golf hole I have ever played.'

The 16th is possibly the only weak hole at Dornoch – it runs uphill all the way – but the cavalier, down-and-up 17th, with its cross bunker and severely sloping green, is one of the very best, and the 18th provides a strong final chapter to this storied and supremely enchanting links.

Hole	Championship	Medal	Par	Stroke Index	Ladies'	Par	Stroke Index
1	332	275	4	7	266	4	7
2	182	167	3	15	163	3	15
3	413	398	4	11	389	4	11
4	418	403	4	3	391	5	3
5	357	318	4	9	311	4	9
6	164	150	3	17	135	3	17
7	463	416	4	1	412	5	1
8	437	385	4	5	380	4	5
9	497	442	5/4	13	435	5	13
Out	3263	2954	35/34		2882	37	
10	150	140	3	16	131	3	16
11	445	434	4	4	426	5	4
12	516	483	5	12	472	5	12
13	168	143	3	18	137	3	18
14	445	435	4	2	401	5	2
15	320	298	4	10	288	4	10
16	400	387	4	6	387	5	6
17	410	389	4	8	384	4	8
18	461	449	4	14	442	5	14
In	3318	3158	35		3074	39	
Out	3263	2954	35/34		2882	37	
Total	6581	6112	70/69		5956	76	

GLENEAGLES (KING'S)

BLOWN, BUFFETED AND BLASTED BY THE WIND: FOR SEVEN DAYS YOU HAVE BEEN TOURING THE GREAT LINKS COURSES OF SCOTLAND. YOU BROUGHT YOUR VERY BEST GOLF GAME THROUGH CUSTOMS, BUT YOU LEFT THE WEATHER BEHIND. YOU PICKED A BAD WEEK.

You, your swing and your pride need soothing. You need a change of scenery; you need to unwind. Go immediately to Gleneagles.

It was christened 'The Scottish Palace in the Glens' when it first opened, and the world fell madly in love with it. Gleneagles is a gorgeous place. Set in the heart of Perthshire, it epitomizes the Scotland you dream about. Gleneagles is bagpipes and tartan, heather-clad hills and mist-covered mountains, whisky, salmon and haggis. The hotel is sumptuous, the surroundings are spectacular and the golf is glorious.

Gleneagles dates from 1910. The visionary who set the ball rolling, so to speak, was Donald Matheson, General Manager of the Caledonian Railway Company. His initial motivation may have been one upmanship, The Glasgow and South Western Railway Company owned the golf links at Turnberry. In 1906 it had unveiled the impressive Turnberry Hotel, and the combination of golf and luxury accommodation was bringing fame – and wealthy customers – to this rival company. Whatever the motivation, once Matheson had wandered across the undulating moorland and surveyed the astonishing 360-degree views, the idea of Gleneagles was born.

James Braid, a renowned architect, as well as Scotland's greatest-ever golfer, was commissioned to design two courses: an eighteen-hole championship layout and a shorter nine-hole course. He was assisted by Major C. K. Hutchinson and by Matheson, who took great interest in every aspect of the construction. The First World War inevitably slowed progress, but in 1919 the twenty-seven holes were ready for play.

The acclaim was instantaneous. Braid himself regarded the eighteen-hole King's Course as the crowning achievement of his career and it was always his personal favourite. The nine-hole Queen's Course was soon extended to eighteen holes and, though not as challenging as the King's in terms of length, was every bit as picturesque and full of character. In June 1921, within two years of opening, Gleneagles staged the first-ever match between British and American professionals. The world-famous Gleneagles Hotel was unveiled in 1924; a third course, designed by Jack Nicklaus, followed in the early 1990s.

The King's Course may be the finest moorland golf course in the world. The design is excellent – blending with rather than imposing itself upon the landscape. And what a landscape! Surely no architect

Birdies at the 17th are occasionally followed by eagles at the par five 18th and much celebrated at the 19th.

1	Championship	362 yards	Par 4
	Medal	362	Par 4
	Ladies'	344	Par 4

2	436 yards	Par 4
	405	Par 4
	376	Par 4

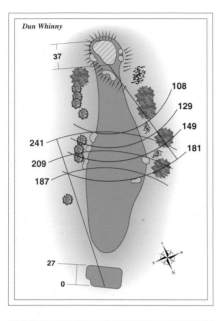

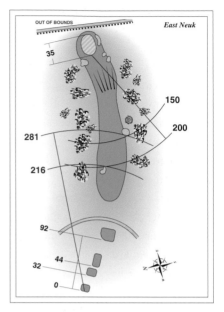

3	Championship	374 yards	Par 4
	Medal	374	Par 4
	Ladies'	344	Par 4

4	466 yards	Par 4
	466	Par 4
	442	Par 5

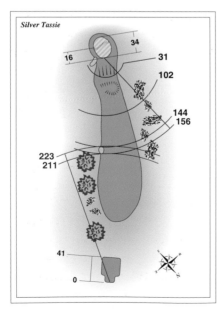

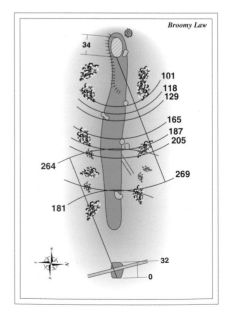

was ever given a more naturally beautiful and rolling piece of terrain to work with. The turf is crisp and springy underfoot. Heather and gorse envelop the rough. Firs, pines, silver birch and rowan adorn the fairways. In fact, everywhere you turn there is a blaze of colour. The golfing stage is encircled by dramatic hills and mountains: the Ochil Hills to the south and east, the Grampians to the north and the peaks of the Trossachs to the west. Concentrating on your game can be difficult at Gleneagles!

Always impeccably groomed, the King's Course features elevated tees, generous tumbling fairways and large sloping greens. There are two or three blind shots – the lie of the land dictated this, and being one of the 'old school' of designers, Braid did not mind – and several holes occupy their own private valley.

Every hole at Gleneagles is named. Apparently you can thank the fertile imagination of Mr Matheson for such King's Course treats as 'Het Girdle', 'Tappit Hen' and 'Wee Bogle'. 'Dun Whinny' can be roughly translated as 'hill of gorse'. This 1st hole reassures, then confounds: a wide fairway welcomes the opening tee-shot, but the approach must climb a very sharp rise to a large plateau green, and the flag is about all you see from the fairway. Two bunkers at the foot of the hill await any shot that fails to make the putting surface.

The 2nd and 3rd combine exhilaration with a hint of eccentricity. The former wriggles downhill all the way to the green. On the 3rd, 'Silver Tassie', you begin with an uphill drive across humps and bumps into a valley fairway. The approach is completely blind, though a marker pole assists, and is hit over a large dune-like ridge to a green tilting severely from front to back – an extremely old-fashioned golf hole.

The 4th is a long par four with a secluded fairway. Then comes the notorious 'Het Girdle'. The 5th is a par three played across a valley to a table green. It has very steep banks all around and four bunkers lurking beneath the rise to the green. It is Braid's 'death or glory' hole and Gleneagles' answer to the 'Postage Stamp' at Troon.

The 6th is the first of the par fives. The hole curves gently to the left along a narrow, turbulent fairway. There is a handsome bunker to the front right and a fall-away towards gorse on the left. The two-shot 7th, 'Kittle Kink', is one of the best designed holes at Gleneagles. From a raised tee, you drive to a fairway that swings to the left as it follows the line of a heathery ridge. The hole is expertly bunkered with twin cross bunkers 75 yards short of the green, two deep greenside traps to the right and another small pot bunker to the left.

Now for 'Whaup's Nest'. If the 5th is a table green, then the one at the short 8th is more akin to a ledge or shelf. The hole is played slightly downhill. There are two bunkers below the front of the green and two at the back: judgment of distance is everything. The front nine concludes with 'Heich o'Fash'. The 9th is a cavalier

33

5	Championship	178 yards	Par 3
	Medal	161	Par 3
	Ladies'	130	Par 3

6	480 yards	Par 5
	476	Par 5
	422	Par 5

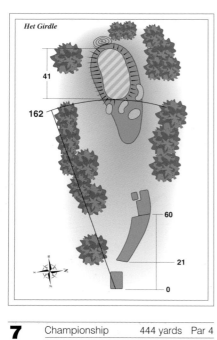

Het Girdle

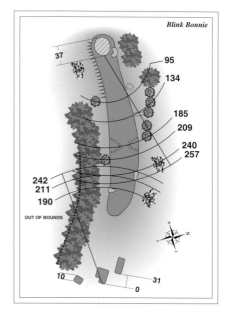

Blink Bonnie

OUT OF BOUNDS

7	Championship	444 yards	Par 4
	Medal	439	Par 4
	Ladies'	423	Par 5

8	178 yards	Par 3
	158	Par 3
	138	Par 3

34

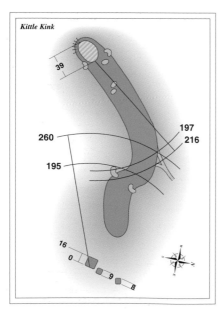

Kittle Kink

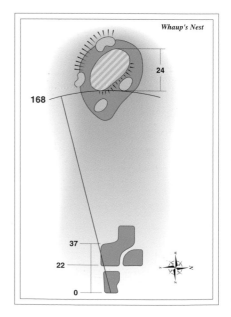

Whaup's Nest

9

Championship	409 yards	Par 4
Medal	354	Par 4
Ladies'	326	Par 4

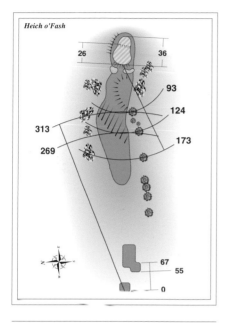

Heich o'Fash

26   36

93

124

313

173

269

67
55

0

10

493 yards	Par 5
441	Par 4
410	Par 5

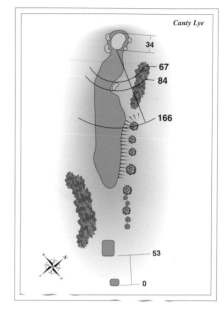

Canty Lye

34

67
84

166

53

0

35

11

Championship	230 yards	Par 3
Medal	230	Par 3
Ladies'	156	Par 3

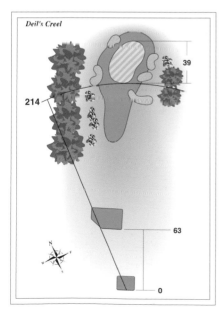

Deil's Creel

39

214

63

0

12

442 yards	Par 4
395	Par 4
346	Par 4

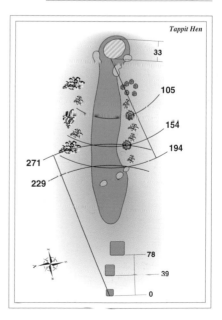

Tappit Hen

33

105

154

194

271

229

78

39

0

13	Championship	464 yards	Par 4
	Medal	448	Par 4
	Ladies'	418	Par 5

14	342 yards	Par 4
	260	Par 4
	241	Par 4

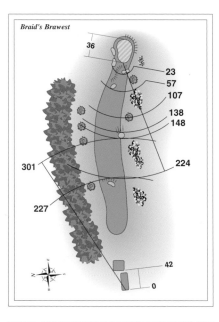

Braid's Brawest

36

23
57
107
138
148

301

224

227

42
0

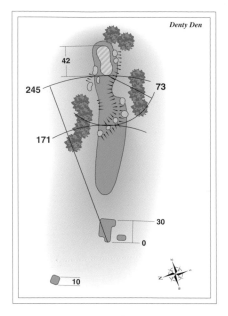

Denty Den

42

245

73

171

30
0

10

15	Championship	459 yards	Par 4
	Medal	459	Par 4
	Ladies'	431	Par 5

16	158 yards	Par 3
	135	Par 3
	123	Par 3

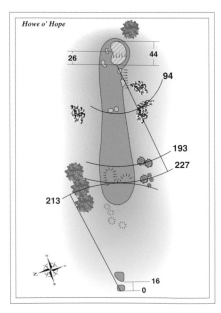

Howe o' Hope

26
44

94

193
227

213

16
0

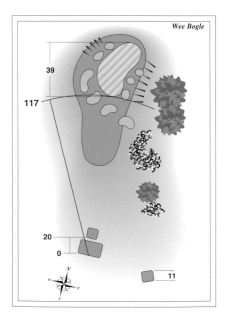

Wee Bogle

39

117

20
0

11

36

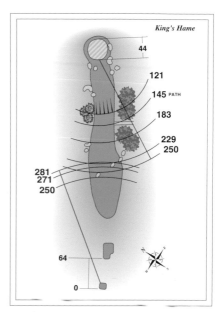

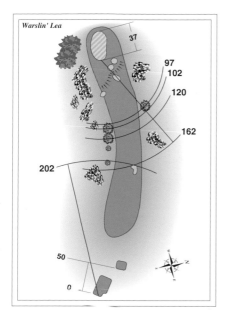

GLENEAGLES (KING'S)

17	Championship	377 yards	Par 4
	Medal	377	Par 4
	Ladies'	359	Par 4

18	525 yards	Par 5
	525	Par 5
	444	Par 5

Warslin' Lea

37
97
102
120
162
202
50
0

King's Hame

44
121
145 PATH
183
229
250
281
271
250
64
0

37

THE GLENEAGLES HOTEL
KING'S COURSE

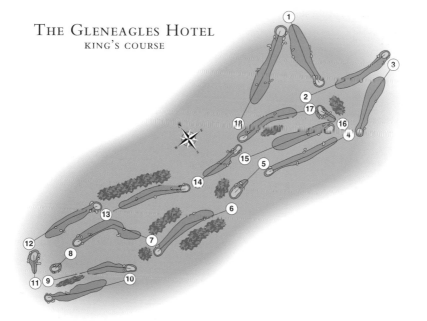

Shades of Troon: the short 5th on the King's Course is called 'Het Girdle' and is Gleneagles' answer to the 'Postage Stamp'.

hole that commences with a downhill charge from the tee; it then tumbles along the floor of a valley before making an abrupt ascent to a two-tiered green. As at the 1st and 5th, the penalty for failing to make the upper level with your approach can be the source of nightmares.

The 10th is more elegant than dramatic. It flows from an elevated tee pretty much in a straight line to a gently raised green. The 11th is the plainest but, at 230 yards from the back tees, easily the longest of the par threes; bunkers guard both sides of the green. The 12th is called 'Tappit Hen'. From the tee there are magnificent views over the Queen's

Course. A wave-like ridge traverses the fairway here and creates a second blind drive over a marker pole. The approach must avoid three very large bunkers.

When you leave the green at the 12th, you are nearing the highest point on the course and you are about to play the greatest hole at Gleneagles. The 13th is 'Braid's Brawest' – Braid's best. It is a very natural looking and mighty par four, measuring 464 yards from the championship marker; even from the most forward men's tee it stretches to 423 yards. The entire hole is visible from the tee. Heather and bracken line both sides of the funnel-shaped rollercoasting fairway. You drive downhill over a ridge, and with

luck avoid meeting up with 'Auld Nick', an horrendously deep bunker on the left side of the fairway. Your second is slightly uphill to a green that slopes from back to front.

A 'Denty Den' is a dainty or pleasant dell, which perfectly describes the sylvan setting of the 14th green. If the hole is treated as a short par four, a dainty tee-shot may suffice; however, it is just possible to drive the green, the route requiring an exciting carry over two separate clusters of pot bunkers. A spinney of tall pines provides a delightful back-drop to the hole.

The 15th is a flattering downhill par four, and the 16th, the wonderfully named and heavily bunkered 'Wee Bogle', is a smidgen of a short hole. The 17th bends around a corner to the left; a high bank of rough prevents you from seeing the flag from the tee, while a narrow left-to-right sloping fairway further complicates the drive. The second shot is to an elevated green and is another of those where you simply cannot afford to be short.

Although 'Braid's Brawest' is undoubtedly the finest hole at Gleneagles, 'King's Hame' is probably the best known. The 18th is a 525-yard par five which (once you have successfully carried a large ridge) sweeps dramatically down to a vast green. Some prodigiously long drives have been recorded: during one of the many televised pro-celebrity series matches, Tom Watson managed to propel his tee-shot 486 yards!

Many important issues have been decided on the 18th green of the King's Course. In the 1930s Gleneagles hosted the Curtis Cup, and today regularly stages major men's and women's amateur and professional tournaments. Until recently, the Scottish Open was played annually over the King's Course; Ian Woosnam is one of several celebrated winners. The most extraordinary finish in that event occurred in 1992, when the Australian golfer Peter O'Malley played the final five holes in an amazing seven under par, scoring eagle–birdie–birdie–birdie–eagle. Jack Nicklaus – the 'Monarch' himself – would have been proud of that.

Hole	Championship	Medal	Par	Stroke Index	Ladies'	Par	Stroke Index
1	362	362	4	6	344	4	6
2	436	405	4	14	376	4	14
3	374	374	4	9	344	4	9
4	466	466	4	2	442	5	2
5	178	161	3	16	130	3	16
6	480	476	5	8	422	5	8
7	444	439	4	4	423	5	4
8	178	158	3	17	138	3	17
9	409	354	4	12	326	4	12
Out	3327	3195	35		2945	37	
10	499	447	5/4	1	410	5	1
11	230	230	3	10	156	3	10
12	442	395	4	13	346	4	13
13	464	448	4	7	418	5	7
14	309	260	4	15	241	4	15
15	459	459	4	3	431	5	3
16	158	135	3	18	123	3	18
17	377	377	4	11	359	4	11
18	525	525	5	5	444	5	5
In	3463	3276	36/35		2928	38	
Out	3327	3195	35		2945	37	
Total	6790	6471	71/70		5873	75	

MUIRFIELD

I T IS DIFFICULT TO JUDGE WHICH IS THE MORE FAMOUS: THE GOLF COURSE OR THE GOLF CLUB. IN ADDITION TO BEING ONE OF THE WORLD'S GREATEST GOLF LINKS, MUIRFIELD IS THE HOME OF THE WORLD'S OLDEST PRIVATE GOLF CLUB.

The Honourable Company of Edinburgh Golfers was founded in 1744; Muirfield, which dates from 1891, is the Company's third home. For nearly a hundred years it had played over the ancient links at Leith before moving to Musselburgh. The Open Championship was held regularly at Musselburgh after 1874 and, as a consequence, the course grew very popular – too popular for the Company's taste. So it decided to look for another, altogether more private home. On the edge of Gullane it discovered a quiet, almost hidden piece of rolling linksland that overlooked the Firth of Forth. This was Muirfield. It was 20 miles from Edinburgh and it became the Honourable Company's Jerusalem.

Within a year of opening (May 1891), Muirfield hosted its first Open Championship. The 1892 Open was won by Harold Hilton and was the first to be contested over seventy-two holes. Initially not everyone was enamoured with Muirfield. One professional described it as 'nothing but an auld watter meddie'. However, many of the negative comments may have been provoked by jealousy, because when the Honourable Company left Musselburgh, it took the staging of the Open Championship with it. The event

returned to Muirfield in 1896, but was never again played at Musselburgh.

The reputation of the new links was enhanced by the deeds of the Great Triumvirate. Harry Vardon won the first of his record six Opens at Muirfield in 1896, defeating the defending champion John H. Taylor in a play-off, and James Braid won the next two Muirfield Opens in 1901 and 1905. In 1910 Bernard Darwin was still grumbling about 'a fatal stone wall that runs around the course, giving the impression of an inland park', but the Muirfield of today bears little resemblance to the Muirfield of the late 19th and early 20th centuries.

In the 1920s Harry Colt and Tom Simpson made substantial revisions to the links. The most important decision was to extend the course into the duneland beyond the stone wall to the north of the property. The wall ran from two-thirds of the way along the present 6th fairway in a fairly straight line towards the 3rd tee. This opened up enormous possibilities, and Colt and Simpson took full advantage. 'Modern' Muirfield is acknowledged as an architectural masterpiece. It is not the most natural golf course in the world nor is it the most spectacular or rugged, but technically and, to use the course critics' jargon, in

1	Championship	447 yards	Par 4
	Medal	444	Par 4
	Ladies'		

2		351 yards	Par 4
		345	Par 4

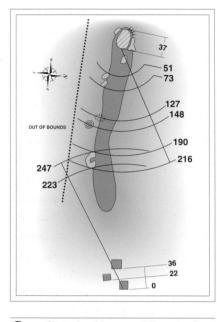

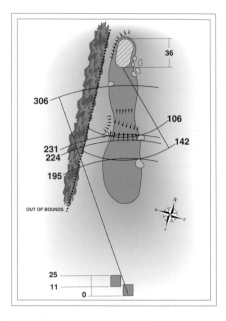

42

3	Championship	379 yards	Par 4
	Medal	374	Par 4
	Ladies'		

4		180 yards	Par 3
		174	Par 3

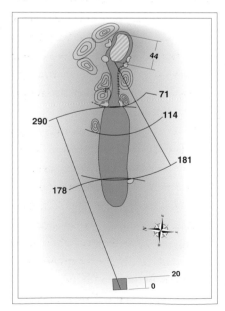

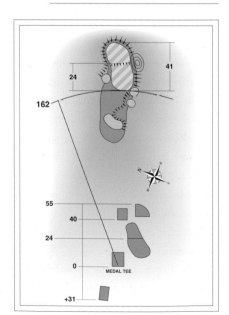

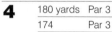

terms of shot values, Muirfield is peerless. The noted Scottish writer and Walker Cup golfer Sam Mckinlay once said of Muirfield, 'If I had to play a match for my life on a course of my choice, I would plump for Muirfield. It is the best and fairest of courses – not, perhaps, the course where I would chose to play all my golf if my activities had to be restricted to one links, for it is a little too fierce, too long, too exposed to the winds that sweep down Gullane Hill or in from the North Sea. But a man who is in command of his game and himself will fare better at Muirfield than almost any other course I know.'

The Firth of Forth provides a serene backdrop to the greens at the par four 11th (foreground) and the par five 5th.

The American journalist Herbert Warren Wind highlighted Muirfield's 'frankness' and its 'honesty': 'there are no hidden bunkers, no recondite burns, no misleading and capricious terrain. Every hazard is clearly visible.'

Muirfield's routing complements and contributes to all the above qualities. The course is laid out in two loops of nine. Broadly speaking, the front nine holes head in a clockwise direction on the outside of an inner loop, the back nine, which runs anti-clockwise. This configuration balances the links, particularly as the two halves are of a similar length, and it ensures that the golfer must confront the prevailing wind from every conceivable angle.

The unceasing wind is, as Mckinlay indicated, a reason why Muirfield is regarded as one of the toughest of the Open Championship courses. There are at least three other major causes: the nature and extent of the bunkering; the severity (at least around the time of an Open) of the rough; and the relatively small size of the greens.

The bunkers are Muirfield's trade mark. There are almost 150 in total and every one of them is capable of affecting play. They are invariably deep (you will rarely be able to reach the green from a fairway bunker), they tend to gather the ball in from the fairway and they are beautifully constructed. In the opinion of Jack Nicklaus, they are 'the most fastidiously built bunkers I have ever seen, the high front walls faced with bricks of turf fitted together so precisely you would have thought a master mason had been called in.' They are punishing but fair. En route to winning the 1959 Open, Gary Player, often regarded as the greatest-ever bunker player, visited twelve greenside traps, yet managed to get up and down to save par on eleven occasions.

For the 1966 Open Muirfield's rough was allowed to grow to an unprecedented height. The American Doug Sanders joked that he would not venture off the fairways without his caddie 'in case there are Apaches out there'. Accurate (as well as long) driving is essential. When Henry Cotton won in 1948, he reputedly missed just four fairways from the tee.

An ability to putt well is a pre-requisite

5	Championship	559 yards	Par 5
	Medal	506	Par 5
	Ladies'		

6	469 yards	Par 4
	436	Par 4

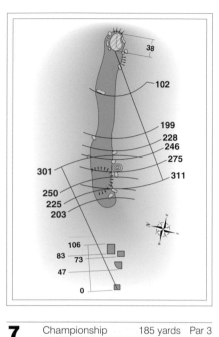

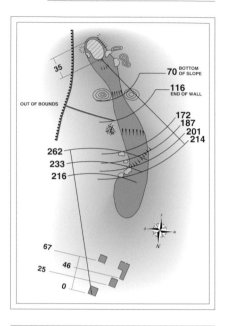

44

7	Championship	185 yards	Par 3
	Medal	151	Par 3
	Ladies'		

8	444 yards	Par 4
	439	Par 4

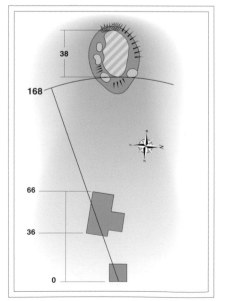

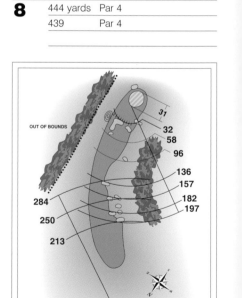

MUIRFIELD

9	Championship	504 yards	Par 5
	Medal	460	Par 4
	Ladies'		

10	475 yards	Par 4
	471	Par 4

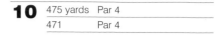

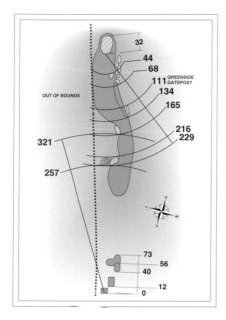

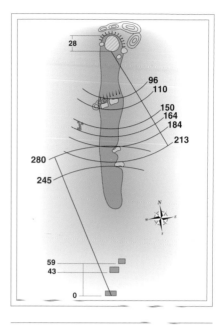

45

11	Championship	385 yards	Par 4
	Medal	350	Par 4
	Ladies'		

12	381 yards	Par 4
	376	Par 4

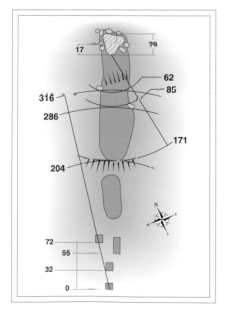

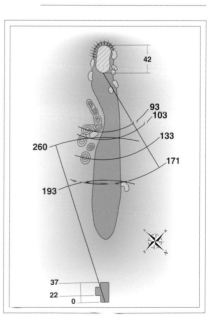

13	Championship	164yards	Par 3
	Medal	146	Par 3
	Ladies'		

14	449 yards	Par 4
	442	Par 4

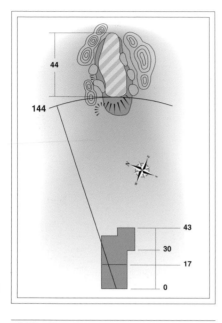

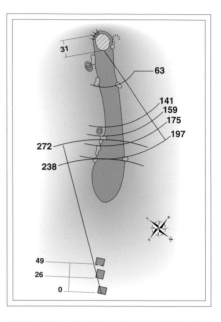

15	Championship	417 yards	Par 4
	Medal	391	Par 4
	Ladies'		

16	188 yards	Par 3
	181	Par 3

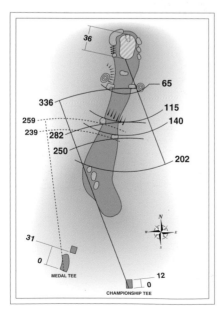

MEDAL TEE

CHAMPIONSHIP TEE

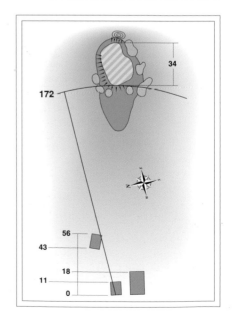

MUIRFIELD

17	Championship	550 yards	Par 5
	Medal	501	Par 5
	Ladies'		

18	448 yards	Par 4
	414	Par 4

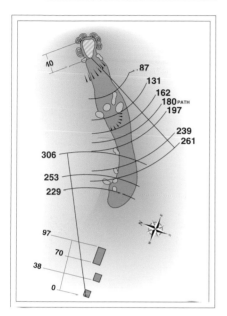

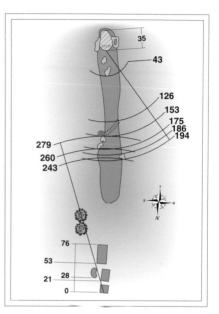

MUIRFIELD

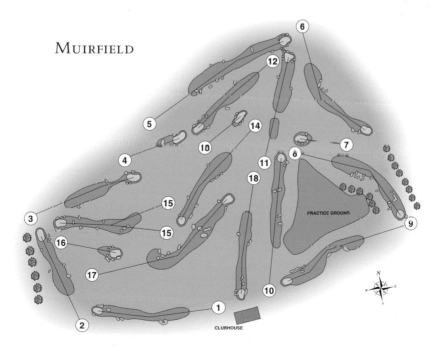

There are nearly 150 bunkers at Muirfield. Perhaps the most unusually shaped lies to the right of the 18th green.

48

for any champion, but Muirfield's greens tend to limit the import-ance of putting, or at least keep it in proportion with other aspects of the game. Skilful pitching and chipping from around the classically sculpted edges of the greens is handsomely rewarded.

Muirfield's great mix of defences can all be experienced on the 1st and 18th holes. Few golf courses in the world start and finish as impressively as Muirfield. The 1st measures 447 yards from the championship tee and dog-legs mildly to the right; the 18th measures 448 yards and dog-legs fractionally left. Both holes have a wasp-waisted fairway and are liberally sprinkled with bunkers. Each also has one bunker that is very distinctive: on the 1st it is a horseshoe-shaped fairway bunker on the left, and at the 18th there is an island of turf in the centre of the greenside bunker to the right.

There are another five lengthy two-shot holes at Muirfield and they are spread throughout the round. Over to the east side of the links and close to Archerfield Wood 'with its trees all bent and twisted in the wind' are the long 6th and 8th. An awkward uphill drive at the left-turning 6th and cross bunkers at the right-turning 8th are their most prominent features. The perfectly straight 10th is played into the prevailing wind and might be considered a bogey five; at the 14th and 15th (more cross bunkers here) the wind is usually blowing over your shoulder, complicating distance judgment.

There are four par fours that might be described as short (although the wind usually has an important bearing on this) and they come in pairs: the downhill undulating 2nd, where everything, including the green, slopes away from you, followed by the 3rd, where your drive must find the centre left of the fairway to give you a clear view of the green through a gap in the dunes; on the back nine there is the 11th, which features Muirfield's only blind tee-shot, and the downhill 12th, with its raised green and deep bunkers.

Muirfield's quartet of short holes are all very good – if just a little too similar – with plateaued greens staunchly defended by pot bunkers and myriad slopes. The 13th is undoubtedly the most attractive par three, with its green neatly wedged between tall dunes, and the exposed 7th is the most difficult when played into the wind.

There can be no criticism of Muirfield's par fives. The 5th is a fine hole and is very heavily bunkered, while the 9th and 17th are both world famous. The 9th calls for a precise tee-shot that must be steered just to the right of the first fairway bunker and a second that must avoid a cluster of bunkers, which begins approximately 50 yards short of the green; Bernard Darwin's favourite stone wall runs all along the left edge of the fairway and threatens the approach. The long dog-legging 17th has determined the outcome of many an Open Championship (Trevino versus Jacklin in 1972, for instance). The temptation to cut the corner of the dog-leg should be resisted – plenty of sand awaits – and four trench-like cross bunkers have to be carried with the second, leaving a pitch to the large dune-framed green.

Of all the current Open venues, Muirfield has consistently produced the greatest championships and the greatest champions. Its post-war roll of honour speaks volumes: Henry Cotton (1948), Gary Player (1959), Jack Nicklaus (1966), Lee Trevino (1972), Tom Watson (1980) and Nick Faldo (1987 and 1992). Muirfield seems to bring out the very best in the best: Cotton's 66 in front of the watching King George VI; Nicklaus becoming (at twenty-six) the youngest-ever winner of all four Majors; Watson's 64 that spread-eagled the field on the third day in 1980; and Faldo's record 66–64 start and 'best four holes of my life' finish to deny John Cook in 1992.

Hole	Championship	Medal	Par	Stroke	Ladies'	Par	Stroke Index
1	447	444	4	5			
2	351	345	4	15			
3	379	374	4	9			
4	180	174	3	13			
5	559	506	5	3			
6	469	436	4	7			
7	185	151	3	18			
8	444	439	4	1			
9	504	460	5/4	11			
Out	3518	3329	36/35				
10	475	471	4	4			
11	385	350	4	17			
12	381	376	4	8			
13	164	146	3	12			
14	449	442	4	2			
15	417	391	4	14			
16	188	181	3	6			
17	550	501	5	16			
18	448	414	4	10			
In	3457	3272	35				
Out	3518	3329	36/35				
Total	6975	6601	71/70				

TURNBERRY (AILSA)

'ON A FRESH DAY, WITH THE SEA TRANQUIL AND DEEPENING IN ITS BLUENESS AS THE SUN RISES HIGHER, OR AT EVENING WHEN THE MOUNTAINS TURN BLACK IN THE FADING LIGHT AND THE SKY IS LIVID WITH COLOUR, TURNBERRY IS INCOMPARABLE'. (PAT WARD-THOMAS, 1976)

Jack Nicklaus versus Tom Watson; Greg Norman's 63 in the wind; Nick Price's eagle putt. The Lighthouse, Bruce's Castle, Ailsa Craig and the Isle of Arran. Turnberry's history is beginning to mirror the transcendent beauty of its setting.

A golfing jewel on the west coast, Turnberry is the Pebble Beach of the British Isles. Or should that be the other way round? The comparisons are mutually flattering. Some are also quite uncanny. In 1972 Pebble Beach staged a first and long overdue US Open, which was won in fine style by Nicklaus; five years later Turnberry belatedly held its first British Open, when Nicklaus and Watson fought their unforgettable 'Duel in the Sun'; and, five years after this, Watson and Nicklaus again commanded centre stage when the US Open returned to Pebble Beach.

Turnberry's recent history is all the more remarkable, considering that twice this century it has been on the verge of extinction. Turnberry was requisitioned by the government for use as an airbase during both World Wars. The links was damaged on each occasion, especially in the Second World War, when several fairways and greens were dug up, land was levelled and vast concrete runways were laid.

When peace came there seemed little hope of saving the links. But the then owners of Turnberry refused to concede defeat, and in 1949 golf architect Philip Mackenzie Ross was appointed and given the mammoth task of rebuilding the links. In fact, Mackenzie Ross's work went far beyond mere restoration. When Turnberry reopened in 1951, the links was much greater than before. In 1961 Turnberry was selected to stage the British Amateur Championship, and this was followed two years later by the Walker Cup. It was now only a matter of time before the links – and Mackenzie Ross – were paid the ultimate compliment.

There are, of course, thirty-six holes at Turnberry, with the Ailsa and the Arran Courses. The latter is a worthy challenge, although it is the Ailsa that everyone wants to play. According to Golf World magazine's recent rankings, it is one of the top three courses in the British Isles. It is hard to argue with this assessment. As beautifully maintained as Muirfield, the Ailsa has a wealth of strong and stirring holes: some are extremely difficult; others encourage attacking play. There is a fine mix of drama and subtlety and, as Donald Steel has remarked, 'there is no trickery or deceit . . . Mackenzie Ross

Opposite: Built on the site of Robert the Bruce's Castle, Turnberry Lighthouse overlooks the 9th green and 10th tee on the Ailsa Course.

1	Championship	350 yards	Par 4
	Medal	358	Par 4
	Ladies'	331	Par 4

2	428 yards	Par 4
	381	Par 4
	360	Par 4

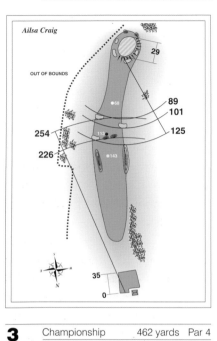

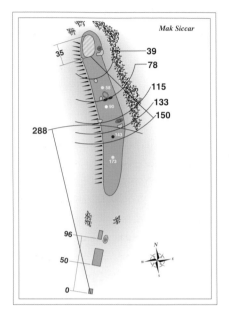

3	Championship	462 yards	Par 4
	Medal	409	Par 4
	Ladies'	390	Par 5

4	167 yards	Par 3
	165	Par 3
	114	Par 3

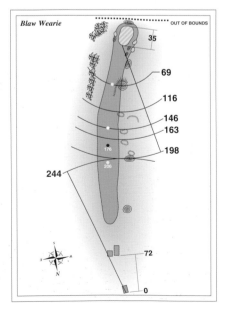

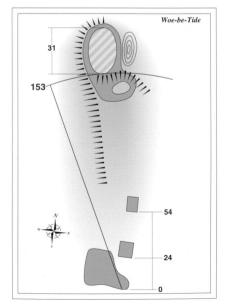

struck the perfect balance between what is challenging and what is unfair'. Perhaps Turnberry is not as breathtakingly rugged as one or two great links – there are no massive sand-hills and no sudden or spectacular changes in elevation – but if there were, would Donald Steel's comment still ring true? Besides, Turnberry is breathtaking in a different way.

In order to best utilize the wonderful stretch of oceanside terrain – in particular to have eight consecutive holes overlooking the sea – it was inevitable that the routing of the Ailsa Course would be more 'out and back' than a 'two loops of nine' configuration. The prevailing wind mainly assists on the front nine. In the final round of the 1979 European Open, Sandy Lyle, the eventual winner, played the first seven holes in six under par. Nothing, however, can explain Greg Norman's amazing round on a very breezy second day of the 1986 Open. Out in 32, despite two dropped strokes, the Australian stood over a 30-foot putt on the 18th green to be home in 29 – a round of 61! He charged the putt four feet past the hole and, unfortunately, missed the return but, still, Norman's 63 (comprising six pars, eight birdies, three bogeys and one eagle) must be considered one of the greatest-ever performances in a Major Championship.

As good as the first three par fours are, it is difficult to avoid feeling that you are simply being manoeuvred towards the shore. The 1st runs gently downhill and dog-legs mildly to the right; at the uphill 2nd you face an attractive approach to a green with a big fall-away to the left; and the 3rd tumbles down to the sea. Then the 'dream sequence' begins.

The 4th is a short hole, yet it requires a carry over some wild marsh-like rough to a green perched high in the dunes. After the 10th, the 5th is possibly the best par four on the course. You must hit a good drive up the centre right of the fairway, otherwise the hole effectively becomes a double dog-leg. Jealously guarded by bunkers, the green is raised and tucked into a corner beneath a high bank of dunes.

Now comes a famous and truly formidable par three. The 6th measures 231 yards from the championship tee and is almost as long from the medal tee. As at the 4th, the green sits up and is rather exposed; unless the wind is helping, you may not get up with a driver. There are three deep pot bunkers to the left and a huge bunker set into the rise on the right. Stray further right and your ball will tumble off down a steep hill, leaving a

53

The spectacular run of holes between the 8th (above) and the 11th is often likened to the great oceanside sequence at Pebble Beach in California.

5	Championship	441 yards	Par 4
	Medal	416	Par 4
	Ladies'	388	Par 5

6	231 yards	Par 3
	221	Par 3
	215	Par 4

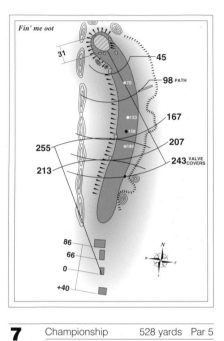

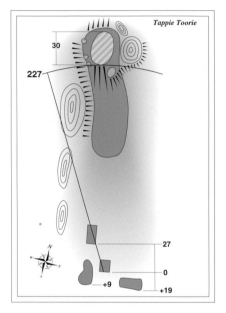

7	Championship	528 yards	Par 5
	Medal	475	Par 4
	Ladies'	415	Par 5

8	431 yards	Par 4
	431	Par 4
	386	Par 5

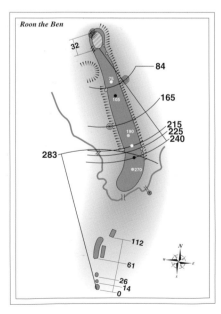

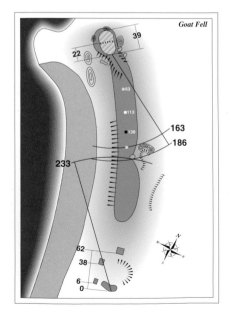

54

9	Championship	452 yards	Par 4
	Medal	411	Par 4
	Ladies'	373	Par 4

10	452 yards	Par 4
	429	Par 4
	336	Par 4

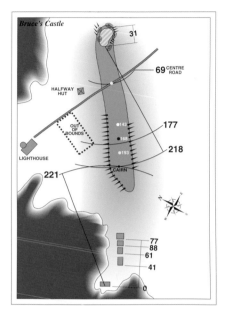

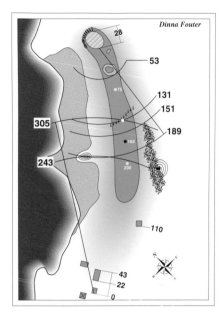

55

11	Championship	177 yards	Par 3
	Medal	161	Par 3
	Ladies'	130	Par 3

12	448 yards	Par 4
	390	Par 4
	354	Par 4

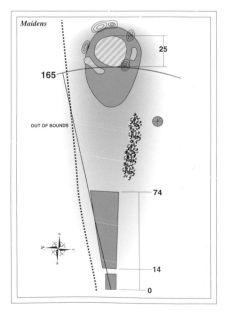

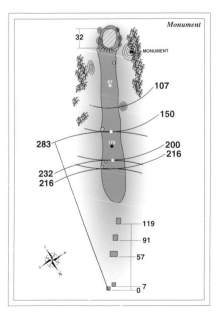

TURNBERRY (AILSA)

13	Championship	411 yards	Par 4
	Medal	379	Par 4
	Ladies'	329	Par 4

14	440 yards	Par 4
	401	Par 4
	384	Par 5

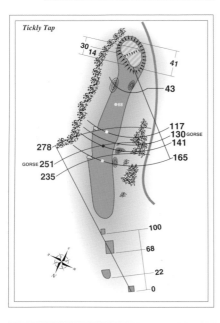

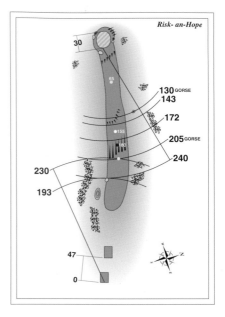

15	Championship	209 yards	Par 3
	Medal	169	Par 3
	Ladies'	160	Par 3

16	410 yards	Par 4
	380	Par 4
	339	Par 4

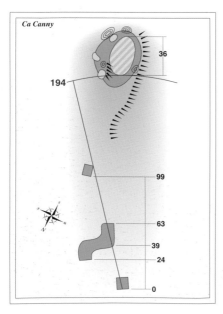

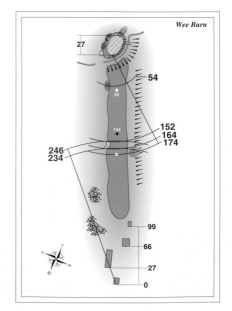

56

17	Championship	498 yards	Par 5
	Medal	487	Par 5
	Ladies'	394	Par 5

18	432 yards	Par 4
	377	Par 4
	359	Par 4

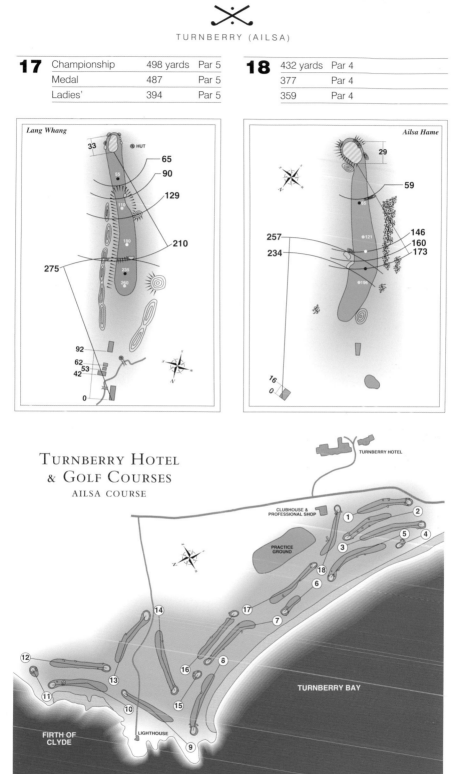

Lang Whang

33
HUT
65
55
90
129
210
275
235
260
92
62 53
42
0

Ailsa Hame

29
59
257
234
121
146
160
173
198
16
0

57

TURNBERRY HOTEL
& GOLF COURSES
AILSA COURSE

TURNBERRY HOTEL

CLUBHOUSE &
PROFESSIONAL SHOP

PRACTICE
GROUND

TURNBERRY BAY

FIRTH OF
CLYDE

LIGHTHOUSE

This fairway bunker at the 10th is not as intimidating as our photographer would have you believe – although the hole itself is a mightily impressive par four.

58

blind pitch back to the green over the top of a big dune.

The 7th is a classic par five. The fairway follows a ridge of dunes, then climbs to a handsome green site, the line for the second being directly towards Turnberry Lighthouse. You continue this gradual climb at the difficult two-shot 8th, where you may be distracted by magnificent views of the Isle of Arran and Ailsa Craig. As you near the green, a sandy beach below gives way to dark craggy rocks and Turnberry starts to resemble Pebble Beach.

The championship tee for the 9th is perched on a pinnacle of rock with the sea crashing below. After an exhilarating drive, which should carry the crest of a hog's back fairway, you play your approach close to the lighthouse. Turnberry's most famous landmark is built beside a much more ancient one –

Bruce's Castle, once the home of Robert the Bruce, King of the Scots in the 14th century. The 10th tee is also adjacent to the lighthouse and castle. The drive is a little less dramatic than on the 9th, but it begins a much better hole. The fairway sweeps down and curves left, hugging the shore for its entire length. Approximately 50 yards short of the green, there is an unusual circular-shaped bunker, the centre of which has been turfed.

The last of the oceanside holes is a picturesque par three; after this the course turns inland and heads for home. The sea is occasionally glimpsed on the inward journey, but from here on reminders of Turnberry's Open Championship history take precedence over the scenery. The 12th, 13th and 14th are par fours that provide plenty of variety, although collectively they serve a similar purpose to the first three holes in

that they pave the way for the Ailsa's superb finish.

The long par three 15th is a marvellous and very dangerous hole, with a deep chasm to the right of the green. It played a crucial role in shaping the outcome of the 1977 'Duel in the Sun' Open. When Nicklaus and Watson left the 12th green, Nicklaus leading by two, Peter Alliss posed the question, 'Who in the world can give Jack Nicklaus two shots over six holes and beat him?' Watson birdied the 13th, but still trailed by one after their tee-shots at the 15th. Nicklaus was in a much better position in the middle of the green, while Watson was at least 60 feet away, just off the fringe close to one of three greenside traps on the left. Watson decided to use his putter and promptly holed out for a two. When Nicklaus failed with his birdie attempt, they were level.

At the 16th, the second is played over Wilson's Burn, which winds across the front of the green, then around to the right. Watson and Nicklaus both managed fours. The par five 17th runs along an undulating dune lined valley. Often it is played into the wind and is almost impossible to reach in two. It was at this hole in the 1994 Open, Turnberry's third, that Nick Price holed a huge curling putt for an improbable eagle three to snatch the title from under the nose of Swedish golfer Jesper Parnevik. In 1977 there was no wind and the fairways were hard and fast. Watson hit a mid-iron on to the green and made a birdie four; Nicklaus missed a short putt and took five – now Watson was one ahead. The 18th is not the most difficult of finishing holes, provided you hit a straight drive. Watson played an iron from the tee and found the centre of the fairway; Nicklaus carved his drive into the rough on the right, his ball stopping close to a gorse bush. It appeared to be all over when Watson struck a magnificent seven iron two feet from the pin, but there was still time for one final twist in the plot. Nicklaus somehow forced his second shot on to the green and then sank an enormous putt for a birdie three. Watson still had to hole his two-footer for victory. But in those days Tom never missed.

Hole	Championship	Medal	Par	Stroke Index	Ladies	Par	Stroke Index
1	350	358	4	9	331	4	9
2	430	381	4	13	360	4	13
3	462	409	4	5	390	5	5
4	165	165	3	17	114	3	17
5	442	416	4	3	388	5	3
6	231	221	3	15	215	4	15
7	529	476	5/4	1	415	5	1
8	431	431	4	11	386	5	11
9	454	411	4	7	373	4	7
Out	3494	3267	35/34		2972	39	
10	452	429	4	6	336	4	6
11	174	161	3	18	130	3	18
12	446	390	4	8	354	4	8
13	412	379	4	14	329	4	14
14	449	401	4	2	384	5	2
15	209	169	3	16	160	3	16
16	409	380	4	10	339	4	10
17	497	487	5	4	394	5	4
18	434	377	4	12	359	4	12
In	3482	3173	35		2785	36	
Out	3494	3267	35/34		2972	39	
Total	6976	6440	70/69		5757	75	

CARNOUSTIE

S̶T ANDREWS HAS HISTORY, PRESTWICK HAS CHARACTER AND DORNOCH HAS CHARM; MUIRFIELD IS CLASSY, TURNBERRY IS PRETTY AND CARNOUSTIE ... ? CARNOUSTIE IS 'A GREAT BIG SHAGGY MONSTER'.

The description – not mine, I hasten to add – is meant as a compliment. Golfers the world over want to play Carnoustie for the same reason that mountaineers seek to scale the highest peaks: it is possibly the ultimate golfing challenge. Hagen thought as much and Hogan proved it.

None of Walter Hagen's four British Open Championships was won at Carnoustie, but this didn't prevent him from regarding it as 'the greatest course in the British Isles and one of the three greatest in the world'. In 1953 Ben Hogan, then at the height of his powers and the best player in the world, competed in his one and only British Open. Hogan had already won the Masters and the US Open that year, and he arrived on the east coast of Scotland determined to complete a unique treble. Carnoustie, hosting its third Open, provided the perfect test, as Hogan rose superbly to the challenge and produced one of the finest-ever performances in a major cham-pionship. It was golf's classic case of *veni vidi vici*.

Golf historians believe the game has been played at Carnoustie since the early 16th century; it was definitely being played on the adjoining Barry links at that time. The first official golf club at Carnoustie was founded in 1842. Golfers played over a ten-hole course laid out by Allan Robertson (the Ben Hogan of his day). Old Tom Morris extended the links to eighteen holes in 1857, and the last major revision was undertaken by James Braid in 1926. Carnoustie's first Open was staged in 1931 when Tommy Armour triumphed, and it returned in 1937, when Henry Cotton claimed the second of his three titles.

Like St Andrews, Carnoustie is a public links. There are, in fact, two courses in addition to the Championship Links, and the small Tayside town near Dundee lives and breathes golf. Carnoustie the town may lack the sophistication and scholarliness of St Andrews, but it is not quite as grey and dour as people imagine. Again, the comment that 'Carnoustie was a good place from which to emigrate' has been taken the wrong way. In the late 19th and early 20th centuries, many people left the east coast of Scotland and headed for the New World. Those who left from Carnoustie were especially gifted at golf and disseminated their talents in America. Stewart Maiden, the famous mentor of Bobby Jones, came from Carnoustie. In more recent times, the incongruous style (and, yes, ugliness) of the main clubhouse building has added to Carnoustie's cold grey image. Fortunately this building's days are numbered, for a new clubhouse

Opposite: The Barry Burn meanders across the 17th fairway and threatens both the drive and the approach at the 18th, giving Carnoustie a decidedly watery conclusion.

1	Championship	410 yards	Par 4
	Medal	401	Par 4
	Ladies'	364	Par 4

2	463 yards	Par 4
	435	Par 4
	382	Par 4

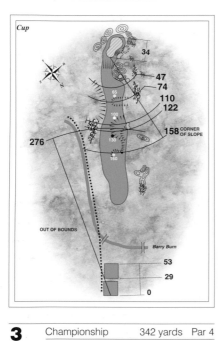

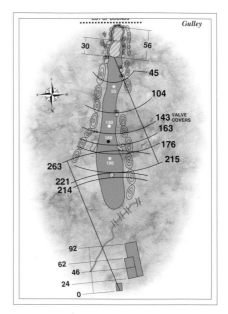

3	Championship	342 yards	Par 4
	Medal	337	Par 4
	Ladies'	301	Par 4

4	413 yards	Par 4
	375	Par 4
	358	Par 4

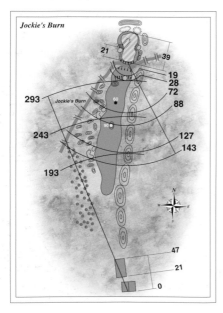

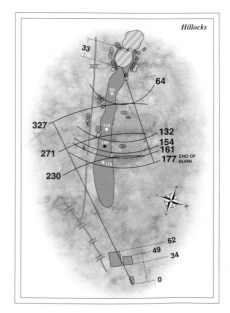

62

will have been built by the time the Open returns to Carnoustie in 1999.

The golf links retains and certainly deserves its reputation as the mightiest of courses. The challenge is epic and relentless. Carnoustie rewards good golf and punishes poor golf better than any course in the British Isles. It is always honest and fair, yet it never attempts to flatter. With no more than two consecutive holes running in the same direction, there is both balance and variety in the challenge.

What makes Carnoustie so difficult? Occupying fairly flat and exposed terrain, the wind often blows fiercely – as it does on every great Scottish links. What distinguishes Carnoustie is its vastness. Everything about the links is big: its overall length (it can be stretched to almost 7,400 yards), the size of the teeing areas, the size of the greens and, most of all, the scale and severity of the hazards.

Carnoustie's bunkers are legendary. There are plenty of them and the majority are very large and deep. Moreover, masochists and students of golf architecture agree that they are brilliantly positioned. As Pat Ward-Thomas once observed, 'Most of the hazards are placed to threaten the stroke that is slightly less than perfect rather than one that is slightly better than awful.'

The other major hazard at Carnoustie is water. Several famous links courses feature a winding burn or stream: St Andrews has its Swilken Burn, Prestwick has the Pow Burn and Royal St George's has 'Suez', but their effect on play is invariably minimal; the same can hardly be said of the Barry Burn and Jockie's Burn at Carnoustie. Those who concur with Walter Hagen's assessment that Carnoustie is Britain's greatest course – and a panel of experts assembled by *Golf Monthly* magazine came to this conclusion in 1993 – will argue that it is this factor that gives Carnoustie an extra dimension. In particular, the manner in which the Barry Burn weaves its way across the 17th and 18th fairways ensures that it has the toughest, most interesting and, potentially, most climactic finish in links golf.

63

The first six and the final six holes reveal the very best of Carnoustie. The only hole that could be described as modest is the short 8th and, if one were being picky, the sequence between the 9th and 12th does have a slightly 'inland' flavour. The 10th, 'South America', is,

Where greens collide; the 4th and 14th holes at Carnoustie share a large double-green.

5	Championship	412 yards	Par 4
	Medal	387	Par 4
	Ladies'	350	Par 4

6	570 yards	Par 5
	520	Par 5
	485	Par 5

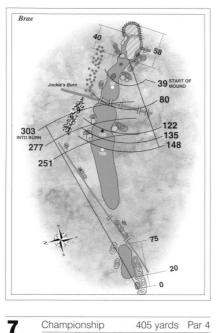

Brae

40

58

39 START OF MOUND

80

Jockie's Burn

122
135
148

303 INTO BURN
277

120

251

150

75

20

0

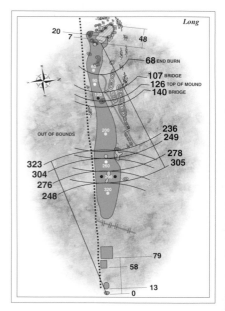

Long

20
7
48

68 END BURN

107 BRIDGE
126 TOP OF MOUND
140 BRIDGE

60

90

OUT OF BOUNDS

200

236
249

278
305

323
304
276
248

280

250

320

79

58

13

0

7	Championship	405 yards	Par 4
	Medal	394	Par 4
	Ladies'	350	Par 4

8	182 yards	Par 4
	167	Par 4
	133	Par 5

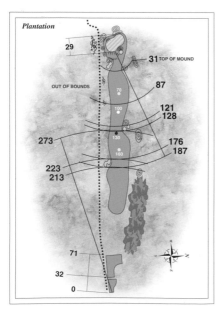

Plantation

29

31 TOP OF MOUND

OUT OF BOUNDS

87

70

121
128

100

273

130

176
187

160

223
213

71

32

0

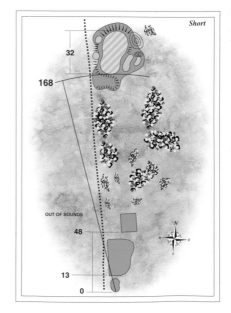

Short

32

168

OUT OF BOUNDS

48

13

0

CARNOUSTIE

9	Championship	474 yards	Par 4
	Medal	413	Par 4
	Ladies'	402	Par 5

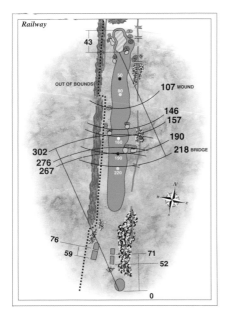

Railway

43

OUT OF BOUNDS

90

80

107 MOUND

146
157

190

180

218 BRIDGE

302
276
267

190

220

76

59

71

52

N

0

10	466 yards	Par 4
	446	Par 4
	332	Par 4

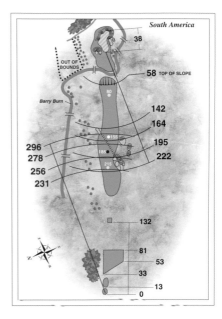

South America

38

OUT OF
BOUNDS

58 TOP OF SLOPE

Barry Burn

80

142

164

155

195

296
278
256
231

186

215

222

132

81
53
33
13

0

65

11	Championship	385 yards	Par 4
	Medal	362	Par 4
	Ladies'	330	Par 4

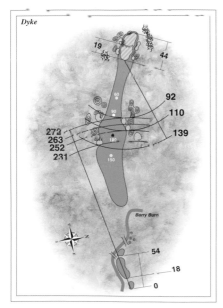

Dyke

19

44

60

92

80

110

272
263
252
231

139

180

150

Barry Burn

54

18

0

12	506 yards	Par 5
	479	Par 5
	395	Par 4

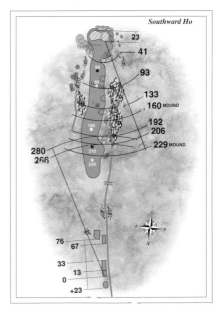

Southward Ho

23

41

60

93

80

133

160 MOUND

192
206

180

229 MOUND

280
266

210

240

76
67

33

13

0

+23

13	Championship	168 yards	Par 3
	Medal	161	Par 3
	Ladies'	118	Par 3

14	516 yards	Par 5
	483	Par 5
	440	Par 5

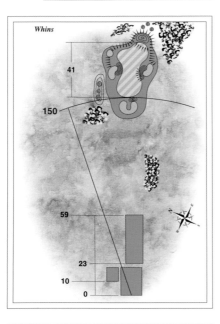

Whins

41

150

59

23

10

0

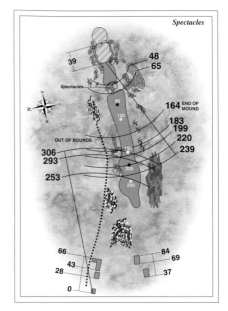

Spectacles

39

48
65

Spectacles

164 END OF MOUND

183
199
220
239

OUT OF BOUNDS

306
293
253

66

84
69

43

28

37

0

15	Championship	464 yards	Par 4
	Medal	459	Par 4
	Ladies'	418	Par 5

16	250 yards	Par 3
	245	Par 3
	212	Par 4

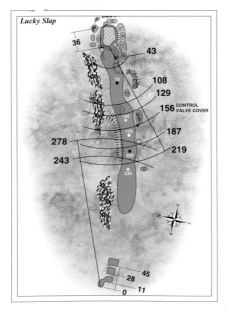

Lucky Slap

36

43

108

129

156 CONTROL VALVE COVER

187

278

219

243

45

28

0 11

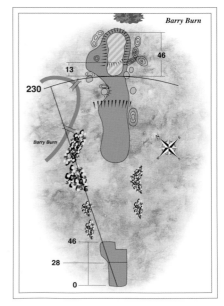

Barry Burn

46

13

230

Barry Burn

46

28

0

17	Championship	457 yards	Par 4
	Medal	433	Par 4
	Ladies'	374	Par 4

18	516 yards	Par 5
	444	Par 4
	383	Par 4

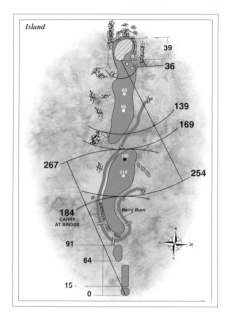

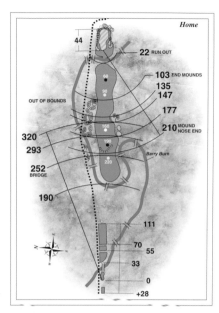

67

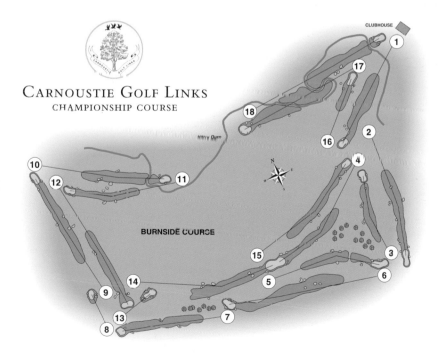

CARNOUSTIE GOLF LINKS
CHAMPIONSHIP COURSE

BURNSIDE COURSE

Carnoustie is acknowledged as the toughest Open Championship venue and is especially famed for its punitive bunkering. This picture was taken from beside the 2nd green.

68

however, a famous hole. With the Barry Burn crossing in front of the green, then wandering around its right side, it can be the most difficult hole of the entire round.

The course starts strongly. A fine 1st hole, where the green sits neatly in a natural bowl, is followed by an even better 2nd. Here you must drive over Braid's Bunker, which is located right in the centre of the fairway, then thread your second along an ever narrowing dune-framed avenue, carefully avoiding a minefield of bunkers. The green is very deep and two-tiered.

The 3rd is an attractive, fairly short par four, and one of the few holes at Carnoustie where you can afford to rest your driver. The key to this hole is the approach, which is played over Jockie's Burn to a heavily contoured green set against a backdrop of firs. The 4th dog-

legs mildly to the right as, in a different direction, does the 5th. This latter hole is every bit as good and demanding as the 2nd: Jockie's Burn reappears approximately 300 yards from the tee, the fairway bunkering is extremely bold, while the green resembles a giant stage that falls, or rather cascades, from back to front. Ben Hogan chipped in for a birdie three at this hole during his final round in the 1953 Open (it was one of the few greens he missed all week) and it effectively sealed his victory.

The combination of an out-of-bounds fence running all the way up the left side and yet more devilish fairway bunkering makes the drive at the par five 6th especially formidable. The second shot is none too easy either, as the fairway tightens at the landing area just as Jockie's Burn makes its final appearance. The green is nicely angled, full of subtle slopes and defended by bunkers at both front and back.

If Hogan was practically 'home and dry' after his three at the 5th, things were very different when the next Open Championship was staged at Carnoustie in 1968. Gary Player left the green at the par three 13th holding a slender two-shot lead, and the man breathing down his neck was playing partner Jack Nicklaus.

The par five 14th at Carnoustie is named 'Spectacles' after the characterful twin bunkers that are set into the rise of a sandy ridge some 50 yards short of the green. It is a blind approach. If you are tempted to go for the green in two – as Player was forced to do when Nicklaus's second finished on the edge of the green – it requires a very courageous shot. Player struck a majestic three wood to within two feet of the flag for an eagle three. Given the circumstances, it was probably the greatest shot of his career. Nicklaus, of course, didn't give up. Over the closing holes he unleashed a series of thunderous strokes, but Player held firm.

Carnoustie's fearsome finish begins at the 15th, a long par four that dog-legs to the left. Its difficulty is compounded by a hog's back-shaped fairway and a sunken green. Then comes 'the world's most difficult short hole'. The 16th measures 250 yards from the championship tee. For most of us it is a par three and a half. The long, thin, shelf-like green has sharp fall-aways on all sides and five deep bunkers guard its entrance. In the final round of the 1968 Open, Nicklaus was the only player to hit his tee-shot beyond the flag – and he used a driver!

In the 1975 Open, Tom Watson the eventual winner, never once achieved a three at the 16th. However, he did successfully negotiate the Barry Burn at the 17th, where its extraordinary meandering creates a near island fairway, and at the 18th, where it must be carried with both the drive and the approach.

After a gap of 24 years, the Open Championship returned to Carnoustie in 1999. It was won in a play-off by Scotland's Paul Lawrie – and it was lost on the 72nd hole by the Frenchman, Jean Van de Velde.

Hole	Championship	Medal	Par	Stroke Index	Ladies'	Par	Stroke Index
1	410	401	4	7	364	4	7
2	463	435	4	3	382	4	3
3	342	337	4	15	301	4	15
4	413	375	4	11	358	4	11
5	412	387	4	13	350	4	13
6	570	520	5	1	485	5	1
7	405	394	4	9	350	4	9
8	182	167	3	17	133	3	17
9	474	413	4	5	402	5	5
Out	3671	3429	36		3125	37	
10	466	446	4	8	332	4	8
11	385	362	4	14	330	4	14
12	506	479	5	4	395	4	4
13	168	161	3	18	118	3	18
14	516	483	5	2	440	5	2
15	464	459	4	12	418	5	12
16	250	245	3	16	212	4	16
17	457	433	4	6	374	4	6
18	516	444	5/4	10	383	4	10
In	3728	3512	37/36		3002	37	
Out	3671	3429	36		3125	37	
Total	7399	6941	73/72		6127	74	

ROYAL TROON (OLD)

T HE MAN STANDING ON THE 8TH TEE WAS A LEGEND. HE WAS SEVENTY-
ONE AND HE SPORTED PLUS-TWOS AND A FLOPPY HAT. IT WAS A
TYPICALLY BREEZY DAY AND, ALTHOUGH HE HAD STRUGGLED A LITTLE OVER
THE FIRST SEVEN HOLES, HE WAS LOOKING FORWARD TO THIS TEE-SHOT.

After all, the short 8th at Troon is one of the most celebrated holes in golf. After some deliberation, he selected a five iron and punched a shot low into the wind. The ball landed on the front of the green, took a couple of hops forward, then rolled neatly into the centre of the cup. Drinks all round.

It is impossible to think of Troon without thinking of the 'Postage Stamp', as the par three 8th on the Old Course is known. It is equally impossible to think of the 'Postage Stamp' without thinking of Gene Sarazen's hole-in-one in the 1973 Open Championship.

The television cameras were present to record Sarazen's amazing feat. The popular American, the first-ever player to win all four of golf's Major Championships, announced that he was having a copy of the film made 'to take with me to heaven so that I can show Walter Hagen and Bobby Jones'. The eyes of the golfing world were focused once again on Troon – Royal Troon since 1978 – when the club hosted its seventh Open Championship in July 1997, victory going to the American golfer, Justin Leonard.

The Ayrshire club hasn't always been so famous. In its early years Troon was greatly overshadowed by neighbouring Prestwick. The club was founded in 1878,

some eighteen years after Prestwick hosted the first Open, and initially there were just five holes. But from modest beginnings, Troon's reputation gradually evolved. Willie Fernie and James Braid were the architects most responsible for extending and improving the links, and by 1923 Troon was considered good enough to stage the Open. Although the championship didn't return until 1950, the Old Course at Troon is now very firmly on the Open Championship rota.

And so it should be. Troon is unquestionably a great links, even if, like Royal Lytham in Lancashire, it is not the kind of links you instantly fall in love with (unless, of course, you happen to do a Sarazen). With the Isle of Arran and Ailsa Craig sitting off the coast, there is an attractiveness in the setting, but this part of Ayrshire is quite industrialized, and Troon is no Turnberry.

The links itself has very masculine traits. On a fine day it appears ruggedly handsome; on a bad day it can look positively dishevelled. There is a wildness about the place. When it is being prepared for an Open Championship, it develops a battleground-like atmosphere – which, of course, is entirely appropriate. At such times Troon provides the perfect stage for acts of triumph and tragedy.

Opposite: A bird's-eye view of one of golf's great battlegrounds. On rare occasions Troon can appear almost benign; typically, however, the links conveys its uncompromising nature.

1

Championship	364 yards	Par 4
Medal	357	Par 4
Ladies'		

2

	391 yards	Par 4
	381	Par 4

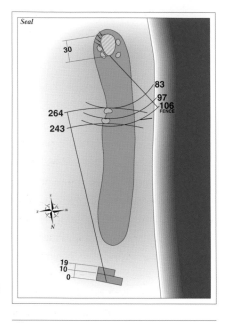

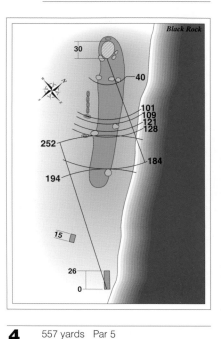

3

Championship	379 yards	Par 4
Medal	371	Par 4
Ladies'		

4

	557 yards	Par 5
	552	Par 5

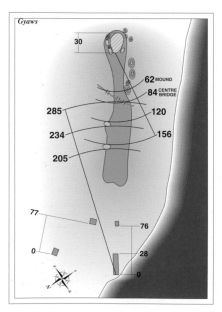

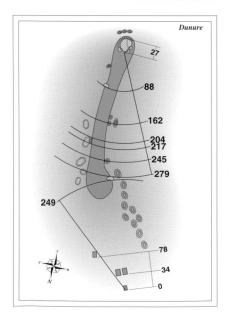

The links has a very traditional 'out and back' layout. Between the 7th and 12th holes, the course wanders in and out of the dunes, but otherwise it heads out along the coast and journeys home on the landward side.

It is often claimed that the front nine offers the better views, while the back nine presents the stiffer challenge. There is certainly some truth in this, for the first three holes are particularly scenic; their fairways run adjacent to the shore, but they are not overly difficult. However, the challenge clearly increases at the 4th, and is firmly established by the par three 5th. The green at the 5th, like the majority of putting surfaces at Troon, is fairly flat and defended by deep bunkers; to land safely upon it you must carry a sea of tangling rough.

The 6th at Troon measures 577 yards and is the longest hole on any of the Open Championship courses. Apart from its great length, it features a collec-tion of fiendishly punishing fairway bunkers. In the third round of the 1982 Open, the American golfer Bobby Clampett came to the par five 6th leading the championship by seven. … and holed out in eight! Clampett was not the first player to overindulge himself in the fair-way bunkers at the 6th.

It has been noted how the course 'goes on walk-about' at the 7th, weaving in and out of the dunes before straightening and heading back towards the clubhouse. As well as signalling a change in direction, the 7th is a classic two-shotter. From a tee situated high above the 6th green, you drive down to a fairway that swings to the right just beyond the landing area. The approach is played to a stage-like green that nestles beneath large flanking dunes and is defended by deep pot bunkers on either side. Then comes the 'Postage Stamp'.

Troon's greatest hole was once described as being 'as full of wickedness as it is of beauty'. The backdrop is decid-

73

The infamous 'Railway' hole: bordered by a stone wall out of bounds to the right and an ocean of gorse to the left, the 11th can easily destroy a promising round.

5

Championship	210 yards	Par 3
Medal	194	Par 3
Ladies'		

6

577 yards	Par 5
544	Par 5

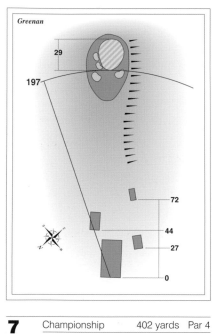

Greenan

29

197

72

44

27

0

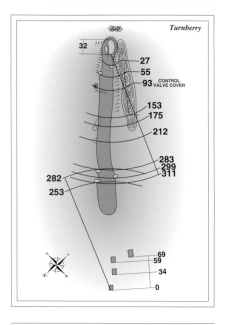

Turnberry

32

27
55
93 CONTROL VALVE COVER

153
175

212

283
299
311

282
253

69
59
34

0

7

Championship	402 yards	Par 4
Medal	381	Par 4
Ladies'		

8

126 yards	Par 3
123	Par 3

74

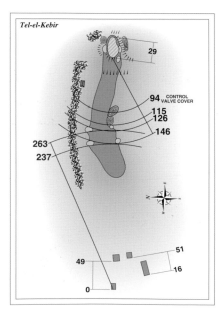

Tel-el-Kebir

29

94 CONTROL VALVE COVER

115
126

146

263
237

51

49

16

0

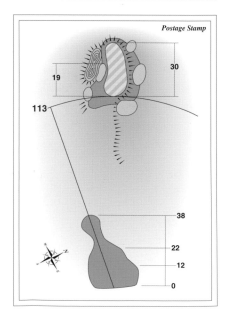

Postage Stamp

30

19

113

38

22

12

0

9	Championship	423 yards	Par 4
	Medal	387	Par 4
	Ladies'		

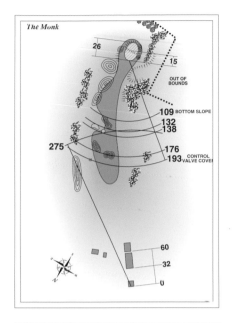

The Monk

26

15

OUT OF
BOUNDS

109 BOTTOM SLOPE
132
138

275

176
193 CONTROL
VALVE COVER

60

32

0

10	438 yards	Par 4
	385	Par 4

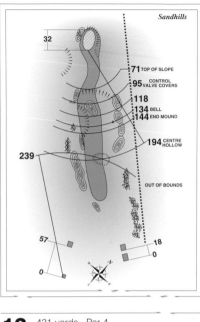

Sandhills

32

71 TOP OF SLOPE
95 CONTROL
VALVE COVERS
118
134 BELL
144 END MOUND

194 CENTRE
HOLLOW

239

OUT OF BOUNDS

57

18
0

0

75

11	Championship	465 yards	Par 4
	Medal	421	Par 4
	Ladies'		

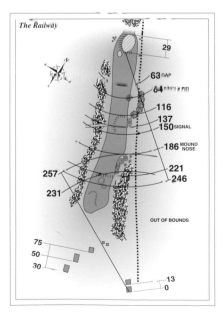

The Railway

29

63 GAP
64 SINGLE FIR

116
137
150 SIGNAL

186 MOUND
NOSE

257

221
246

231

OUT OF BOUNDS

75
50
30

13
0

12	431 yards	Par 4
	427	Par 4

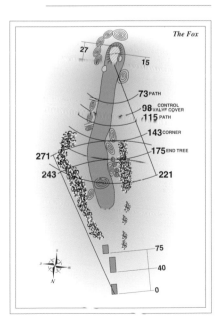

The Fox

27
15

73 PATH

98 CONTROL
VALVE COVER
115 PATH

143 CORNER

175 END TREE

271
243
221

75

40

0

13

Championship	465 yards	Par 4
Medal	411	Par 4
Ladies'		

14

179 yards	Par 3
175	Par 3

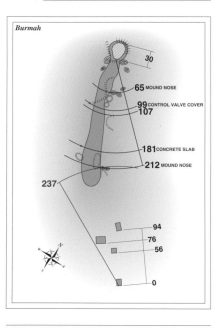

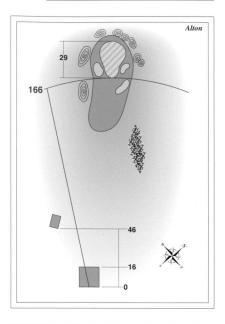

15

Championship	457 yards	Par 4
Medal	445	Par 4
Ladies'		

16

542 yards	Par 5
533	Par 5

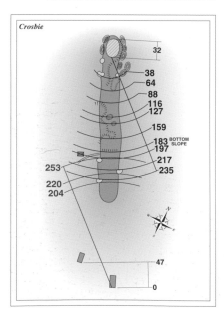

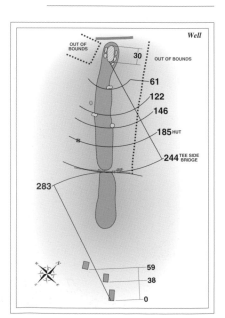

17	Championship	223 yards	Par 3
	Medal	210	Par 3
	Ladies'		

18	452 yards	Par 4
	374	Par 4

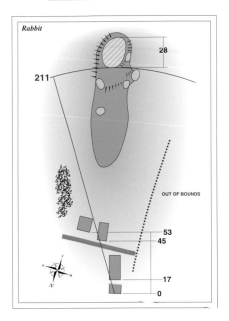

Rabbit

28

211

OUT OF BOUNDS

53
45

17

0

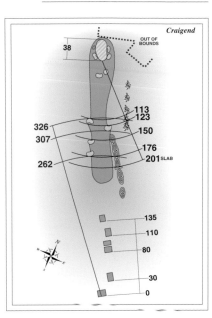

Craigend

38

OUT OF BOUNDS

113
123
150

326
307

176
201 SLAB

262

135

110

80

30

0

77

ROYAL TROON
GOLF CLUB

PORTLAND COURSE

PORTLAND CLUBHOUSE

HOTEL

CLUBHOUSE & PRO-SHOP

The calm before the storm. The opening hole at Troon is a straightaway par four; the challenge increases over the next few holes and the gauntlet is firmly laid down at the short 5th.

78

edly beautiful but, yes, miss the green with your tee-shot and it can be an extremely wicked hole. Herman Tissies, a German amateur playing in the 1950 Open, took fifteen strokes at the 8th after he missed the green. The potential for catastrophe exists, not because the target is so minute, but because the green is table-shaped, with very steep sides tumbling down into very deep bunkers. Tissies spent several frustrating moments trying to extricate himself from one of these bunkers. When he finally succeeded, his ball ran across the green and fell into an equally horrid trap on the other side. He then repeated the trick before returning to the first bunker for an encore performance. One only hopes his playing partner remained silent throughout.

The 9th hole dog-legs mildly to the right and the 10th turns sharply to the left. The former features a very narrow entrance to a sunken two-tiered green, but the 10th is the better hole. It is called 'Sandhills', because this is what you must play over – or through – from the tee. This is the most rugged part of the course; the 10th has a flavour of Royal County Down about it, with rampant gorse, a tumbling fairway and a wonderfully natural green site.

The par five 11th is another notorious hole, more feared than loved. A railway line runs all the way up the right side of the fairway and, just like the 1st at Prestwick, only a stone wall stands between it and the edge of the green. If you venture too far left, your ball will likely vanish in the gorse.

The 1989 Open champion, Mark Calcavecchia, has special memories of the 12th. From a wretched lie in the rough at the back of the green, he pitched straight into the hole for a birdie three. That shot,

together with further birdies at the 16th and 18th holes, enabled him to catch Greg Norman, who earlier in the day had birdied each of the first six holes in a brilliant round of 64.

Turning for home, the 13th rivals the 7th as the best par four at Troon. The championship tee at both holes is very elevated, although in other respects they are quite different. The 13th is straight, rather than dog-legged, and generally plays much longer. Its characterful dune-lined fairway is also much more turbulent, and there are no greenside bunkers – not that it needs any.

The 14th is possibly the easiest and least interesting of the par threes, but another testing par four immediately follows. The 15th is an unusual hole in that the first part of the fairway is quite level; it then becomes every bit as crumpled as the 13th, only for the green (which is partially hidden by mounds) to be as flat as any you are ever likely to putt on.

The last 'obvious' birdie opportunity comes at the par five 16th, provided you can avoid Gyaws Burn and a nasty fairway bunker, which is strategically positioned 60 yards short of the green. The 17th is a very demanding 223-yard par three. In truth, it is not as difficult as the 16th at Carnoustie, with which it is occasionally compared, although it is well bunkered and birdies are extremely rare.

If we are making comparisons, then the 18th at Troon bears more than a passing resemblance to the 18th at Lytham. Birdies are not too common here either, even if Mark Calcavecchia managed two

in a day when he defeated Norman and third-round leader Wayne Grady in the 1989 Open play-off. Norman's hopes of victory disappeared when his drive at the final hole flew more than 300 yards, but came to rest against the face of a fairway bunker. From there things went from bad to worse. Calcavecchia joined Royal Troon's distinguished roll of post-war Open champions, namely Bobby Locke, Arnold Palmer, Tom Weiskopf and Tom Watson. But poor Norman! Six birdies in a row, a course record of 64, two more birdies at the start of the four-hole play-off and then … disaster! If ever a golfer mixed triumph with tragedy, it was the 'Great White Shark' at Troon that day.

Hole	Championship	Medal	Par	Stroke Index	Ladies'	Par	Stroke Index
1	364	357	4	16			
2	391	381	4	7			
3	379	371	4	11			
4	557	522	5	4			
5	210	194	3	14			
6	577	544	5	2			
7	402	381	4	9			
8	126	123	3	18			
9	423	387	4	5			
Out	3426	3260	36				
10	438	385	4	10			
11	465	421	4	1			
12	431	427	4	6			
13	465	411	4	12			
14	179	175	3	15			
15	457	445	4	3			
16	542	533	5	8			
17	223	210	3	13			
18	452	374	4	17			
In	3652	3381	35				
Out	3429	3260	36				
Total	7081	6641	71				

LOCH LOMOND

Y OU COULD TRAVEL THE WORLD, SAIL THE SEVEN SEAS AND EXPLORE THE FIVE CONTINENTS, AND NEVER FIND A MORE EXQUISITE PLACE THAN LOCH LOMOND. ANY SCOTSMAN WILL TELL YOU THIS, AND EVERY BUDDING ULYSSES WILL CONFIRM IT.

And to think that a golf course, a wonderful one at that, now graces the legendary bonnie banks – golf must be the loveliest and luckiest of games.

Loch Lomond Golf Club is a dream that nearly didn't happen. It took the original developer the best part of a decade to obtain planning permission; it took just one trip to America to snare the architects but then some three years to build the course. Just when all appeared to be falling neatly into place, along came the recession of the early 1990s. Loch Lomond tumbled into receivership and the project was placed on hold. As dormant months became dormant years, the architects, Tom Weiskopf and Jay Morrish, feared Loch Lomond might never be accomplished. The feelings of despair and frustration must have been immense, since both were convinced that this was the finest course they would ever design.

Then, at last, Weiskopf found a white knight. He persuaded Lyle Anderson, a highly successful businessman and founder of the Desert Mountain and Desert Highlands golf communities in Arizona, to visit Loch Lomond. Anderson was captivated by what he described as 'the spirit of Loch Lomond'. As he hails from Phoenix, perhaps he was fated to cause Loch Lomond to 'rise from the ashes'.

Today Lyle Anderson is the President of Loch Lomond Golf Club owned jointly by his company and DMB Associates, a dynamic, growing US-based company. The golf course flourishes and amazes (Golf Magazine recently ranked it among the top fifty courses in the world – remarkable for such a young course), and membership of the exclusive internationally oriented club has become a prized possession.

The staging of a major annual golf event has always formed part of Anderson's grand scheme. His goal is to create a tournament that mirrors the international flavour and quality of the club. The inaugural Loch Lomond World Invitational was held in September 1996. Denmark's rising star, Thomas Bjorn, was the winner, and eight different nationalities were represented among the top ten finishers. The reigning US Masters champion, Nick Faldo, and the European number one, Colin Montgomerie, both competed and were quick to lavish praise on the layout. Faldo described it as 'absolutely fabulous' and suggested the course was 'as good as any I've seen'. He later added, 'in terms of conditioning, it has to be by far the best course in the British Isles.' Montgomerie called it 'faultless'.

Opposite: A view looking back down the fairway at the dog-legged par four 7th; both the tee and the green are adjacent to the loch.

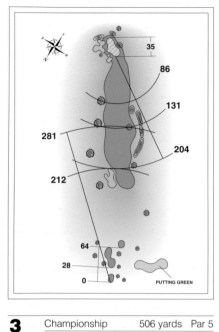

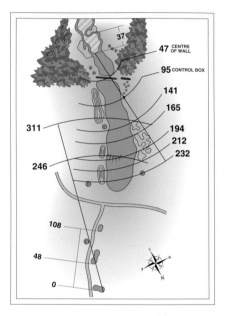

LOCH LOMOND

1

Championship	426 yards	Par 4
Medal	398	Par 4
Ladies'	362	Par 4

35
86
131
281
204
212
64
28
0
PUTTING GREEN

2

	460 yards	Par 4
	412	Par 4
	352	Par 4

37
47 CENTRE OF WALL
95 CONTROL BOX
141
165
311
194
212
232
246
108
48
0

82

3

Championship	506 yards	Par 5
Medal	468	Par 5
Ladies'	407	Par 5

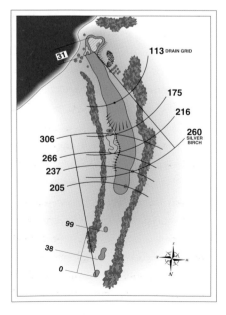

31
113 DRAIN GRID
175
216
260 SILVER BIRCH
306
266
237
205
99
38
0

4

	388 yards	Par 4
	358	Par 4
	313	Par 4

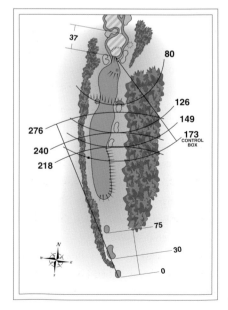

37
80
126
149
276
173 CONTROL BOX
240
218
75
30
0

In 1997 the tournament was scheduled for the week preceding the Open Championship at Royal Troon – a marvellous fortnight for Scottish golf and a wonderful double for Weiskopf. Troon was the scene of his greatest triumph in 1973. Is Loch Lomond now his greatest triumph? Weiskopf thinks it might be: 'it is my lasting memorial to golf.'

It isn't difficult to comprehend what so enchanted Weiskopf, and later Anderson. Practically encircled by mountains and hills, the beginning of the Scottish Highlands, there is no golf course in the world with a more beautiful or more romantic lakeside setting. The great advantage Loch Lomond has is that it is laid out in the midst of an historic 800-year-old estate. Loch Lomond occupies part of the ancient lands of Luss, the ancestral home of the Clan Colquohoun, who fought with Robert the Bruce. The estate is blessed with an extraordinary wealth of trees, including many giant pines and an ample sprinkling of stately oaks, some as much as 800 years old; rhododendrons and azaleas provide seasonal splashes of colour. There is an 18th-century Georgian mansion, Rossdhu House (now the club's palatial 19th hole), a ruined 15th-century castle and, of course, the odd internationally oriented ghost.

The design takes good advantage of the lakeside setting. Either the tee or green (or both) is adjacent to the loch on no fewer than eight holes; a stream or burn affects another four. If water is not a significant hazard, then Loch Lomond's distinctive marshes or a host of dazzling white jigsaw-shaped bunkers invariably are. The presence and strength of the wind is a further factor. It doesn't blow as fiercely as on a links, but with the course being situated beside the loch, it has a far greater influence than on most parkland layouts. Perhaps more than anything though, it is a very strategic golf course. You have to think your way around. Selecting the best side of the fairway from the tee and then finding the correct area of the green from the fairway is the key to playing well at Loch Lomond.

According to Weiskopf, the 1st is a 'pretty doggone tough starting hole'. With your back to the mountains, you play a mild dog-leg left towards the loch. The large jigsaw bunkers quickly introduce themselves: there is one on the angle of the dog-leg and two more to the left of the green. You are teased by glimpses of the loch for the next three holes. The 2nd and 4th greens back on to one another, actually joining to form an undulating double green. The approach to the 2nd is over a low wall (shades of North Berwick) to a fairly receptive green, whereas at the shorter 4th, with its stunning Ben Lomond back-drop, you hit to a raised crown-like surface closely guarded by bunkers with a steep fall-away to the right. Linking these two holes is the glorious par five 3rd. Here you drive to a crest of fairway that swings to the left; another perfectly positioned bunker discourages an overly ambitious drive. The second shot is hit slightly downhill with a pond (inhabited by some colourful rhododendron bushes) to the right of the green and

83

5	Championship	191 yards	Par 3
	Medal	173	Par 3
	Ladies'	116	Par 3

6	626 yards	Par 5
	579	Par 5
	461	Par 5

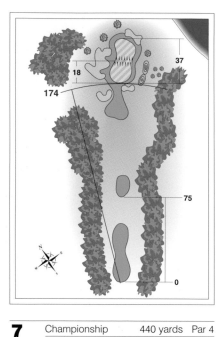

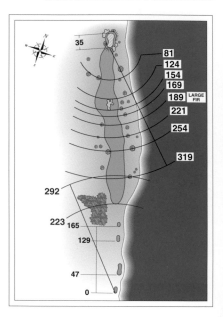

7	Championship	440 yards	Par 4
	Medal	440	Par 4
	Ladies'	361	Par 4

8	156 yards	Par 3
	156	Par 3
	120	Par 3

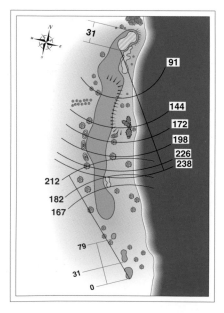

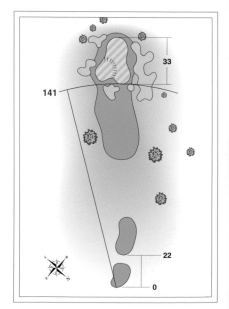

9

Championship	339 yards	Par 4
Medal	323	Par 4
Ladies'	289	Par 4

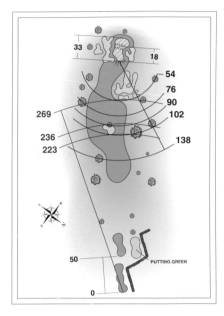

10

456 yards	Par 4
426	Par 4
385	Par 5

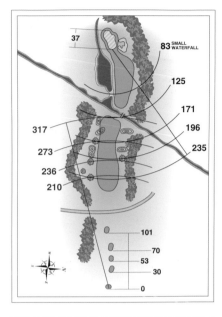

11

Championship	236 yards	Par 3
Medal	236	Par 3
Ladies'	148	Par 3

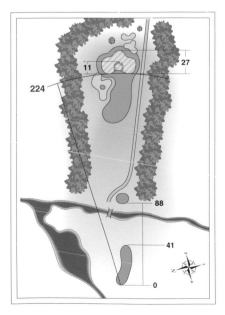

12

416 yards	Par 4
380	Par 4
310	Par 4

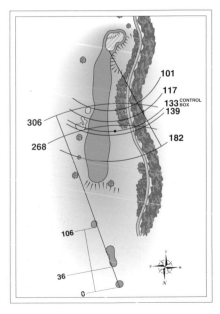

85

LOCH LOMOND

13	Championship	561 yards	Par 5
	Medal	530	Par 5
	Ladies'	496	Par 5

14	357 yards	Par 4
	331	Par 4
	254	Par 4

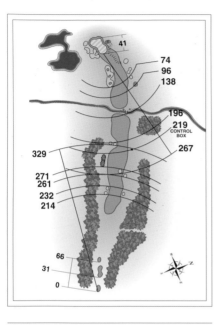

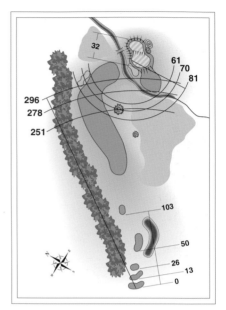

15	Championship	415 yards	Par 4
	Medal	385	Par 4
	Ladies'	337	Par 4

16	468 yards	Par 4
	501	Par 5
	426	Par 5

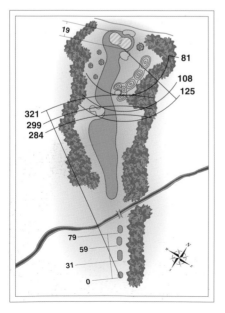

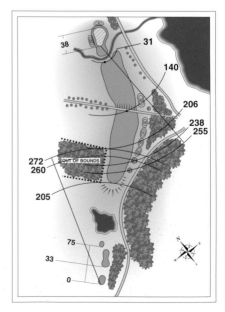

17	Championship	207 yards	Par 3
	Medal	185	Par 3
	Ladies'	140	Par 3

18	435 yards	Par 4
	417	Par 4
	358	Par 4

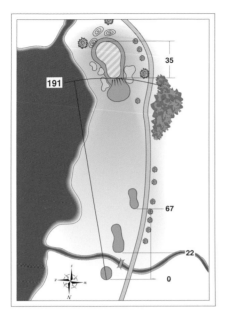

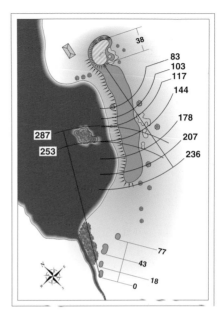

87

THE LOCH LOMOND
GOLF CLUB

The bonnie bunkers of Loch Lomond? Nick Faldo explodes from sand at the par three 5th during the inaugural Loch Lomond World Invitational tournament.

a large bunker to the left. Beyond the bunker is the loch.

The photogenic 5th is the first of Loch Lomond's impressive quartet of short holes. Aiming straight at the loch, you must first carry some marshes and then – whatever else – avoid missing the green on the left where trees and an especially large bunker await. The next two holes run right alongside the loch.

The 6th is a gargantuan par five, the longest hole in Scotland. A vast cross bunker dictates the strategy for the second shot and the approach is anything but straight-forward, as the green is small, tightly trapped and significantly raised above the level of the fairway. The 7th is a beautiful left-to-right dog-leg that first

drifts away from the shore, then sweeps back to a magnificently sited green perched on the water's edge. The left side of the fairway gives the best angle for attacking the flag. Sand dominates the remaining two holes of the front nine. Overlooked by Rossdhu House, the short 8th is surrounded by bunkers, and at the 9th you are tempted to drive over a nest of fairway traps. The green can be driven from the forward tee, but the more conservative route is often better rewarded.

The second nine begins with an exhilarating downhill tee-shot. The loch temporarily disappears from view, as mountains and hills dominate the scenery. The long approach to the par four 10th is played across the Arn Burn, with the left of the fairway threatened all the way to the green by a pond. An extremely demanding uphill par three follows. There are days when the 11th is out of range with a driver. The green sits at the top of a fairly steep incline and is backed by a bank of trees. It is a near perfect arena and its vast stage (the green) slopes in several directions.

Notwithstanding a massive oak on the left edge of the fairway, the 12th is possibly the least picturesque hole at Loch Lomond. However, it does feature some classic golf architecture with an angled, bunkerless green falling away sharply to the front and right. There is a hint of déjà vu about the drive at the par five 13th. Dramatically downhill, it is very similar to the tee-shot at the 10th. If anything, this is an even better hole. The 14th, a drivable par four, is known as 'Tom and Jay's Chance'. For those not wishing to take on a 230-yard-plus carry over marsh and water to a three-tiered green, there is an alternative fairway. But you cannot completely avoid the water: if the hole is played as a conventional two-shotter, you must still execute a very precise pitch over the Arn Burn.

The par four 15th heralds the start of an exceptional finish. From an elevated tee, the fairway flows down towards a shallow, sloping green beautifully framed by dark woods. The 16th is a sweeping par five. A wide expanse of fairway greets the drive; thereafter you must elect whether to lay up short of Port Burn, which crosses in front of the green, or throw caution to the wind and attempt the carry. Many golfers leave this green

wondering if the final two holes can possibly match the first sixteen. In fact, the best is saved for last.

The 17th and 18th return to the edge of the loch. The 17th is a challenging par three with a tee-shot across marshes to a well bunkered green, reputed to be Weiskopf's favourite hole. The 18th curves spectacularly around Rossdhu Bay. The fairway tilts from right to left towards the water, and several bunkers police the right side of the fairway; a brave drive will seek to cut off as much of the bay as possible. Just behind the green are the ruins of Rossdhu Castle – and a haunting conclusion to a heavenly round.

Hole	Championship	Medal	Par	Stroke Index	Ladies'	Par	Stroke Index
1	425	400	4	9	360	4	9
2	455	410	4	5	350	4	5
3	505	465	5	7	405	5	7
4	385	360	4	11	315	4	11
5	190	175	3	15	115	3	15
6	625	580	5	1	460	5	1
7	440	440	4	3	360	4	3
8	155	155	3	17	120	3	17
9	340	340	4	13	290	4	13
Out	3520	3325	36		2775	36	
10	455	425	4	2	385	5	2
11	235	215	3	18	150	3	18
12	415	380	4	8	305	4	8
13	560	560	5	4	495	5	4
14	345	330	4	14	255	4	14
15	415	385	4	10	335	4	10
16	480	510	4/5	12	400	5	12
17	205	185	3	16	140	3	16
18	430	415	4	6	355	4	6
In	3540	3405	35/6		2820	37	
Out	3520	3325	36		2775	37	
Total	7060	6730	71/72		5595	73	

PRESTWICK

After St Andrews, Prestwick is the most important golf course in the British Isles. It is the birthplace of the Open Championship. According to some, the links is now an anachronism, a golfing museum where blind shots, awkward stances and outrageously contoured greens still rule the day.

Prestwick Golf Club was founded in 1851. The game had been played over the hilly Ayrshire linksland for many years, but on an informal basis only. One of the first actions of the club was to persuade Tom Morris to move down from St Andrews. 'Old Tom', as he became universally known, was asked to lay out a twelve-hole course. Within nine years of its formation, Prestwick pioneered the first Open Championship. Eight people contested the inaugural event; they played the twelve holes three times on the same afternoon. The winner, Willie Park, earned himself temporary possession of a red Moroccan leather belt. Tom Morris finished runner-up; he then won the championship four times in the next seven years.

Old Tom became the game's first legendary figure, but it was his son who became golf's first truly great player. Tom Morris, jun., 'Young Tom', gained his first victory in the Open in 1868 at the age of seventeen, and won again the following year. In 1860 it had been decided that if anyone should win the championship three times in succession they would keep the belt outright. Young Tom won the 1870 Open by twelve strokes. His record total of 149 included a first round score of 47, a remarkable 'one under fours'.

No championship was held the year following Young Tom's hat trick. It was revived in 1872, but Prestwick was no longer the sole host. For the next twenty years the Open rotated between Prestwick, St Andrews and Musselburgh.

In 1883 the links was extended to eighteen holes, with Old Tom once again the architect. The Open was staged at Prestwick a year later, when Willie Campbell looked a likely winner until he took four shots to extricate himself from the fairway bunker at the 16th. In the 1925 Open, Jim Barnes, 'an American Cornishman', edged out Macdonald Smith, 'an American Scot' A large crowd had turned up hoping to cheer Smith to victory; not only did they fail to see this happen, but their unruliness also highlighted the fact that Prestwick could no longer cope adequately with the large galleries the championship had begun to attract It was Prestwick's twenty-fourth and final Open.

Even if Prestwick's halcyon days were over, important events continued to be played over the famous links. In 1934 Lawson Little won the Amateur Championship here.

Opposite: The Cardinal bunker traverses the 3rd fairway.

1

Championship	346 yards	Par 4
Medal	346	Par 4
Ladies'		

2

167 yards	Par 3
167	Par 3

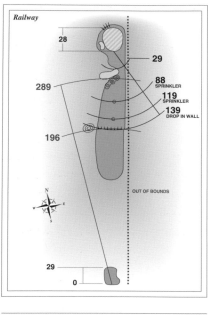

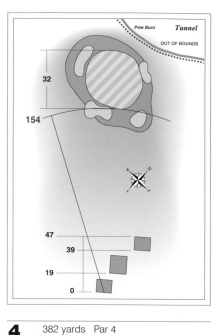

92

3

Championship	500 yards	Par 5
Medal	482	Par 5
Ladies'		

4

382 yards	Par 4
382	Par 4

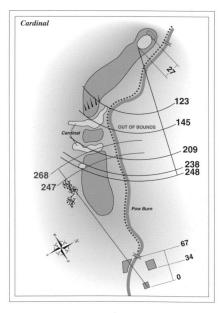

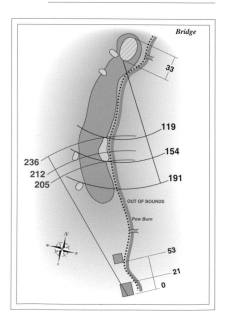

Although necessarily longer, the course today has barely altered since 1934. Indeed, the character of Prestwick has never changed: seven of the present greens formed part of the 1860 layout.

The 1st at Prestwick is a strong opening hole. This is the notorious 'Railway' with its stone wall out of bounds running all the way up the right-hand side. The 2nd is an underrated, heavily bunkered par three. Then you come to three of the most celebrated holes in golf. The par five 3rd features the vast Cardinal bunker, its steep face shored up with railway sleepers aeons before they became fashionable in America. The 4th dog-legs around the Pow Burn, and the 5th is the infamous 'Himalayas', a blind par three played over a towering sand-hill.

The loop between the 6th and 9th might never be described as vintage Prestwick, but it comprises four interesting and varied par fours. The 10th hole is, however, clearly superior to any within the loop. It is a stirring two-shotter, with a drive from an elevated tee that provides commanding views of the Isle of Arran and Ailsa Craig.

Six deep pot bunkers defend a slightly sunken green at the short 11th. The par five 12th can be reached with two hefty blows, but immediately following this is 'Sea Headrig', a formidable par four. The second part of the bumpy, hillocky 13th fairway is shared with the 16th. Putting is always an adventure, as the green is not so much two-tiered as two-storeyed. The 14th shouldn't pose too many problems; there then begins a classic finish.

The 15th sports a remarkably narrow fairway, on either side of which lurk two cavernous bunkers, and a green that rivals the 13th for its eccentricity. The 16th fairway hiccups all the way to yet another fascinating green, and at the 17th you confront the mighty 'Alps', as you tackle one of the world's great blind par fours. After an exciting downhill drive, you must play your approach over a mountainous heather-clad dune; the saucer-shaped green is situated 40 yards beyond the dune, and in between the two is the giant and seemingly magnetic Sahara bunker. The 18th eases you back towards the comforts of the 19th hole.

Hole	Championship	Medal	Par	Stroke Index	Ladies'	Par	Stroke Index
1	346	346	4	8			
2	167	167	3	18			
3	500	482	5	2			
4	382	382	4	14			
5	206	206	3	10			
6	400	362	4	4			
7	484	430	5/4	16			
8	431	431	4	6			
9	458	444	4	12			
Out	3374	3250	36/35				
10	454	454	4	1			
11	195	195	3	17			
12	513	513	5	7			
13	460	460	4	3			
14	362	362	4	9			
15	347	347	4	13			
16	298	288	4	11			
17	391	391	4	5			
18	284	284	4	15			
In	3304	3294	36				
Out	3374	3250	36/35				
Total	6678	6544	72/71				

5	Championship	206 yards	Par 3
	Medal	206	Par 3
	Ladies'		

6	400 yards	Par 4
	362	Par 4

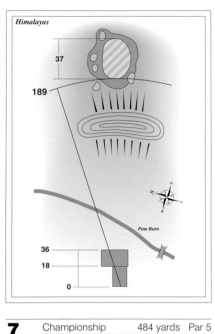

Himalayas

37
189
36
18
0

Pow Burn

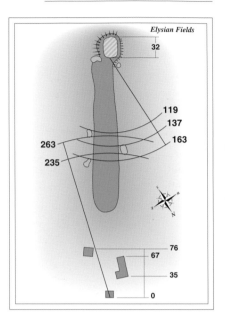

Elysian Fields

32
119
137
163
263
235
76
67
35
0

94

7	Championship	484 yards	Par 5
	Medal	430	Par 4
	Ladies'		

8	431 yards	Par 4
	431	Par 4

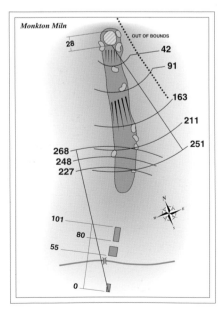

Monkton Miln

28
OUT OF BOUNDS
42
91
163
211
251
268
248
227
101
80
55
0

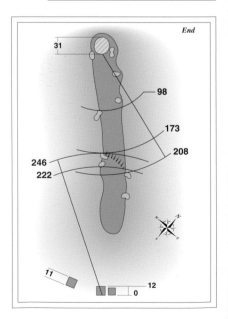

End

31
98
173
208
246
222
11
12
0

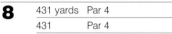

9	Championship	458 yards	Par 4
	Medal	444	Par 4
	Ladies'		

10	454 yards	Par 4
	454	Par 4

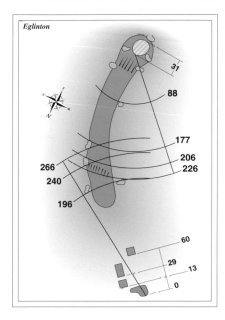

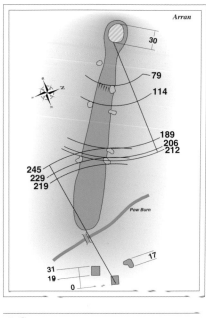

95

11	Championship	195 yards	Par 3
	Medal	195	Par 3
	Ladies'		

12	513 yards	Par 5
	513	Par 5

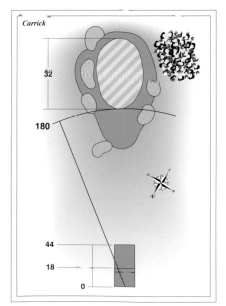

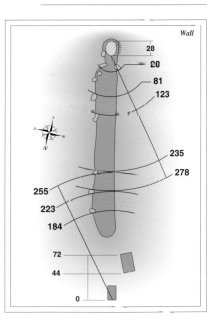

13	Championship	460 yards	Par 4
	Medal	460	Par 4
	Ladies'		

14	362 yards	Par 4
	362	Par 4

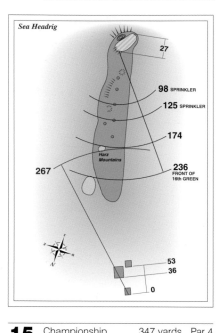

Sea Headrig

27

98 SPRINKLER

125 SPRINKLER

174

Harz Mountains

267

236 FRONT OF 16th GREEN

53
36

0

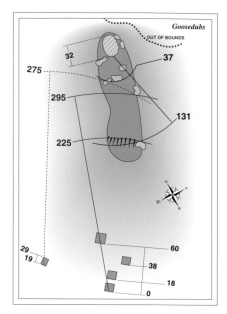

Goosedubs

OUT OF BOUNDS

32

37

275

295

131

225

29
19

60

38

18

0

96

15	Championship	347 yards	Par 4
	Medal	347	Par 4
	Ladies'		

16	298 yards	Par 4
	298	Par 4

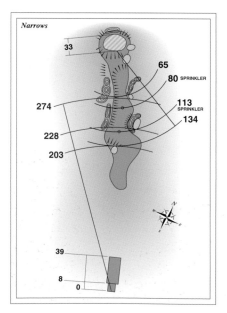

Narrows

33

65

80 SPRINKLER

274

113 SPRINKLER

134

228

203

39

8

0

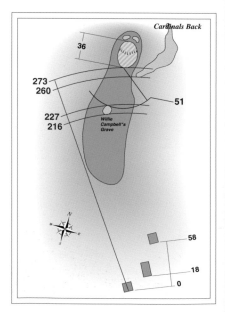

Cardinals Back

36

273
260

51

227
216

Willie Campbell's Grave

58

18

0

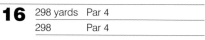

17	Championship	391 yards	Par 4	**18**	284 yards	Par 4
	Medal	391	Par 4		284	Par 4
	Ladies'					

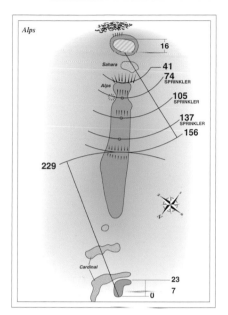

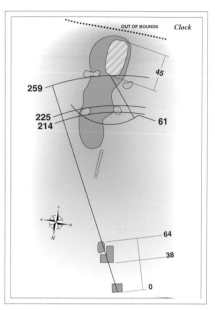

97

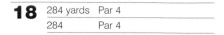

Prestwick Golf Club

PORTMARNOCK

Henry Longhurst once concluded 'Some of the Irish links, I was about to write, stand comparison with the greatest courses in the world.

They don't, they are the greatest courses in the world, not only in layout but in scenery and "atmosphere" and that indefinable something which makes you relive again and again the day you played there.'

In terms of stature in the golfing world, Portmarnock is the greatest links in Ireland. Romantics, particularly American romantics, may regard Ballybunion as more worthy of a pilgrimage – although no one outside County Kerry had heard of it thirty years ago – but Portmarnock is the true home of Irish golf. The World Cup and the Walker Cup have been played there and the Ryder Cup should have been played there.

Portmarnock is located eight miles north of Dublin. The links occupies a sandy peninsula and is surrounded by water on three sides. It was 'discovered', so legend has it, by two men in a boat. One day in 1893, W. L. Pickeman, a golf-mad Scot who was living in Dublin, gazed at the wild-looking strip of land across the estuary from Sutton and began to wonder if it might make suitable golfing country. Eventually curiosity got the better of him, and he persuaded his friend George Ross to accompany him as he rowed across the water on a 'voyage of discovery'. They found the peninsula inhabited by a small community of farmers and fishermen, but Pickeman liked what he saw. How or whether he converted the natives to golf is not clear, but Portmarnock Golf Club was soon up and running.

It seems – for records are rather sketchy – that Pickeman also played a prominent role in laying out the course. One thing we do know, thanks to a famous painting by Harry Rountree, is that at low tide it was just possible to reach the club by horse-drawn carriage, but this didn't discourage the more intrepid members from rowing across the estuary for decades to come.

Nowadays Portmarnock is hardly isolated and yet, when you stand on the 1st tee, with the water immediately off to your right, there is a sense of being marooned on an island; also, when the wind hammers across the course, or when you repeatedly stray from the fairways, Portmarnock can still seem a wild and desolate place.

But it is not an especially rugged links. If you want to play such a course when you are in Dublin, visit the nearby Island Golf Club at Donabate, a few miles further north. The dunes at Portmarnock resemble those at Muirfield: that is, they are sufficiently large to provide definition, though not so vast to afford much

Opposite: The par three 15th at Portmarnock is the most celebrated hole on the most famous links in Ireland. When the wind is blowing fiercely off the Irish Sea, it presents an extremely demanding tee-shot.

1

Championship	355 metres Par 4
Medal	340	Par 4
Ladies'		

2

	346 metres Par 4
326	Par 4

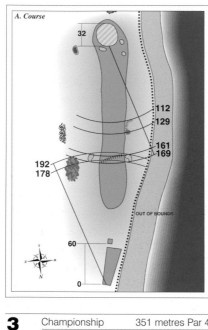

3

Championship	351 metres Par 4
Medal	345	Par 4
Ladies'		

4

	403 metres Par 4
398	Par 4

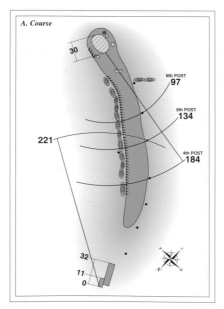

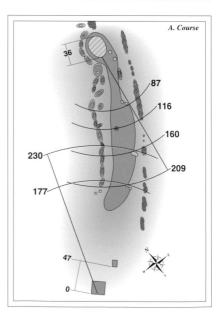

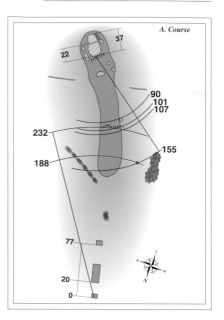

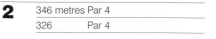

100

protection from the elements. Portmarnock, in fact, is often compared with Muirfield. Both links are regarded as very demanding – Portmarnock measures in excess of 7,100 yards from its championship tees – yet very 'fair': each has only one blind tee-shot (the 5th at Portmarnock); their fairways do not undulate significantly, thus awkward stances are the product of poor golf rather than poor fortune; and both courses are arranged in two loops of nine, ensuring that their routings maximize the potential for variety and balance in wind direction. Portmarnock is expertly bunkered – perhaps not so expertly or fearsomely as Muirfield, but as strategically soundly as any course in Ireland. The greens are invariably in excellent condition, and the green complexes mix boldness with subtlety. In short, Portmarnock has many strengths and no apparent weaknesses.

In a similar vein to Royal Troon, you set off with three par fours, each measuring less than 400 yards. An easy beginning? Yes, so long as you can avoid slicing into the aforementioned water at the 1st; provided you are not fooled by the two-tiered green at the 2nd; and assuming you stay clear of the marshy ground to the right and a steep bank of

Water lilies on a links?
A small pond lurks to the left of the fairway at the par five 6th, threatening wayward second shots.

rough to the left of the pencil-thin 3rd. The course steps up a gear at the 4th. The following five holes probably comprise the best and most interesting sequence at Portmarnock, although the two classics are undoubtedly the 14th and 15th.

A long drive up the right side of the fairway is necessary at the 4th if you are to have any prospect of reaching the green in two; don't venture too far right, however, for a series of pot bunkers patrols the edge of the rough. There are also some impressive dunes to the left of the fairway that increase in size half-way along the hole, eventually semi-circling the green and creating a wonderful natural arena. A four can prove equally elusive at the 5th, with its blind drive over a big sand-hill and an approach that must carry a ridge in front of an angled green.

The 6th is one of the world's greatest par fives: even for the professionals it is a genuine three-shot hole, and from the back tee it measures over 600 yards. As at the 4th, the right side should be favoured from the tee. There are no fairway bunkers to navigate until you near the green, but the rough is very severe. Ideally, the second shot should be positioned close to the pond (best check your Strokesaver!), leaving a pitch up to a superbly sited plateau green. Two pot

101

PORTMARNOCK

5	Championship	364 metres Par 4
	Medal	347	Par 4
	Ladies'	

6	550 metres Par 5
	533	Par 5

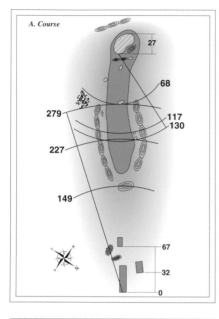

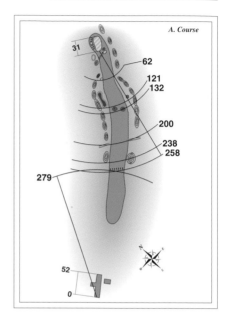

102

7	Championship	168 metres Par 3
	Medal	156	Par 3
	Ladies'	

8	364 metres Par 4
	346	Par 4

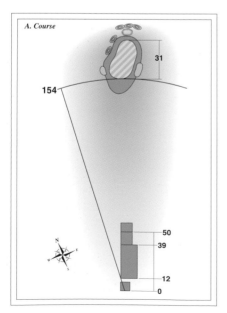

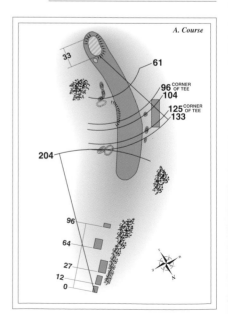

PORTMARNOCK

9	Championship	399 metres Par 4
	Medal	381	Par 4
	Ladies'	

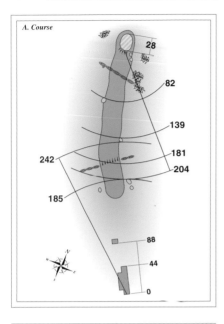

A. Course

10	341 metres Par 4
	333	Par 4

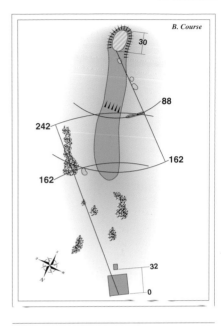

B. Course

103

11	Championship	389 metres Par 4
	Medal	379	Par 4
	Ladies'	

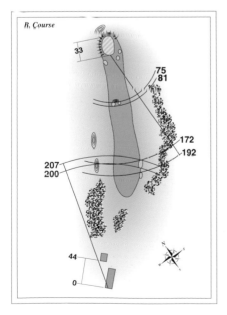

B. Course

12	139 metres Par 3
	129	Par 3

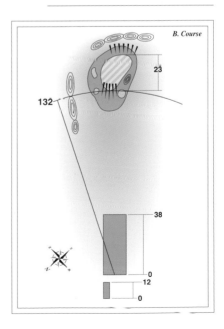

B. Course

13

Championship	516 metres	Par 5
Medal	502	Par 5
Ladies'		

14

	350 metres	Par 4
	343	Par 4

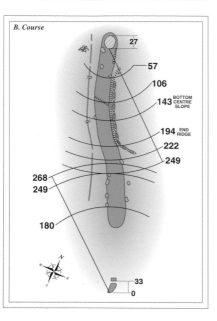

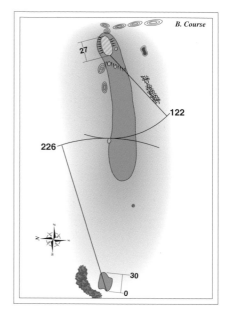

15

Championship	173 metres	Par 3
Medal	167	Par 3
Ladies'		

16

	480 metres	Par 5
	470	Par 5

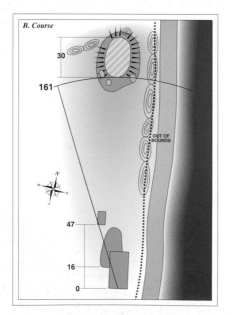

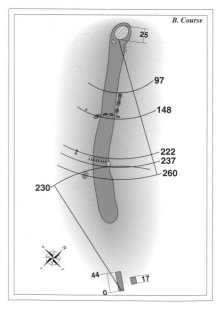

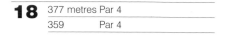

PORTMARNOCK

17

Championship	429 metres Par 4
Medal	397	Par 4
Ladies'	

18

377 metres Par 4
359	Par 4

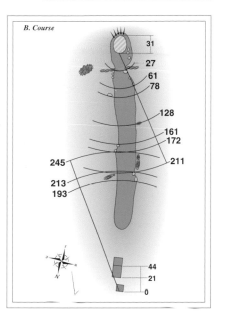

B. Course

31
27
61
78
128
161
172
245
211
213
193

44
21
0

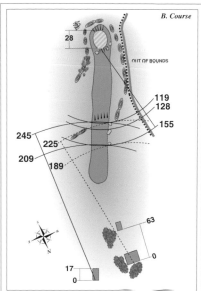

B. Course

28
OUT OF BOUNDS
119
128
155
245
225
209
189
63
0
17
0

105

PORTMARNOCK
GOLF CLUB

1 · 2 · 3 · 4 · 5 · 6 · 7 · 8 · 9 · 10 · 11 · 12 · 13 · 14 · 15 · 16 · 17 · 18

PRACTICE GROUND

CLUBHOUSE

○ **CHAMPIONSHIP COURSE**

○ **C. COURSE**

One final test: a golfer faces an awkward downhill chip from the rough beside the 18th green.

106

bunkers and a large grass bunker defend its entrance.

Next comes an attractive par three played from an elevated tee. The green at the 7th blends very naturally into the surrounding dunes. The 8th, though, is surely the most underrated hole at Portmarnock. The fairway swings to the left, and while it is important to try and find the right half of it with your drive, it is even more vital that you hit the target with your second. The green is more table-shaped than plateaued; a deep bunker guards the front left approach (needless to say, the pin is often tucked immediately behind it) and there are sharp fall-aways to the back and right. If you do miss the green at the 8th, you will face some very difficult chipping.

By comparison, the 9th is an uneventful march back towards the clubhouse. The 10th, however, is quite similar to the 8th. It is a straighter hole, but again there is a steep fall off to the right of the green, with a cunningly placed bunker threatening the approach – this time looming just short and right of the putting surface.

The 11th is often played directly into the wind and can be the hardest hole on the course, while the par three 12th might be described as dangerously seductive. It only requires a short iron to find what appears to be a reasonably sized green, beautifully framed by dunes. True, the green isn't small, but it tilts dramatically from back to front, making putting extremely tricky. Yawning bunkers eat into either side of the front, there is a hidden depression at the back and another bunker lurks half-way up the green to the left – more fives than twos are recorded at this hole.

Two similar par fives, the 13th and 16th, top and tail Portmarnock's most famous duo; they run in the same direction. The 13th is the stronger hole, since it is slightly longer and, unlike the 16th, you drive from a spectacular tee overlooking the sea and an inviting beach.

The 14th bristles with character. Henry Cotton regarded it as one of the greatest two-shot holes in golf. You head towards the sea along a gently curving, tumbling fairway; a pair of cross bunkers have been carved into the face of a rise in the fairway some 20 yards short of the green, although they appear to be much closer from the fairway. As for the green, it occupies a narrow shelf and is surrounded by little humps and hollows. The 15th has attracted equally exalted praise. Ben Crenshaw, a winner of the Irish Open at Portmarnock, described it as 'one of the greatest short holes on Earth', and Arnold Palmer was of the same opinion. It is played parallel to the shore; if the wind is whipping in off the Irish Sea, you may have to start your tee-shot out over the beach – an alarming prospect. The shot is all carry, as there is no fairway to speak of; moreover, the green is shaped like an inverted saucer and is jealously protected by three bunkers … but it is a beautiful hole!

For all the charm of the 14th and 15th, it is the 17th that has tended to determine the outcome of the many tournaments held at Portmarnock. It is a long and brutally tough par four. The route to the green is fraught with danger, for you must somehow thread a long iron shot – or more likely a wood – between a minefield of bunkers. The 17th green is also partially concealed by mounds, but the 18th is quite different. This is a very elegant closing hole, the principal feature being the handsome approach which is played to a large amphitheatre green – a perfect golfing stage. Among the great champions who have taken a bow on the 18th green are Palmer and Sam Snead (when winning the 1960 World Cup for America), the US Walker Cup team after their emphatic triumph in 1991 and an illustrious quartet of European golfers, all of whom captured Irish Open titles on the links: Seve Ballesteros, Bernhard Langer, Ian Woosnam and José-Maria Olazabal.

Hole	Championship	Medal	Par	Stroke Index	Ladies'	Par	Stroke Index
1	355	340	4	13			
2	346	326	4	15			
3	351	345	4	11			
4	403	398	4	1			
5	364	347	4	5			
6	550	533	5	9			
7	168	150	3	17			
8	364	346	4	7			
9	399	381	4	3			
Out	3300	3172	36				
10	341	333	4	8			
11	389	379	4	2			
12	139	129	3	18			
13	516	502	5	14			
14	350	343	4	6			
15	173	167	3	12			
16	480	470	5	16			
17	429	397	4	4			
18	377	359	4	10			
In	3194	3079	36				
Out	3300	3172	36				
Total	6494	6251	72				

ROYAL COUNTY DOWN

IF AUGUSTA IS 'THE CATHEDRAL IN THE PINES' AND CYPRESS POINT 'THE SISTINE CHAPEL OF GOLF', WHAT EPITHET COULD POSSIBLY DO JUSTICE TO NEWCASTLE, TO THE GOLFING SHRINE THAT IS ROYAL COUNTY DOWN?

Of all the world's great golf destinations, Newcastle was the acknowledged favourite of the esteemed English golf writer Peter Dobereiner, who thought it 'exhilarating, even without a club in your hand'. As for the degree of challenge presented by the links, Dobereiner's American counterpart, Herbert Warren Wind, declared it to be 'the sternest examination in golf I have ever taken'. At one time or another, Royal County Down has been adjudged more beautiful than Turnberry, more spectacular than Ballybunion, more natural and more charming than Royal Dornoch and more punishing than Carnoustie.

The golf, then, is extraordinary. The accompanying scenery adds a touch of majesty and romance. Newcastle is where, in the immortal words of Percy French, 'the Mountains of Mourne sweep down to the sea'. Soaring, smoky blue peaks and a glistening turquoise ocean – or, when the elements are stirred, forbidding mist-covered mountains and a wild, turbulent sea. Situated some 30 miles south of Belfast and fringed by the impressive sweep of Dundrum Bay, here is where towering sand-hills appear wrapped in bright yellow gorse during spring and early summer and in September are liberally sprinkled with purple heather. On such a stage and amid such splendour weave the emerald fairways of Royal County Down. Newcastle may be the greatest links on earth.

Open any book entitled *Great Golf Courses of the World* and chances are that it will include a photograph of Royal County Down – probably an image taken from the top of the hill at the 9th or from the championship tee of the 4th. The first time you see such a picture you fall immediately under the spell, and you make a vow: 'one day I will stand on that exact spot and drink in that view'.

In fact, pictures seldom do the scene justice. For one thing, the Mountains of Mourne are much closer and rise far more dramatically than people imagine; also, the colours are even more vivid than the best tricks a modern camera can effect.

So the scenery and the setting can exceed expectations, but is the golf links really 'more beautiful than Turnberry' and 'more spectacular than Ballybunion'? ... Even on a dull day when clouds envelop the mountains and hills, Royal County Down is a stunning place. This is because the golf course itself is stunning. There is no famous lighthouse and no Ailsa Craig sitting off the coast of Dundrum Bay, nor is there a sequence of oceanside holes like the 4th to the 10th at Turnberry or ones that resemble the rollercoasting 11th and 17th at

---

Opposite: Could this be the greatest links on earth? Royal County Down has it all – including, when the elements are stirred, 'forbidding mist-covered mountains and a wild, turbulent sea'.

1	Championship	506 yards	Par 5
	Medal	502	Par 5
	Ladies'	482	Par 5

2	421 yards	Par 4
	385	Par 4
	344	Par 4

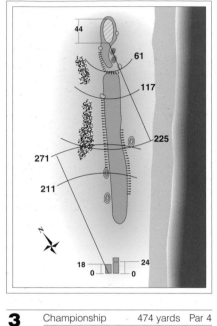

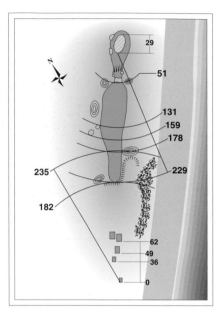

110

3	Championship	474 yards	Par 4
	Medal	474	Par 4
	Ladies'	435	Par 5

4	212 yards	Par 3
	212	Par 3
	144	Par 3

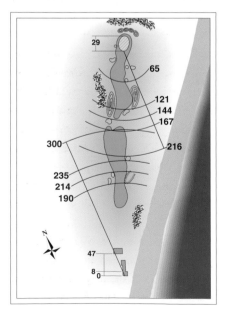

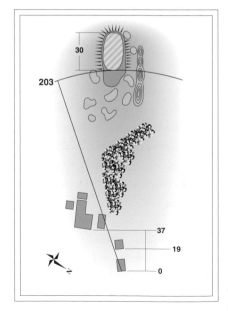

The view from the championship tee at the 3rd. Royal County Down has many formidable two-shot holes, but none is more challenging than the 3rd.

Ballybunion, but Newcastle doesn't want for them. It has several holes capable of sending the pulse into overdrive.

After hearing the crash of the sea as you walk along the first and second fairways, pause on the very back tee of the 3rd: you are as close to the ocean as you could ever wish to be on a golf course, and what a thrilling hole confronts you! The 3rd at Royal County Down has featured in many a panel's 'greatest eighteen holes'. For its entire length it runs parallel to the shore and is distinguished by an ever-narrowing split-level fairway – when the wind is against, it is a ferociously difficult par four. Then, honouring that vow, climb to the top tee of the 4th to savour one of the world's finest short holes, where a sea of heather and gorse (never mind ten bunkers!) awaits the miss-hit shot; be teased by the sharply dog-legging 5th; enjoy the

wonderful sea views from the 6th tee; and permit your jaw to drop with dignity at the 9th. At this instant you will be completing what no less a judge than Tom Watson reckons to be 'as fine a nine holes as I have ever played'. The five-time Open champion, like everyone, of course, was particularly struck by the 9th. Here is where an exhilarating uphill tee-shot must be targeted at the mighty peak of Slieve Donard – 'undisputed king' of the Mountains of Mourne and followed (assuming the drive has successfully flown the hill and descended into the valley below) by a long second to a plateau green. On the back nine, clamber up the giant hill at the 11th to experience the relief of seeing your ball nestling safely in the middle of the fairway; prepare to be amazed by the character and challenge of the long, curving 13th, with its splendid amphitheatre green –

5

Championship	438 yards	Par 4
Medal	416	Par 4
Ladies'	394	Par 4

6

396 yards	Par 4
369	Par 4
338	Par 5

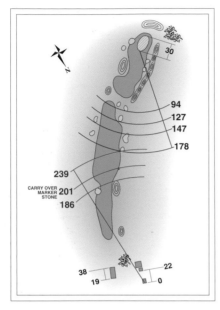

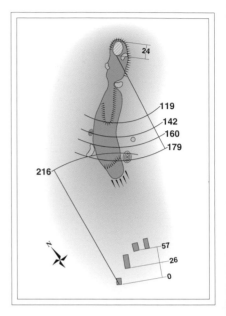

7

Championship	145 yards	Par 3
Medal	135	Par 3
Ladies'	116	Par 3

8

429 yards	Par 4
425	Par 4
403	Par 5

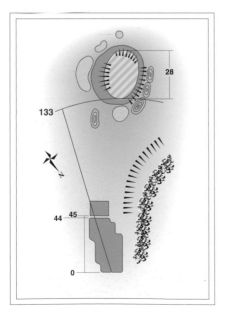

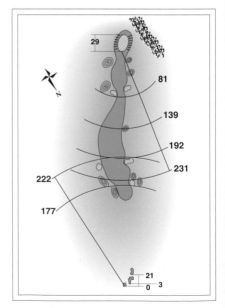

9	Championship	486 yards	Par 5
	Medal	425	Par 4
	Ladies'	424	Par 5

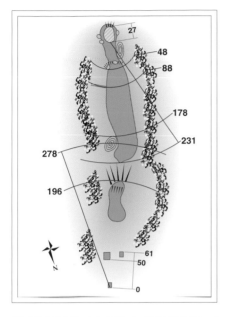

10	197 yards	Par 3
	189	Par 3
	173	Par 3

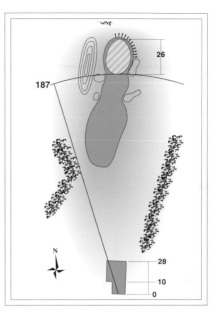

113

11	Championship	438 yards	Par 4
	Medal	425	Par 4
	Ladies'	384	Par 4

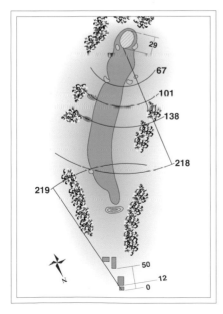

12	525 yards	Par 5
	479	Par 5
	456	Par 5

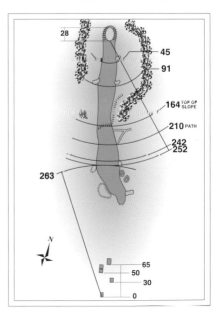

13	Championship	443 yards	Par 4
	Medal	421	Par 4
	Ladies'	406	Par 5

14	213 yards	Par 3
	203	Par 3
	195	Par 3

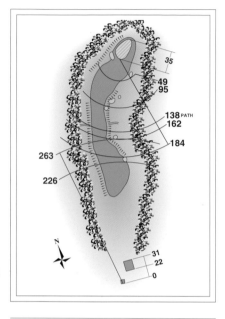

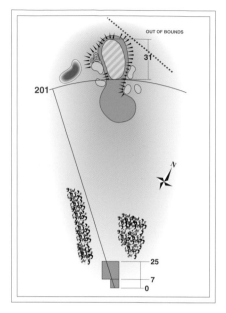

15	Championship	464 yards	Par 4
	Medal	450	Par 4
	Ladies'	407	Par 5

16	276 yards	Par 4
	265	Par 4
	241	Par 4

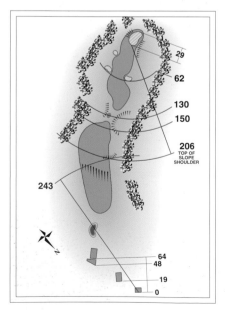

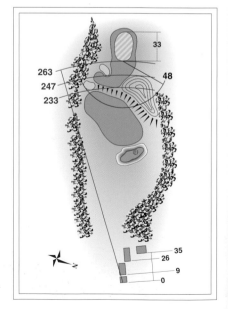

17	Championship	427 yards	Par 4
	Medal	400	Par 4
	Ladies'	369	Par 4

18	547 yards	Par 4
	547	Par 4
	479	Par 5

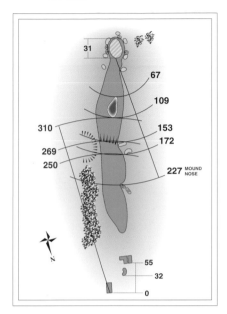

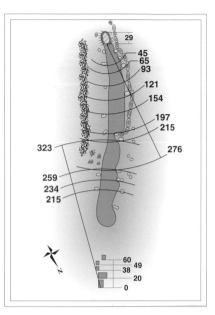

THE ROYAL
COUNTY DOWN
GOLF CLUB

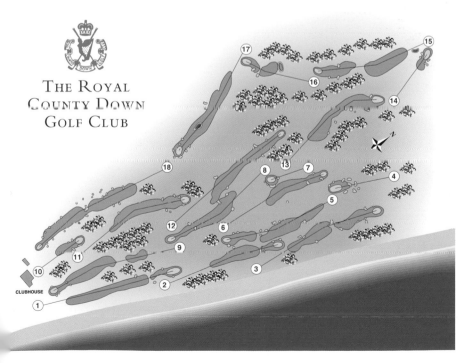

CLUBHOUSE

The exhilarating 9th brings to a dramatic conclusion what Tom Watson once described as
'as fine a nine holes as I have ever played'.

another of the links' world famous two-shotters; dare to go for the flag at the precipice-style 15th and attempt to drive the green at the chasmic 16th!

The sand-hills at Newcastle are not merely exceptionally rugged, but (unlike Ballybunion and Turnberry) they are attractively cloaked in gorse and heather. And then there are the extraordinarily distinctive bunkers with their steep faces framed by wild tussocky grasses. Yes, all very beautiful and very spectacular: in the words of Bernard Darwin, 'the kind of golf that people play in their most ecstatic dreams'.

What of the claim that Royal County Down is 'more natural and more charming than Royal Dornoch'? ... Well, Newcastle undoubtedly has mesmeric qualities. Sir Peter Allen, a lifelong admirer of the links, once described Slieve Donard as a 'perpetual gazingstock' and, sure enough, when you play the course for the first time, it is tempting to walk the first three fairways backwards, so enchanting is the view over your shoulder. The full Ancient Mariner treatment comes with the next tee-shot.

As befits a golf course orig-inally laid out by Old Tom Morris, there are many charming features of the design and many charming holes. The 2nd is one obvious example, with its central fairway bunker seemingly wedged between two large sand-dunes; the short, impish 7th is another, as is the almost eccentric shape of the 13th.

The notorious blind shots at Newcastle could also be described as both

charming and eccentric. Much is made of them (and the comments are usually negative), but as they are all tee-shots, and none is at a par three, it could be argued that their effect on play is limited. In any event, the first time you play at Newcastle you are likely to so spellbound, you will want to forgive its every blemish, including the blindness, and once you get to know the course, the blindness becomes irrelevant. As Tommy Armour once famously put it, 'There is nothing blind to any man with a memory.'

It is said that the ghost of Old Tom still wanders the fairways and haunts the rough at Royal County Down. Perhaps the club should have paid him a little more than four guineas for his work! Of course, what such a modest fee indicates is that there was not a great deal Old Tom felt he needed to do. One only has to reflect on the superb collection of natural green sites to appreciate that Mother Nature was the principal architect at Newcastle.

Finally, is Royal County Down truly 'more punishing than Carnoustie'? ... Measuring almost 7,000 yards from the championship tees, it is of a similar length. The finishing three holes are not as tough as those on the famous Scottish links (they couldn't be). Whether those characterful tussock-faced bunkers – there are approximately 130 in total – are as destructive as the vast cavernous pots of Carnoustie is difficult to judge. But, certainly, its fairways are far more undulating and generally narrower. Moreover, the average size of the greens at Newcastle is markedly smaller; indeed, the putting

surfaces are frequently dwarfed by the surrounding dunes and, with the exception of the 17th, they are not inclined to gather the ball. Those blind shots are none too friendly either!

This shouldn't lead one to the conclusion that Newcastle is overly penal. There are some subtle, even graceful, holes, such as the very underrated 8th and the beautifully flowing 12th, and many that are highly strategic in nature. When all is said and done, perhaps you cannot fairly compare Royal County Down with any other of the world's great links, for it is too different, too special. It is, to adopt a great 'Irishism', so very unique.

Hole	Championship	Medal	Par	Stroke Index	Ladies'	Par	Stroke Index
1	506	502	5	13	482	5	13
2	421	385	4	9	344	4	9
3	474	474	4	3	435	5	3
4	212	212	3	15	144	3	15
5	438	416	4	7	394	4	7
6	396	369	4	11	338	4	11
7	145	135	3	17	116	3	17
8	429	425	4	1	403	5	1
9	486	425	5/4	5	424	5	5
Out	3507	3343	36/35		3080	38	
10	197	189	3	14	173	3	14
11	438	425	4	8	384	4	8
12	525	479	5	10	456	5	10
13	443	421	4	2	406	5	2
14	213	203	3	12	195	3	12
15	464	450	4	4	407	5	4
16	276	265	4	18	241	4	18
17	427	400	4	16	369	4	16
18	547	547	5	6	479	5	6
In	3530	3379	36		3110	38	
Out	3507	3343	36/35		3080	38	
Total	7037	6722	72/71		6190	76	

BALLYLIFFIN (GLASHEDY)

CLOSE YOUR EYES AND THINK OF DONEGAL. IMAGINE A SECRET PLACE WITH A THOUSAND ACRES OF CLASSIC GOLFING TERRAIN, AN ENDLESS RANGE OF SAND-DUNES HIDDEN FROM THE OUTSIDE WORLD BY TOWERING MOUNTAINS AND HEATHER-CLAD HILLS, WHERE THE ONLY OTHER BOUNDARY IS A SOMETIMES STORMY, SOMETIMES SPARKLING ATLANTIC OCEAN.

Ballyliffin enjoys such a setting. Ireland's most northern golf club is situated near Malin Head on Donegal's Inishowen Peninsula. The links hugs the shore beside Pollan Bay and overlooks a vast stretch of sand. At one end of the bay are the ruins of Carrickabraghy Castle, and at the other the small village of Ballyliffin nestling beneath the slopes of Binion Hill. Just off the coast, and surveying everything, is Glashedy Rock, Ballyliffin's own Ailsa Craig.

A golfing paradise? No doubt if this were the east coast of Scotland, the game would have been played here for centuries. In fact, golf didn't come to Ballyliffin until after the Second World War, and even then it began inauspiciously. In 1947 a crude nine-hole course was laid out on poor ground close to the village. A few dedicated members cut the greens and several dedicated sheep tended the fairways. Little changed for more than twenty years, until the club resolved to purchase some of those endless acres of classic golfing terrain.

The par three 7th on the Glashedy Links is played from the top of an enormous sand-hill down to a green sited 100 feet below.

Ballyliffin's first eighteen-hole links was indeed a classic. Not too many people outside Ballyliffin got to hear about it, but it was a classic nonetheless. The most distinctive feature of the course was its amazing rippling fairways – the handiwork, of course, of Mother Nature.

Another twenty years slipped by until, one sunny day in June 1993, a helicopter landed beside the clubhouse and out jumped Nick Faldo. The then reigning British Open champion dropped in en route to defending his Irish Open title at Mount Juliet. He played eighteen holes with his friends, was wined and dined in true Donegal fashion and left raving about those rippling fairways and generally singing Ballyliffin's praises from the hilltops. Faldo promised he would return and, sure enough, within three years (and as the reigning Masters champion), he did. By which time Ballyliffin had thirty-six holes.

In August 1995 the Glashedy Links was unveiled. Designed by Tom Craddock and Pat Ruddy, the club's

Opposite: Glashedy Rock, Ballyliffin's version of Ailsa Craig, provides a stunning backcloth to the 13th hole, a massive, rollercoasting par five.

1	Championship	426 yards	Par 4
	Medal	420	Par 4
	Ladies'	325	Par 4

2	432 yards	Par 4
	423	Par 4
	350	Par 4

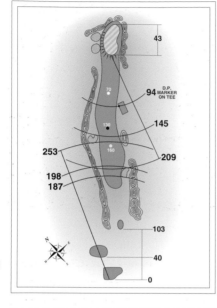

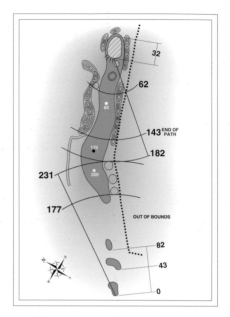

3	Championship	428 yards	Par 4
	Medal	408	Par 4
	Ladies'	336	Par 4

4	479 yards	Par 5
	476	Par 5
	426	Par 5

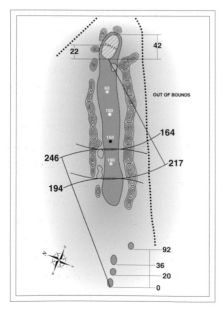

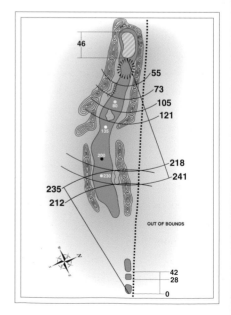

The downhill par 3 14th is one of the most exhilarating short holes in Irish golf.

second eighteen holes have been carved out of predominantly more rugged duneland beyond the (now named) Old Links. Since the day it opened, the new course has been showered with accolades. The proverbial ribbon was cut by Declan Howley, President of the Golfing Union of Ireland, and in his words, 'It is a truly wonderful links. Rarely do you ever see a course without a weak hole or two, and here we have no weak holes. I don't think the club should wait too long before bidding for a championship event.' In November 1996 *Golf World* magazine rated the Glashedy Links 'the best new links in Ireland' and 'one of the top six new courses in the British Isles', while in a recent article for a leading American publication, John Hopkins, golf correspondent, compared Ballyliffin favourably with the mighty Ballybunion (see page 127).

The Glashedy Links fits harmoniously into its landscape and, in a manner reminiscent of Royal Birkdale, the fairways flow along natural valleys beneath the dunes. It has been built on an heroic scale with vast undulating greens – several of which are two-tiered – and deep revetted bunkers. As the links can be stretched to 7,102 yards, it presents a formidable (and potentially overwhelming) challenge.

The course sets off very boldly with three mighty par fours, each measuring in excess of 420 yards from the back tees. Their combined effect is to lead the golfer away from the clubhouse and deep into the dunes. The green at the 1st is perched, rather enticingly, between two large sandhills. The threat of hitting out of bounds looms at the 2nd – as does an alarmingly cavernous bunker in front of the green – and the landing area appears painfully narrow from the elevated tee at the 3rd.

5

Championship	177 yards	Par 3
Medal	173	Par 3
Ladies'	143	Par 3

6

361 yards	Par 4
348	Par 4
305	Par 4

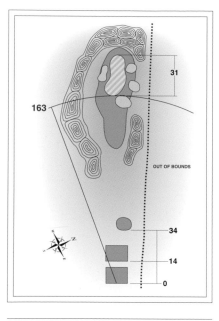

31
163
OUT OF BOUNDS
34
14
0

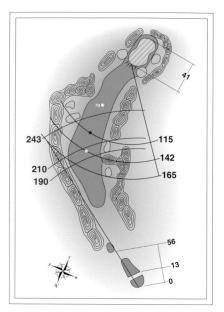

41
70
243
115
142
210
190
165
56
13
0

122

7

Championship	174 yards	Par 3
Medal	162	Par 3
Ladies'	116	Par 3

8

422 yards	Par 4
419	Par 4
337	Par 4

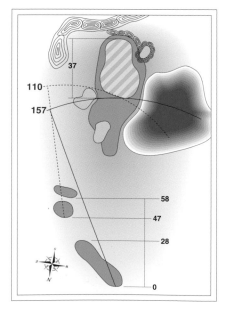

37
110
157
58
47
28
0

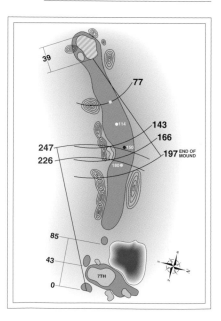

39
77
114
143
166
247
150
197 END OF MOUND
226
180
85
43
0
7TH

9

Championship	382 yards	Par 4
Medal	372	Par 4
Ladies'	313	Par 4

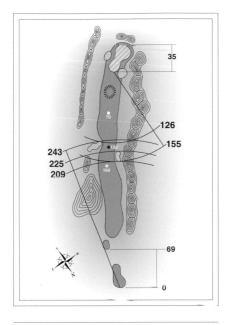

10

397 yards	Par 4
376	Par 4
349	Par 4

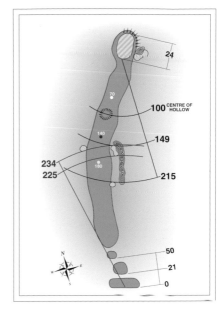

123

11

Championship	419 yards	Par 4
Medal	379	Par 4
Ladies'	316	Par 4

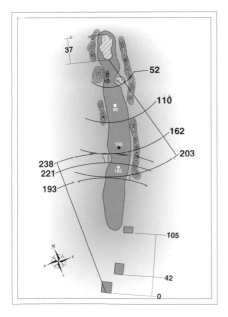

12

448 yards	Par 4
414	Par 4
391	Par 4

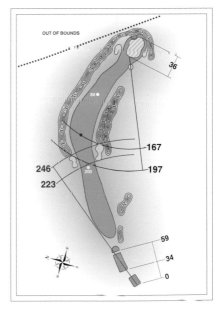

13	Championship	572 yards	Par 5
	Medal	564	Par 5
	Ladies'	474	Par 5

14	159 yards	Par 3
	135	Par 3
	110	Par 3

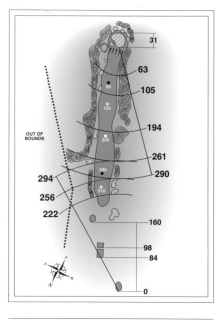

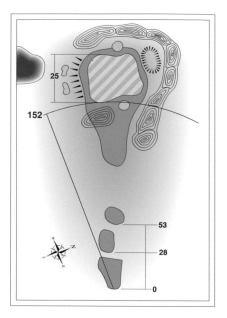

15	Championship	440 yards	Par 4
	Medal	430	Par 4
	Ladies'	359	Par 4

16	426 yards	Par 4
	416	Par 4
	389	Par 4

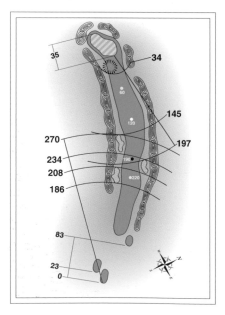

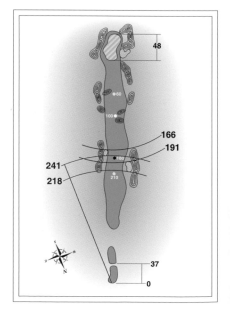

17	Championship	549 yards	Par 5
	Medal	542	Par 5
	Ladies'	465	Par 5

18	411 yards	Par 4
	380	Par 4
	357	Par 4

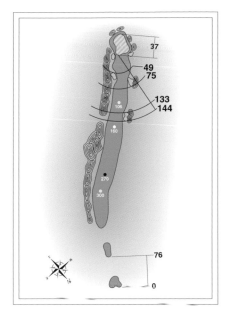

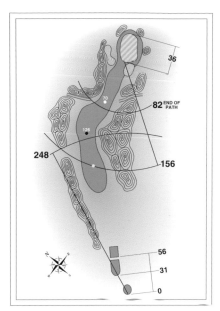

125

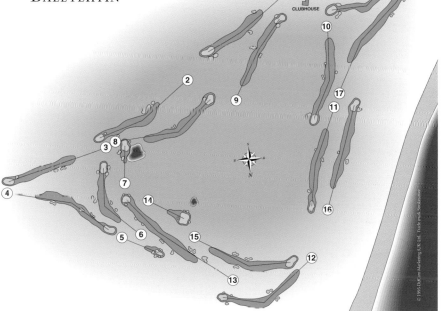

BALLYLIFFIN

'The Dornoch of Ireland' or 'the Ballybunion of the North'? Ballyliffin has thirty-six holes:
the classic, charming Old Links and the rugged majestic new Glashedy Links.

The dunes increase in size as you approach the dog-leg at the par five 4th and, just as the fairway swings to the right and a cross bunker reveals itself, Glashedy Rock comes fully into view directly behind the green. It is a magical moment.

Glashedy becomes an almost constant companion for the remainder of the round. It dominates the backdrop to the 5th, the first of the short holes. Stand on the tee of this hole on a lovely summer's evening with the sun reflecting off the sea and you may think Ballyliffin the most heavenly place on earth … at least, until your ball plummets into one of a series of deep bunkers that practically encircle the green. The 6th is perhaps the most gentle of the par fours. After a vertigo-inducing

tee-shot at the 7th, where you play from the top of an enormous sand-hill to a green sited almost 100 feet below, the course flows gracefully back to the clubhouse.

Each of the holes on the Glashedy Links has been given a Gaelic name. Thus you tee off with 'Creig a'Bhainne' (the 1st), return to the clubhouse via 'Bárr na Gaoithe' (the 9th), set off again along 'Stúca Buí' (the 10th) and sink your final putt on the green of 'Gort na Móna' (the 18th).

The second nine on the Glashedy Links is the longer and tougher of the two halves. Holes 10 and 11 weave a path through the Old Links and head back out towards the higher, wilder duneland behind the great sand-hill. Now begins a

marvellous sequence of holes: the 12th is a fearsome dog-leg right, probably the most difficult two-shotter of the entire round, and the 13th a massive par five – uphill and breathtaking in both senses of the word. The fairway at this hole is framed by huge sand-dunes and sweeps uphill in dramatic rollercoasting fashion, eventually meeting up with a severely sloping green that is defended by a mischievous assortment of bunkers. Five is a very good score at the 13th! The seductive 14th is arguably the best of the short holes – like the 5th it affords stunning views of the ocean and Glashedy Rock. The 15th is the longest of the par fours. It is another of the Glashedy Links' sweeping dog legs and calls for a downhill drive followed by a searching second to a raised green.

From the 16th tee, the course returns towards the clubhouse. It is an examining and potentially perilous journey home: an arrow-straight par four into the prevailing wind, a second par five that seems to stretch forever and a day and, finally, a superb finishing hole. The 18th is a classic right-angled dog leg, where the approach must be threaded along a corridor of sentinel-like dunes and between two reverted bunkers – miss the green to the left or right and you may have to display your short game skills in front of a packed clubhouse.

While some may consider it a little premature to judge the quality of the new course, no one can deny that the Glashedy Links is both beautiful and dramatic. There seems every possibility that it will one day take its place alongside Royal Portrush and Royal County Down as one of the three great links courses in the North of Ireland.

'I have found the new Ballybunion,' enthused John Hopkins, in the lengthy article he provided for *Links* magazine. 'Its name is Ballyliffin and, like Ballybunion, it has two links courses. One, the Old Links, looks so natural it could have been laid out hundreds of years ago; the other, the Glashedy Links, opened in 1995 and may be the best new links course to have been built this century. It is good enough to stage the British Open.' Agreed. If only it were situated on the east coast of Scotland.

Hole	Championship	Medal	Par	Stroke Index	Ladies'	Par	Stroke Index
1	426	420	4	11	325	4	11
2	432	423	4	7	350	4	7
3	428	408	4	2	336	4	2
4	479	476	5	13	426	5	13
5	177	173	3	15	143	3	15
6	361	348	4	18	305	4	18
7	174	162	0	9	116	3	9
8	422	419	4	4	337	4	4
9	382	372	4	6	313	4	6
Out	3281	3201	35		2651	35	
10	397	376	4	8	349	4	8
11	419	379	4	14	316	4	14
12	448	414	4	3	391	4	3
13	572	564	5	10	474	5	10
14	159	135	3	17	110	3	17
15	440	430	4	1	359	4	1
16	426	416	4	5	389	4	5
17	549	542	5	12	465	5	12
18	411	380	4	16	357	4	16
In	3821	3636	37		3210	37	
Out	3281	3201	35		2651	35	
Total	7102	6837	72		5861	72	

LAHINCH

I**N 1892 OFFICERS OF THE FAMOUS BLACK WATCH REGIMENT STATIONED IN LIMERICK CAME UPON A VAST WILDERNESS OF DUNELAND TWO MILES FROM THE SPECTACULAR CLIFFS OF MOHER.**

Being good Scotsmen, they knew at once that they had found the perfect terrain for a golf links. On Good Friday 1893, Lahinch Golf Club was duly founded.

The obvious choice as architect was Old Tom Morris of St Andrews. He accepted the challenge, but other than laying out the tees and greens, he felt there was little he could do. He commented: 'I consider the links is as fine a natural course as it has ever been my good fortune to play over.' More praise was to follow. In 1927 Dr Alister Mackenzie was invited to make a number of adjustments to the links. On completion he remarked, 'Lahinch will make the finest and most popular course that I, or I believe anyone else, ever constructed.' Not perhaps the most modest statement ever made, but coming from a man who would very shortly design Cypress Point on the Monterey Peninsula and later help to create the legendary Augusta, it can hardly be taken lightly.

In fact, Mackenzie was not too wide of the mark. Lahinch is undoubtedly one of the world's classic links. It has all the ingredients of greatness: a glorious setting, a rich history, superb natural terrain and, where man has 'intervened', it has been through the hand of an outstanding architect. It also has a pair of notorious blind holes, a ruined castle and goats that roam freely on the dunes.

Lahinch has much in common with the Old Course at Ballybunion. The sand-hills are similarly huge (if not as extensive) and on both links the golfer is sent on an exhilarating rollercoaster journey through the dunes and along the edge of the Atlantic Ocean – breathtaking golf. There is an abundance of natural green sites, with several of the greens sitting atop plateaux and others nestling slightly below the level of the fairway. In a hole-by-hole analysis, Lahinch compares favourably with Ballybunion, until the 15th hole at least. The two areas where golf course critics find fault with Lahinch are in its closing holes and in the two blind holes, 'Klondyke' (the 5th) and 'The Dell' (the 6th).

What is considered so ordinary about the last four holes? The player may have emerged from the most rugged part of the links, but the fairways and greens retain much of their character. With two big par fours either side of a downhill par three, and a 520-yard par five finishing hole, there is both challenge and variety in the closing stretch at Lahinch.

The 5th and 6th are the only holes that Mackenzie was forbidden to touch. Having won four British Open Championships at Prestwick, Old Tom clearly relished the blind shot and in the 1890s they were, to adopt a late 19th-

LAHINCH

1	Championship	352 metres Par 4
	Medal	343	Par 4
	Ladies'	335	Par 5

2	468 metres Par 5
	455	Par 5
	421	Par 5

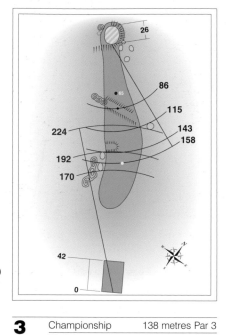

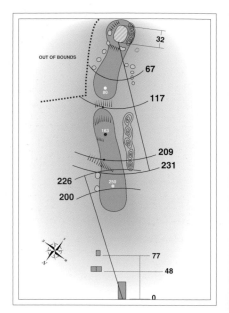

3	Championship	138 metres Par 3
	Medal	135	Par 3
	Ladies'	110	Par 3

4	391 metres Par 4
	380	Par 4
	314	Par 5

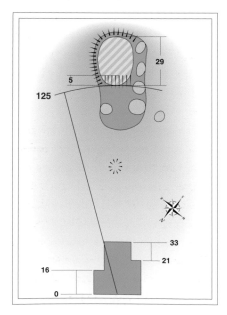

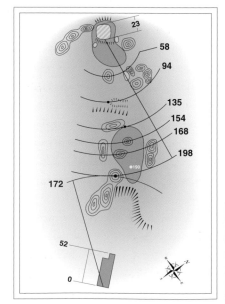

The par three 6th, 'The Dell', is a hole you either love or hate. Its pencil-thin green is wedged between two large dunes and is completely invisible from the tee.

century architectural term, 'all the rage'. Not too many people quibble with the 5th – after all, it is a par five – but the 6th is a blind par three and as such has the modernists tearing their hair out. Presumably the same people must wince at the prospect of confronting the 'Cardinal' (3rd), 'Himalayas' (5th) and 'The Alps' (17th) at Prestwick? Where is their sprit of adventure and their sense of history? The American writer Herbert Warren Wind summed it up nicely when he wrote of the 5th and 6th at Lahinch, 'These may be defective holes in this day and age but at Lahinch they are absolutely right. two living museum pieces, two perfect Irish holes.'

The 1st tee is situated immediately adjacent to the clubhouse, which can be either reassuring or very intimidating. The opening drive is uphill, making the hole play longer than the card suggests,

and the approach is to a table green with a serious fall away, as well as two bunkers to the right: a four is a good start. The par five 2nd encourages you to open your shoulders, as it runs downhill back towards the clubhouse. Then there is a rather plain-looking short hole. But beware – the 3rd green is another with sharp fall-aways, this time to the back and left, while (hidden from the tee) at the front and right of the green are no fewer than six pot bunkers.

The 4th is the first of Lahinch's great holes. For its entire length it runs parallel to the shore and yet is as challenging as it is scenic. First you must hit a good drive to reach the top of an enormous hill, then on a higher level and in a world of prodigious sand-hills, you play over a wilderness of rough to a beautifully situated green. Now comes the dastardly duo, 'Klondyke' and 'The Dell'.

5

Championship	441 metres Par 5
Medal	435	Par 5
Ladies'	380	Par 5

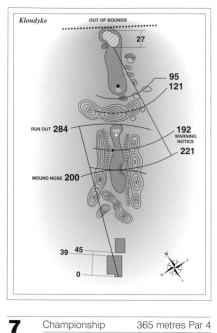

Klondyke

OUT OF BOUNDS

27

95
121

70

RUN OUT 284

192
WARNING
NOTICE

162

221

MOUND NOSE 200

39 45

0

N

6

| 142 metres Par 3 |
| 137 | Par 3 |
| 132 | Par 3 |

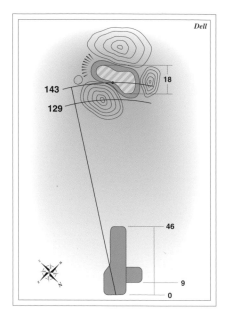

Dell

18

143

129

46

9

0

7

Championship	365 metres Par 4
Medal	350	Par 4
Ladies'	227	Par 4

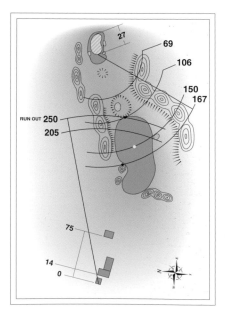

27

69

106

150
167

RUN OUT 250

205

75

14
0

8

| 320 metres Par 4 |
| 318 | Par 4 |
| 271 | Par 4 |

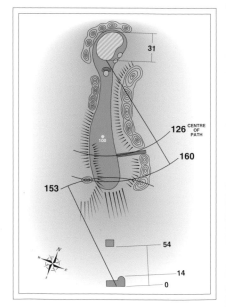

31

126 CENTRE
OF
PATH

100

160

153

54

14

0

9	Championship	351 metres Par 4
	Medal	322	Par 4
	Ladies'	226	Par 4

10	412 metres Par 4
	385	Par 4
	320	Par 4

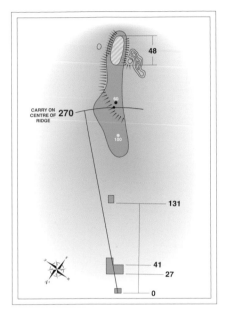

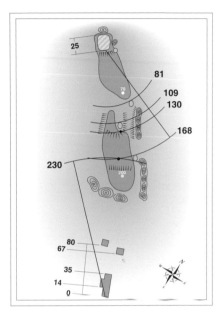

133

11	Championship	126 metres Par 3
	Medal	122	Par 3
	Ladies'	112	Par 3

12	423 metres Par 4
	418	Par 4
	368	Par 4

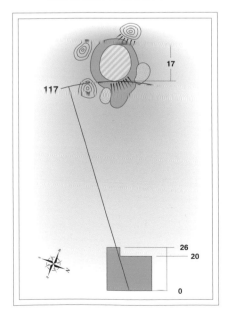

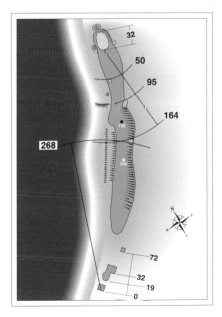

13	Championship	250 metres	Par 4
	Medal	244	Par 4
	Ladies'	220	Par 4

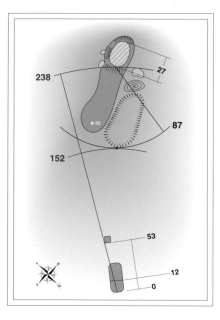

14	446 metres	Par 5
	440	Par 5
	392	Par 5

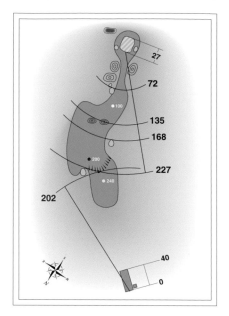

15	Championship	422 metres	Par 4
	Medal	403	Par 4
	Ladies'	347	Par 5

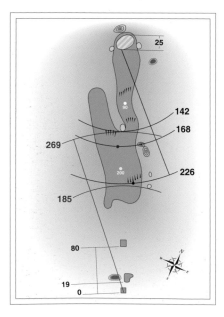

16	178 metres	Par 3
	164	Par 3
	124	Par 3

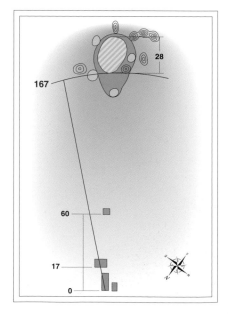

17	Championship	400 metres	Par 4
	Medal	382	Par 4
	Ladies'	320	Par 4

18	487 metres	Par 5
	457	Par 5
	328	Par 4

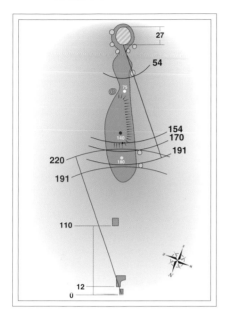

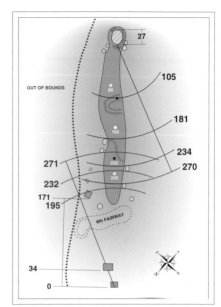

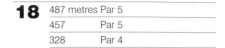

135

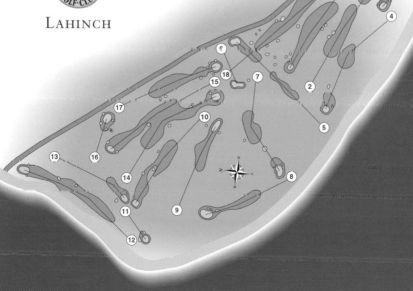

LAHINCH

A wonderfully natural green site distinguishes the short 11th. It was conceived by master architect Alister Mackenzie who, in the 1920s, revised Old Tom Morris's original layout

The 5th tee overlooks the sea, but you must turn and face a giant ridge of dunes, 250 yards or more distant, and drive down an extraordinary valley fairway. It is a bit like playing a hole at Birkdale, only with a 'dead-end' dune rather than a welcoming green looming up ahead. Of course, there is a green, but the only route to it is a blind shot directly over the top of the sandy ridge, from which point you still have 200 yards to travel.

The green at the 6th is long, very narrow and laid across the direction of the tee-shot; it is also completely hidden in a gully between two steep dunes. All you see from the tee is a white marker stone placed on the front hill in a spot indicating the current pin position. Love it or hate it, no one could deny that the 6th at Lahinch has enormous character.

A brilliant run of holes begins at the 7th. For all the talk – good and bad – of 'Klondyke' and 'The Dell', the 7th to the 12th comprise the heart and strength of Lahinch. This is where the course resembles, and some believe surpasses, the best of Ballybunion. The 7th descends dramatically from high ground to low and heads directly towards the sea. After driving to a crest of fairway, you face a thrilling downhill second shot over wildly turbulent terrain. The 8th hugs the shore.

Whereas at the 4th your drive had to climb a giant hill, here it must carry a ravine. A narrow neck of fairway leads to a green guarded by bunkers and framed by massive sand-hills. Holes 9 and 10 run in opposite directions; the former is played from a very elevated tee – the views across the entire links are amazing – to a green perched precariously on a shelf, and the 10th has perhaps the most elegantly fashioned green site of all, a classic plateau green.

The 11th is a charming par three. It is very short and very natural looking, with the green blending perfectly into a 'quiet' corner of the dunes. From the subtlety of the 11th, you then switch to the drama of the 12th. This is the longest and is rated the toughest of the par fours at Lahinch. The hole curves gently to the left and is bordered all along its left edge by water – not the Atlantic on this occasion, but an estuary. A series of bunkers rein you in on the right and exacerbate the difficulty of the drive. A ruined castle may attract your attention and, if you are lucky, you may also glimpse one of Lahinch's famous goats.

The 13th is a teasingly short par four. It is possible to drive the green, but a deep chasm short right of the green awaits any shot that fails to make the grade. The green is well bunkered and two-tiered. The 14th is a par five that sweeps downhill, but requires the second shot to be threaded between two patrolling dunes. Then comes that unjustly maligned finish. Each hole has individuality and merit: the 15th features

a fiendishly positioned fairway bunker and a raised green; the 16th green enjoys another attractive and natural setting; the 17th clambers over some dunes to an unusually shaped fairway; and the 18th undulates, twists and tumbles all the way home.

Lahinch's clubhouse is a marvellously intimate building and certainly an excellent place to adjourn should the heavens suddenly decide to open. Actually, you will have ample warning of the impending doom, for legend has it that the goats will always beat an early retreat towards the shelter of the 19th. One can safely assume, then, that jackets and ties are not obligatory.

Hole	Championship	Medal	Par	Stroke Index	Ladies'	Par	Stroke Index
1	352	343	4	4	335	5	4
2	468	455	5	14	421	5	14
3	138	135	3	16	110	3	16
4	391	380	4	2	314	5	2
5	441	435	5	12	380	5	12
6	142	137	3	18	132	3	18
7	365	350	4	6	227	4	6
8	320	318	4	10	271	4	10
9	351	322	4	8	226	4	8
Out	2968	2875	36		2466	38	
10	412	385	4	3	320	4	3
11	126	122	3	17	112	3	17
12	434	418	4	1	368	4	1
13	250	244	4	11	220	4	11
14	446	440	5	13	392	5	13
15	422	403	4	5	347	5	5
16	178	164	3	15	124	3	15
17	400	382	4	7	320	4	7
18	487	457	5	9	328	4	9
In	3155	3015	36		2531	36	
Out	2968	2875	36		2466	38	
Total	6123	5890	72		4997	74	

THE K CLUB

D R MICHAEL SMURFIT, CHAIRMAN OF IRELAND'S LARGEST AND MOST SUCCESSFUL COMPANY, HAD A DREAM. HE DREAMED OF CREATING A UNIQUE COUNTRY CLUB WITHIN STRIKING DISTANCE OF DUBLIN.

This club would comprise a 'world-class' five-star hotel and unrivalled sporting facilities; in particular, it would boast an exceptional championship golf course, the venue for major international tournaments.

Dr Smurfit has the uncanny habit of living his dreams (however grandiose) which explains why he was soon exploring the grounds of an ancient estate at Straffan in County Kildare, just 25 miles south-west of the capital. There, in addition to a wealth of mature woodland, he discovered vast acres of gently rolling terrain, through which (most conveniently) flows the River Liffey. Standing proudly in the heart of the estate was a very handsome – if slightly dilapidated – 19th-century country house ... This was just the site he had been looking for.

The estate at Straffan was duly acquired in 1988, and Straffan House carefully restored to its former glory. The building was then extended and converted into a lavish hotel. Today the five-star hotel of the Kildare Country Club – everyone calls it The K Club – is possibly the finest in Ireland and among the most striking in Europe. But what of those plans to build an exceptional championship golf course?

The ambitious Dr Smurfit had envisaged a layout capable of testing the very

best golfers in the world; one that was not only supremely challenging, but also thrilling to play and spectacular in appearance. Four leading golf course architects submitted proposals, and yet it seems that only one plan was given serious attention – the one bearing the signature of Arnold Palmer.

When golf's most charismatic and cavalier champion stopped winning tournaments all over the world, he became involved in course design. A man of his character was never destined to design humdrum golf courses; indeed, those that Arnold Palmer creates tend to be the sort that any golfer with high blood pressure should steer well clear of. Palmer had already designed one course in Ireland, the dramatic links at Tralee in County Kerry, thus Dr Smurfit had no hesitation in asking him to demonstrate his swashbuckling design theories on an inland site close to Dublin.

The course opened in July 1991. If ever an architect fulfilled his brief, it was Arnold Palmer at The K Club. It is an exceptional championship golf course, already the venue for major international tournaments and, yes, The K Club is both thrilling and spectacular, as well as supremely challenging.

Notwithstanding its youth, The K Club has become the home of the

Opposite: Night descends on The K Club. Although opened as recently as July 1991, in 2005 the club will host the Ryder Cup.

THE K CLUB

1	Championship	584 yards	Par 5
	Medal	561	Par 5
	Ladies'	405	Par 5

2	408 yards	Par 4
	382	Par 4
	289	Par 4

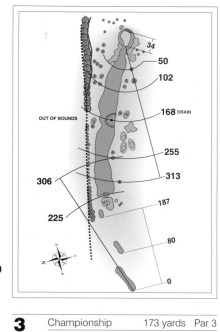

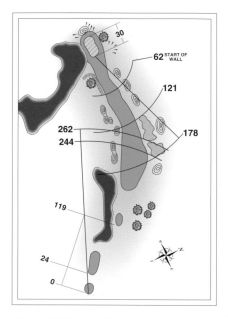

3	Championship	173 yards	Par 3
	Medal	164	Par 3
	Ladies'	122	Par 3

4	402 yards	Par 4
	386	Par 4
	287	Par 4

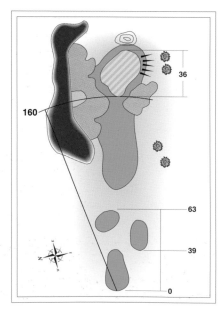

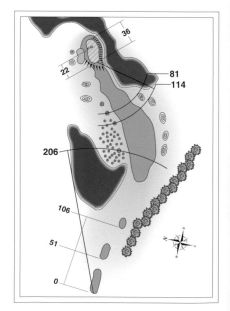

European Open, one of the most prestigious events on the PGA European Tour.

Even more remarkably, The K Club will host the Ryder Cup is 2005. It will be the first time the Ryder Cup has been played on Irish soil, and while some have criticised the decision to select an inland rather than a links course, The K Club will provide a dramatic venue.

The course starts (as well as ends) with a par five. – at least it breaks you in gently! Your tee-shot at the 1st must carry a cluster of central fairway bunkers; thereafter, the hole sweeps down towards a green which has a fairly narrow entrance. A more fearsome proposition, however, is the 2nd, a sharp dog-leg left, where water threatens both the drive and the approach. In fact, the second shot to the 2nd is one of the most exacting and exhilarating of the entire round, being downhill to a smallish green guarded by trees on one side and a pond on the other. The putting surface, like many at The K Club, is heavily contoured and tilts towards the water. The 3rd is a par three and it introduces the first of The K Club's distinctive 'beach-like' bunkers, where the sand literally runs into the water's edge. One factor that separates this course from almost every other is the impressive and original nature of its hazards.

The 4th, 5th and 6th take the golfer far away from the clubhouse. They comprise a classic 'bite off as much as you dare' hole at which, once again, water laps the edge of the green, a long par three played directly towards the ruins of an ancient church and a very testing par four that features a difficult second to a green partially hidden by grassy hummocks and sloping severely from front to back.

Throughout the first six holes there are watery duels, sometimes with ponds, sometimes with small lakes. Now the golfer must confront the River Liffey. Starting from a most attractive teeing area, the par five 7th double-dog-legs its way over sand, rough and water and in between an amazing mix of trees and shrubs. The sanctuary-like green occupies its own little island, sandwiched between two arms of the River Liffey. A quaint 19th-century iron bridge transports players to and from the island.

Each hole at The K Club has a name. The 8th is called 'Half Moon', derived from the shape of the fairway which, for its entire length, accompanies a bend in the River Liffey. It has been described as an old-fashioned golf hole because its challenge and charms are entirely natural. The long, two shot 9th leads back to the clubhouse. The hole isn't quite as difficult as its name, 'The Eye of the Needle', implies, but with a giant tree standing defiantly in the centre of the fairway,

141

A ribbon of fairway separates a giant lake front and left of the 18th green from a sea of sand to the front and right; the bold approach is to attempt to carry everything.

5	Championship	213 yards	Par 3
	Medal	197	Par 3
	Ladies'	151	Par 3

6	446 yards	Par 4
	407	Par 4
	362	Par 4

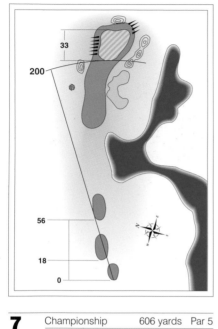

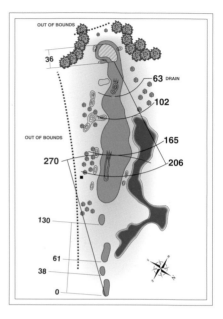

7	Championship	606 yards	Par 5
	Medal	581	Par 5
	Ladies'	501	Par 5

8	375 yards	Par 4
	332	Par 4
	296	Par 4

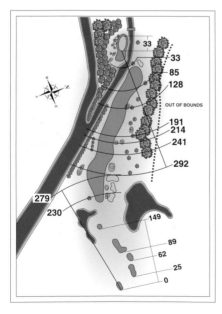

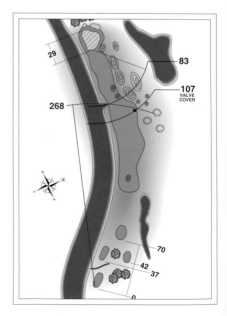

THE K CLUB

9	Championship	434 yards	Par 4
	Medal	427	Par 4
	Ladies'	384	Par 4

10	418 yards	Par 4
	401	Par 4
	298	Par 4

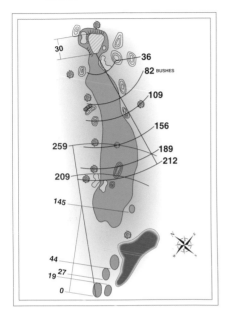

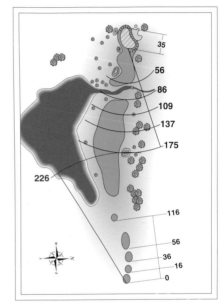

143

11	Championship	413 yards	Par 4
	Medal	399	Par 4
	Ladies'	292	Par 4

12	170 yards	Par 3
	157	Par 3
	109	Par 3

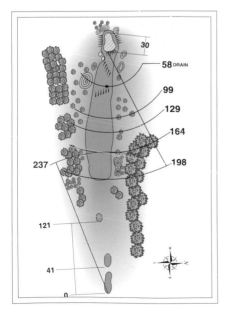

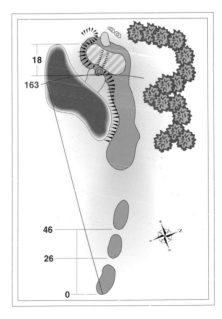

THE K CLUB

13	Championship	568 yards	Par 5
	Medal	545	Par 5
	Ladies'	456	Par 5

14	416 yards	Par 4
	397	Par 4
	310	Par 4

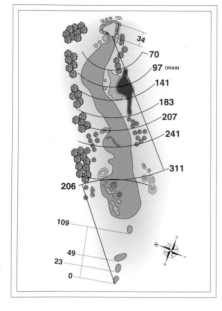

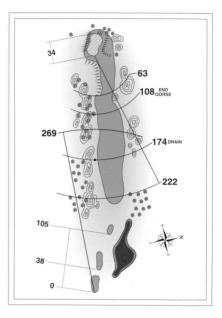

144

15	Championship	472 yards	Par 4
	Medal	412	Par 4
	Ladies'	298	Par 4

16	395 yards	Par 4
	371	Par 4
	301	Par 4

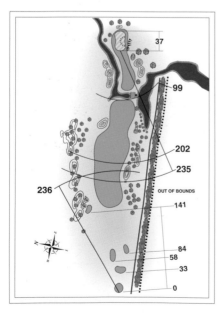

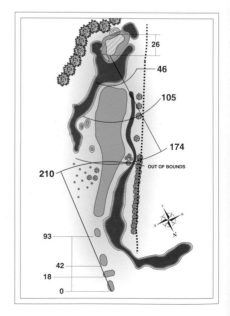

THE K CLUB

17	Championship	173 yards	Par 3
	Medal	155	Par 3
	Ladies'	134	Par 3

18	518 yards	Par 5
	502	Par 5
	441	Par 5

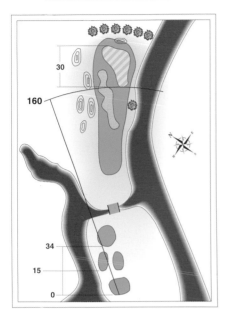

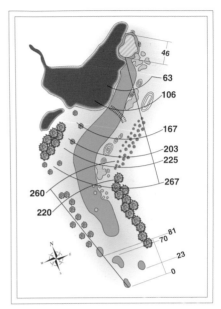

145

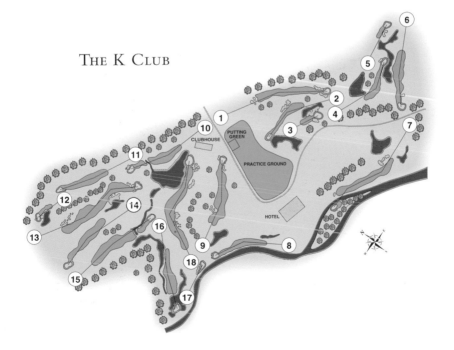

The K Club

The 16th hole, 'Michael's Favourite', exemplifies the do-or-die nature of the Arnold Palmer designed layout: water intimidates the drive – and terrorizes the approach.

146 there isn't a great deal of room for golfers (never mind camels).

The second nine commences with a drive from a spectacularly sited tee. Towering pines extend for quite a way down the right-hand side of the 10th fairway; off to the left there is water, the same water that later fashions the thrilling approach to the final hole. The par four 11th is perhaps the most subtle hole at Straffan. The fairway climbs gently uphill along a secluded valley. There are twin bunkers set into a rise in the fairway and a hidden gully just short of what is a fairly small plateau green.

The mood changes again at the 12th. This is the shortest hole and, in a manner reminiscent of the fabled 12th at Augusta, is played over water to a shallow angled green. Judgment of distance is everything: one of the aforementioned beach-like bunkers occupies much of the area between the green and the hazard, the putting surface sports a pronounced ridge and is devilishly quick, while looming beyond and to the side of the green is a mischievous assortment of trees.

The 13th, 'Arnold's Pick', is another excellent par five. It is a very strategic hole, offering various options, yet, at the same time, it seems to demand a bold approach. The courageous route is to drive left of centre over a nest of bunkers to find a concealed portion of the fairway. From here a steep incline catapults the ball downhill. A very long tee-shot can set up the prospect of going for the green in two, although whichever way the hole is played, the myriad bunkers, trees and water must all be negotiated. The green is large but slopes in every conceivable direction.

If the wind is against, the 14th can be brutally tough. It is long and runs uphill all the way; moreover, the rough is extremely punishing. Water doesn't affect the hole, nor are there any greenside traps to avoid – presumably the architect feared he might be adding insult to injury!

Up to this point the story of the back nine has been as follows: a spectacular drive; a subtle approach; a penal hole followed by a strategic one; a brutal challenge. … What could possibly come next? The word is 'heroic'. The four finishing holes at The K Club – and there is a real sense of turning for home at the 15th – build to a thunderous climax.

The crescendo begins with the 15th, a real rollercoaster of a hole that charges dramatically downhill from the tee. The second shot is extremely testing, as to reach the green you have to play across water, often from an uneven lie, and normally with a wood or long iron. A small bale-out area exists just short of the 15th green, but there is no such luxury at the 16th. Officially, this hole is called 'Michael's Favourite'; unofficially, it has several (mostly unprintable) names. It is a breathtaking, all-or-nothing two-shotter, where an accurate drive must be followed by an even more precise second to an island green. A watery grave is not inevitable, but countless promising rounds have been shipwrecked at the 16th.

Next comes an exquisite par three. Nestling beside the banks of the Liffey, and with a splendid backdrop of trees, the 17th resembles a scene from a Constable painting. As a golf hole it is not quite so serene, as a large bunker runs

diagonally across the entrance to the green. Nor is it easy to ignore the close proximity of the river!

And so to The K Club's crowning glory – not only is the 18th brilliantly conceived, but it is also the perfect finishing hole. As at the 13th, there is more than one way to play the hole, but its very shape encourages – and rewards – a daring strategy. It dares you to drive over the top of a bunker-strewn hill and, after allowing a moment to savour the incredible prospect ahead, dares you to fire straight at the flag as you attempt to carry the water that eats into the heart of the vast, stage-like green. Heroic? Certainly. It is an Arnold Palmer golf hole.

Hole	Championship	Medal	Par	Stroke	Ladies	Par	Stroke Index
1	584	561	5	5	405	5	11
2	408	382	4	9	289	4	7
3	173	164	3	17	122	3	17
4	402	389	4	7	287	4	3
5	213	197	3	15	151	3	15
6	446	407	4	11	362	4	5
7	606	581	5	3	501	5	1
8	375	332	4	13	296	4	13
9	434	427	4	1	384	5	9
Out	3641	3440	36		2797	37	
10	418	401	4	6	298	4	0
11	413	399	4	12	292	4	14
12	170	157	3	18	109	3	16
13	568	545	5	4	456	5	2
14	416	397	4	14	310	4	12
15	472	412	4	2	298	4	4
16	395	371	4	10	301	4	10
17	173	155	3	16	134	3	18
18	518	502	5	8	441	5	8
In	3543	3339	36		2639	36	
Out	3641	3440	36		2797	37	
Total	7184	6779	72		5436	73	

ROYAL PORTRUSH (DUNLUCE)

IT IS A BEAUTIFUL DAY AND YOU ARE TRAVELLING ALONG ONE OF THE MOST DRAMATIC STRETCHES OF COAST IN THE WORLD. THE STUNNING ROADWAY TAKES YOU RIGHT ALONGSIDE THE ATLANTIC AND WINDS ITS WAY THROUGH HISTORIC VILLAGES AND SMALL TOWNS, PAST THE RUINS OF AN HEROICALLY PERCHED CASTLE AND THE SPOT WHERE A GOLD-LADEN GALLEON WAS WRECKED BY A FEROCIOUS STORM.

It takes you past the world's oldest whiskey distillery and within a few yards of the 'eighth natural wonder of the world'. After a few more twists in the road you will be confronted by a golfing spectacle second to none – a magnificent stretch of perfect links terrain with thirty-six flags fluttering in the breeze.

You are on the Antrim Coast of Northern Ireland. The castle you passed is called Dunluce Castle, the home of the Irish MacDonnels until another of those storms blew the kitchen (and all its cooks) into the sea; the wrecked galleon was Spanish and the distillery – almost as old as the Armada – bears the name of Bushmills. As for the 'eighth wonder' it is, of course, the Giant's Causeway, and the perfect links terrain you are approaching is the home of Royal Portrush, one of the natural wonders of the golfing world.

Royal Portrush Golf Club celebrated its centenary in May 1988. A 'Royal' club since 1892, it has enjoyed a rich history. It has hosted both men's and ladies' British Amateur Championships, it has held the British Seniors Open and it is the only golf club in Ireland to have staged the Open Championship. Max Faulkner won the 1951 Open at Portrush finishing two strokes ahead of Argentina's Tony Cerda; no British golfer then won the championship until Tony Jacklin in 1989.

The richness of the club's history is matched by the beauty and grandeur of its setting – among current Open Championship venues only Turnberry's scenery can hold a candle to Portrush – and the beauty and grandeur of the setting is matched by the majesty and quality of the links.

The 'thirty-six fluttering flags' comprise the Dunluce Course and the Valley Course, the former being the championship links. Harry Colt was the architect of the Dunluce layout. Construction of the golf course took place at intervals between 1929 and 1933. On completion Colt considered it his masterpiece and during the 1951 Open Bernard Darwin wrote in *The Times*, 'It is truly magnificent and Mr H. S. Colt, who designed it in its present form, has thereby built himself a monument more enduring than brass.'

The Dunluce Course meanders along natural valleys and through large tumbling dunes. Many of the holes occupy slightly elevated ground and thus enjoy commanding views. Portrush is a

Opposite: The 5th green on the Dunluce Course is precariously perched on the edge of the links: an overly bold approach may find its way to the shores of Scotland.

1	Championship	389 yards	Par 4
	Medal	381	Par 4
	Ladies'	325	Par 4

2	497 yards	Par 5
	493	Par 5
	455	Par 5

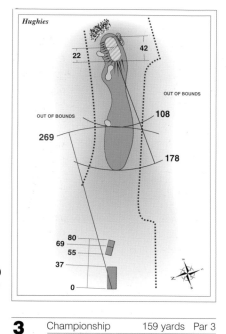

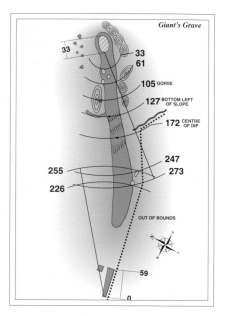

3	Championship	159 yards	Par 3
	Medal	150	Par 3
	Ladies'	130	Par 3

4	455 yards	Par 4
	454	Par 4
	422	Par 5

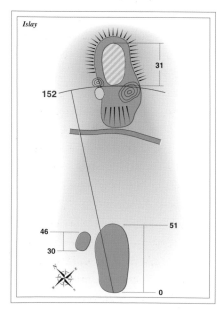

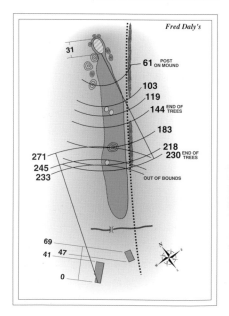

150

ROYAL PORTRUSH (DUNLUCE)

There is no gentle introduction at Portrush: the 1st hole features an out of bounds,
a steep rise to the green and two cavernous bunkers.

pure links; there are no trees and, in a sense, there is no rough – just tees, fairways, greens and sand-dunes. If you stray from the fairways, and they are not overly generous, you are in the dunes. Solid driving is the key to playing well at Portrush, not merely because the fairways are narrow, but because the layout includes an abundance of dog-legged holes to both left and right. In fact, of the two-shot holes on the Dunluce links, only three could properly be described as straight. You will invariably see a part of the flag from the tee, teasingly peeping over the top of a dune or mound, but in order to gain a full view of it for your approach, you must drive to the correct area of the fairway. Most of the greens are fairly small, subtly contoured and defended more often by mounds, hummocks and swales than by bunkers. In fact, no fewer than five holes have no

bunkers at all. Colt utilized the contours of the land to great effect and the natural, often understated appearance of the green complexes is perhaps his finest architectural achievement.

The 1st hole guides you into the dunes and is a formidable opening hole. It runs uphill, rising sharply to a large sloping green and has an out of bounds all along the left. A deep bunker lurks to the left side of the fairway, while an even deeper and larger trap guards the front of the green. The 2nd, an undulating par five with a plateau green, is a much gentler hole. Then comes an attractive par three and the first wonderful panorama.

The Antrim Coast is visible in all its glory from the 3rd tee: the White Rocks, the castle ruins, the nearby hills and, offshore, Rathlin Island, the Skerries and the darker, more distant shape of Scotland's Mull of Kintyre.

5	Championship	384 yards	Par 4
	Medal	386	Par 4
	Ladies'	342	Par 4

6	193 yards	Par 3
	191	Par 3
	161	Par 3

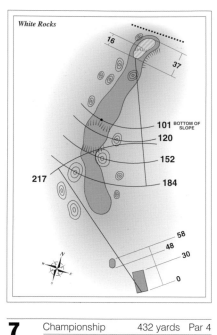

White Rocks

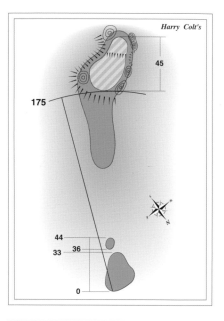

Harry Colt's

7	Championship	432 yards	Par 4
	Medal	420	Par 4
	Ladies'	412	Par 5

8	376 yards	Par 4
	365	Par 4
	335	Par 4

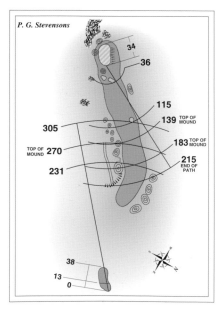

P. G. Stevensons

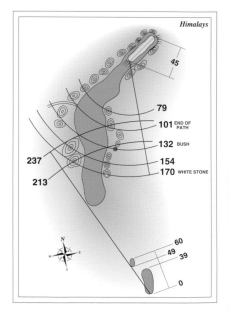

Himalays

9	Championship	478 yards	Par 5
	Medal	476	Par 5
	Ladies'	423	Par 5

10		480 yards	Par 5
		477	Par 5
		452	Par 5

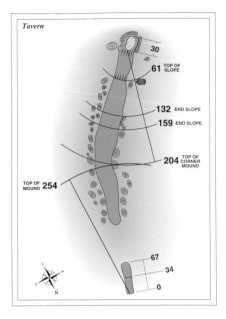

Tavern

30
61 TOP OF SLOPE
132 END SLOPE
159 END SLOPE
204 TOP OF CORNER MOUND
TOP OF MOUND 254
67
34
0

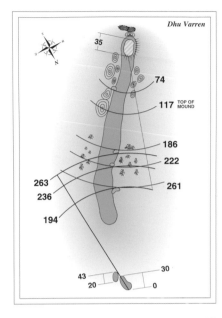

Dhu Varren

35
74
117 TOP OF MOUND
186
222
263
261
236
194
43
30
20
0

153

11	Championship	166 yards	Par 3
	Medal	166	Par 3
	Ladies'	137	Par 3

12		395 yards	Par 4
		389	Par 4
		362	Par 4

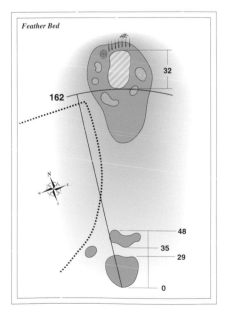

Feather Bed

32
162
48
35
29
0

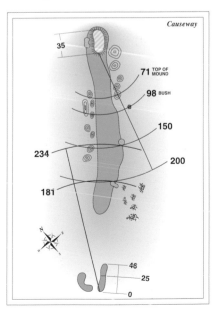

Causeway

35
71 TOP OF MOUND
98 BUSH
150
234
200
181
46
25
0

13	Championship	371 yards	Par 4
	Medal	366	Par 4
	Ladies'	352	Par 4

14	213 yards	Par 3
	205	Par 3
	166	Par 3

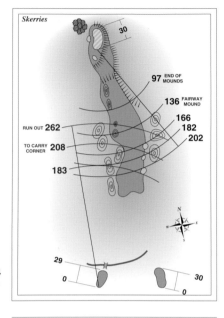

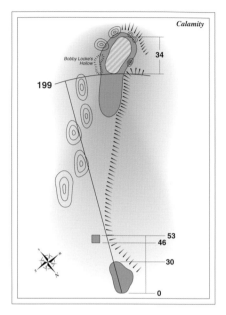

15	Championship	366 yards	Par 4
	Medal	361	Par 4
	Ladies'	333	Par 4

16	432 yards	Par 4
	415	Par 4
	396	Par 5

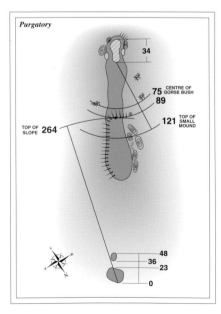

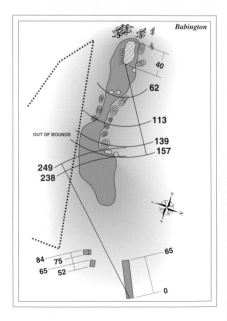

ROYAL PORTRUSH (DUNLUCE)

17	Championship	517 yards	Par 5	**18**	479 yards	Par 4
	Medal	508	Par 5		457	Par 4
	Ladies'	490	Par 5		436	Par 5

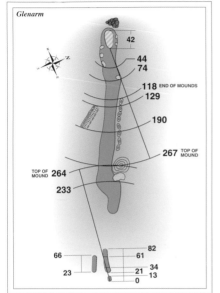

Glenarm

42

44
74

118 END OF MOUNDS
129

190

267 TOP OF MOUND

TOP OF MOUND 264
233

82
66   61
          34
23   21 13
          0

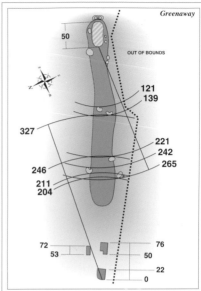

Greenaway

50

OUT OF BOUNDS

121
139

327

221
242
265

246

211
204

72   76
53   50
          22
          0

155

ROYAL PORTRUSH
GOLF CLUB
DUNLUCE LINKS

6
7 9
14
5
8
13
15
10
4
16
3
12
11
17
1
2
18
CLUBHOUSE

Notwithstanding its former name ('Primrose Dell'), the 4th is a strong par four that features another intimidating drive. Again there is a deep fairway bunker to avoid on the left, and there is also an out of bounds, although this time it is to the right; in between the bunker and the out of bounds there is not a great amount of fairway. The second shot must be targeted between a gap in the dunes to a handsome bowl-shaped green. 'White Rocks' is the next hole – one of the most celebrated par fours in golf.

Some of that wonderful scenery you drank in on the 3rd tee threatens to come into play at the 5th. The tee-shot is severely downhill, straight at the sea … or at least you are tempted to aim straight at the sea. The fairway actually dog-legs from left to right and some horribly wild country awaits the player who tries to cut off too much of the corner. The green is dramatically perched on the edge of the links, overlooking the sea. There are no bunkers, but the green is full of significant slopes and there is a sharp fall-away to the right. There is also a sharp fall-away at the back – 40 feet down to the sea!

The 6th and 7th complete a superb run of holes. The 6th is called 'Harry Colt's' and, fittingly, it is a classically designed, bunkerless par three. The green is two-tiered, angled from front left to back right and surrounded by dunes and swales. As for the 7th, it rivals the 4th as the pick of the long par fours. Curving mildly to the left, the second shot is played to a beautifully raised green. A pair of deep cross bunkers have been cannily positioned 20 yards short of the putting surface.

If you are hoping to make a good score at Portrush, then the time to capitalize is between the 8th and 13th. The 8th is a shortish par four, a swinging dog-leg that has been carved out of particularly rugged terrain. It is followed by back-to-back par fives. The 9th and 10th run in the same direction as one another and, given a favourable wind, can be reached with two good blows. The 11th is a tightly bunkered downhill par three; the 12th is a medium length par four – another classic Colt green here – and the 13th, 'Skerries', an exhilarating drive-and-pitch hole that lures you

The par three 14th is called 'Calamity' for good reason: miss the green to the right and you could be playing your second shot from 50 feet below the hole.

back towards the sea. 'Calamity' and 'Purgatory' await. The 14th at Portrush is one of the great 'white knuckle' holes of golf: a 200-yard par three where the direct route to the green requires a huge carry over an enormous ravine. If you miss-hit the shot, you could be playing your second from 50 feet below the hole: 'Calamity' is an appropriate name. 'Purgatory' is perhaps a little excessive for a par four that swoops spectacularly downhill, although seemingly good drives at the 15th do have a nasty habit of kicking off the fairway into the dunes on the left. An exacting two-shotter, a big par five with a bunker reminiscent of the colossus on the 4th at Sandwich and a long par four bring you back to the clubhouse.

Should you play the Dunluce Course in the morning, you might try to arrange a game on the Valley Course after lunch. You will not be disappointed. If you are planning on spending some time in the area, you could also inspect the nearby championship links courses at Portstewart and Castlerock. And you must visit the Giant's Causeway. A geologist will probably attempt to persuade you otherwise, but those in the know can confirm that it was built by one Finn McCool.

Finn was the great warrior giant who commanded the armies of the King of All Ireland. He inhabited an Antrim headland not far from Portrush. By all accounts he was an extraordinary individual; after all, not too many beings can pick thorns out of their heels while

running and rip up vast chunks of rock and hurl them 50 miles out into the sea (this apparently is how the Isle of Man came to be). One day Finn fell madly in love with a lady giant who lived on the Hebridean island of Staffa and he determined to build a bridge to bring her across the water to Ireland. The Giant's Causeway was the start of this romantic crusade. It seems that after work had already commenced, Finn discovered that his love was unrequited and so, with a heavy heart, he abandoned the project. Still, the Giant's Causeway remains a splendid monument to the ardour of one mighty big fellow.

Hole	Championship	Medal	Par	Stroke Index	Ladies'	Par	Stroke Index
1	389	381	4	7	325	4	7
2	497	493	5	11	455	5	11
3	159	150	3	17	130	3	17
4	455	454	4	3	422	5	3
5	384	386	4	9	342	4	9
6	193	191	3	15	161	3	15
7	100	420	4	1	412	5	1
8	376	365	4	13	335	4	13
9	476	476	5	5	423	5	5
Out	3361	3316	36		3005	38	
10	480	477	5	10	452	5	10
11	166	166	3	18	137	3	18
12	395	389	4	2	362	4	2
13	371	366	4	6	352	4	6
14	213	205	3	16	166	3	16
15	366	361	4	12	333	4	12
16	432	415	4	4	396	5	4
17	517	508	5	8	490	5	8
18	481	477	5	14	436	5	14
In	3421	3364	37		3124	38	
Out	3361	3316	36		3005	38	
Total	6782	6680	73		6129	76	

DRUIDS GLEN

YOU SAW ALL THE SIGHTS IN DUBLIN AND YOU WENT TO
CONNEMARA; YOU SANG AND DANCED IN GALWAY AND YOU
WENT TO COUNTY KERRY. BUT DID YOU VISIT COUNTY
WICKLOW? DID YOU SEE 'THE GARDEN OF IRELAND'?

On arriving in Dublin golfing visitors to Ireland have traditionally sought to arrange a game at Portmarnock – Royal Dublin too perhaps, but have then hurried off to the glorious South West. Nowadays they should consider spending a little more time closer to the capital. County Wicklow is a beautiful county – it isn't called 'the Garden of Ireland' for nothing – and it is right on Dublin's doorstep. In the past decade three outstanding new golf courses have been built in County Wicklow: Powerscourt, Rathsallagh and, best of all, Druids Glen near the village of Kilcoole.

With such a mystical name, Druids Glen was always likely to be special; it is situated within the grounds of the former 400-year-old Woodstock Estate, a beautiful domain even by County Wicklow's standards. Being well-wooded, spectacularly yet not severely undulating and crossed by two mountain streams, the site was ideal for a golf course.

It is impossible to visit Druids Glen and not be reminded of Augusta. This was by no means the architects' – Tom Craddock and Pat Ruddy's – only influence, but Druids Glen resembles Augusta more than any other golf course outside North America. The extraordinary beautification of the (already beautiful) landscape bears testimony to this.

Jack O'Connor, a renowned landscape gardener and nurseryman, was commissioned to 'add background colour' to the golf course. In fact, O'Connor went brilliantly berserk. At any time of the year, even in midwinter, Druids Glen is a riot of colour. In spring and summer, it is positively kaleidoscopic. O'Connor planted literally hundreds of thousands of flowers and shrubs; scores of trees have also been brought on to the site – not that it lacked plenty to begin with. And the variety is as staggering as the amount.

Many of the world's finest golf courses begin benignly (in relative terms), then build to a dramatic climax. Druids Glen adopts a different approach. It starts strongly – the downhill, beautifully flowing par four 1st and the short 2nd are two of the best holes on the course – and it finishes in a blaze of glory. In between there are two purple patches: one on the front nine, from the 7th to the 9th, and another on the back nine, from the 12th to the 14th – 'the Amen Corner of Ireland'.

The first purple patch is unexpected simply because the sequence between the 3rd and 6th comprises four good holes.

The principal feature of the 7th is the thrilling, if intimidating, nature of the tee-shot. The drive is dramatically down-

159

Opposite: The 18th-century Woodstock House overlooks the 18th green.
The closing hole at Druids Glen presents a fitting climax to a thrilling course.

DRUIDS GLEN

1	Championship	445 yards	Par 4
	Medal	427	Par 4
	Ladies'	329	Par 4

2	190 yards	Par 3
	174	Par 3
	122	Par 3

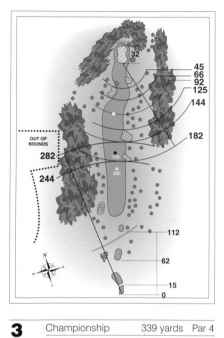

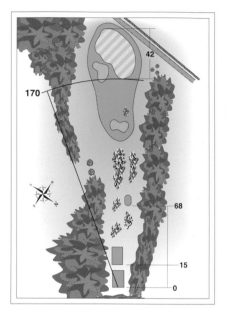

3	Championship	339 yards	Par 4
	Medal	330	Par 4
	Ladies'	299	Par 4

4	446 yards	Par 4
	417	Par 4
	317	Par 4

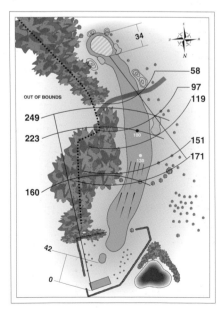

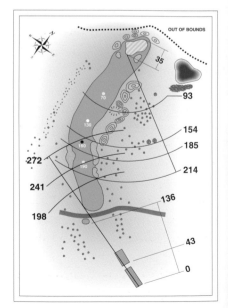

hill; off to the left there is dense woodland and water which accompanies you all the way to the green. The par three 8th is a gorgeous hole. It is also strikingly similar to the short 16th at Augusta. As on the famous American course, there is water to the front and left of the green and the putting surface slopes from right to left, towards the water's edge; a backdrop of trees creates an amphitheatre effect. As you might imagine, Jack O'Connor couldn't wait to exercise his trowel and his imagination on this hole. At the 9th you drive across a deep ravine, then walk over a suspension bridge to reach the fairway. The approach is gently uphill to a nicely contoured green.

The 12th is a second outstanding par three. The tee-shot is played down across water to a green semi-circled by a vast bank of trees and shrubs. If the 8th green is an amphitheatre, this one is cathedral-like – as it should be, for overlooking the green is the place where the druids built their altar, after which the club is named.

One wonders what the druids would have made of the goings-on at the 13th. Here the designers insisted that a mountain of granite be blasted away from the rockface to allow golfers a better view of the fairway. Mind you, it has made the 13th an awesome golf hole. You drive from a very elevated tee down to the lowest level of the course. The fairway is bisected by a stream and runs through a steep-sided valley; you have to carry the stream from the tee, and again – if you dare – with your second. Another bold stroke is required from the tee at the 14th,

followed by a deft pitch to a raised green The 15th and 16th occupy flatter, more open ground. Then comes that finishing blaze of glory.

The 17th at Druids Glen is a potentially terrifying par three. From the championship tee it requires a 200-yard carry across sand and water to an island green, the first of its kind in Ireland. Water threatens again at the par five 18th, this time in the shape of three small lakes close to the green which, in the manner of a waterfall, cascade over weirs, one into the other. It is a sensational finish to a sensational golf course – not that you would expect anything less from the Augusta of Ireland.

Hole	Championship	Medal	Par	Stroke Index	Ladies'	Par	Stroke Index
1	445	427	4	3	329	4	4
2	190	174	3	7	122	3	18
3	339	330	4	16	299	4	14
4	446	417	4	6	317	4	8
5	517	492	5	17	424	5	6
6	476	456	4	2	358	5	15
7	405	392	4	5	346	4	3
8	166	152	3	10	125	3	10
9	389	369	4	15	354	4	2
Out	3373	3209	35		2674	36	
10	440	401	4	9	268	4	12
11	522	512	5	12	389	5	7
12	174	155	3	11	119	3	11
13	471	461	4	1	347	5	1
14	399	333	4	13	270	4	16
15	456	395	4	8	315	4	5
16	538	481	5	18	367	5	17
17	203	178	3	4	108	3	9
18	482	472	5	14	393	5	13
In	3685	3388	37		2576	38	
Out	3373	3209	35		2674	36	
Total	7058	6597	72		5250	74	

5	Championship	517 yards	Par 5
	Medal	492	Par 5
	Ladies'	424	Par 5

6	476 yards	Par 4
	456	Par 4
	358	Par 5

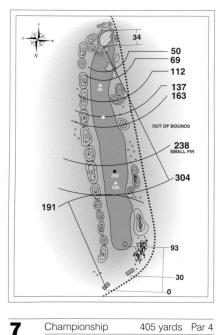

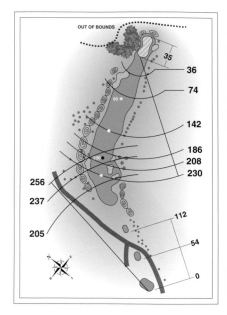

162

7	Championship	405 yards	Par 4
	Medal	392	Par 4
	Ladies'	346	Par 4

8	166 yards	Par 3
	152	Par 3
	125	Par 3

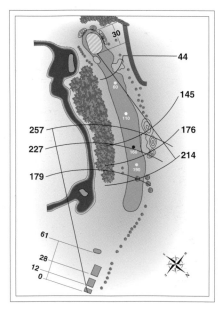

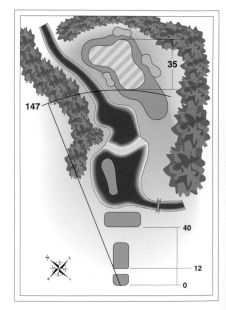

9	Championship	389 yards	Par 4
	Medal	369	Par 4
	Ladies'	354	Par 4

10	440 yards	Par 4
	401	Par 4
	268	Par 4

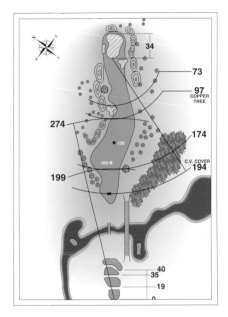

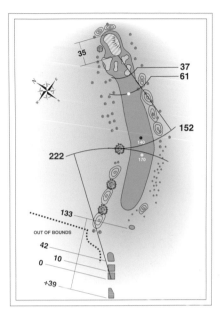

163

11	Championship	522 yards	Par 5
	Medal	512	Par 5
	Ladies'	389	Par 5

12	174 yards	Par 4
	155	Par 4
	119	Par 5

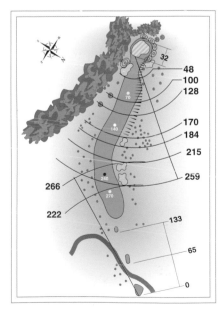

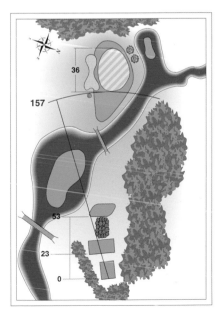

13	Championship	471 yards	Par 4
	Medal	461	Par 4
	Ladies'	347	Par 5

14	399 yards	Par 4
	333	Par 4
	270	Par 4

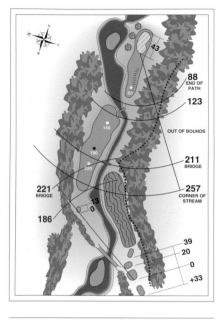

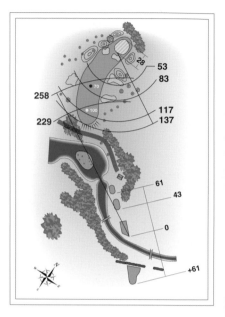

15	Championship	456 yards	Par 4
	Medal	395	Par 4
	Ladies'	315	Par 4

16	538 yards	Par 5
	481	Par 5
	367	Par 5

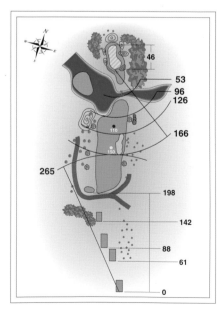

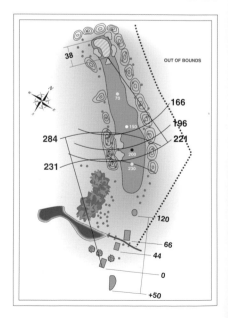

DRUIDS GLEN

17	Championship	203 yards	Par 3
	Medal	178	Par 3
	Ladies'	108	Par 3

18	482 yards	Par 5
	472	Par 5
	393	Par 5

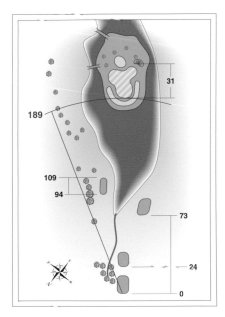

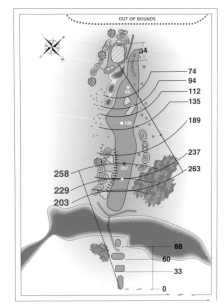

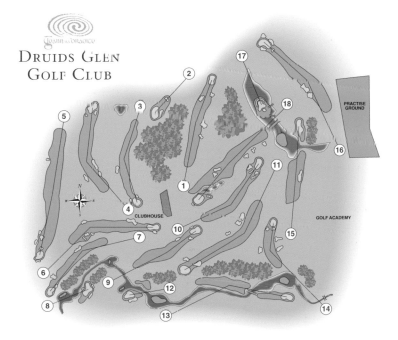

DRUIDS GLEN
GOLF CLUB

PRACTISE GROUND

GOLF ACADEMY

CLUBHOUSE

ROYAL ST GEORGE'S

As they walked side by side down the 18th fairway, the cheers of the massive gallery ringing in their ears, Bernhard Langer turned to Greg Norman and said, 'Well done. That was the best golf I have ever seen. You deserve to win.'

It was the day Norman emphatically silenced his critics and the end of a week when Royal St George's firmly re-established its proud reputation.

The patron saint of English golf has experienced a remarkably colourful, and in some ways chequered, existence. It all started over a century ago, following a rather bizarre journey of discovery. Within a few years of opening, St George's was being heralded as 'the finest links in Christendom'; it staged many Open Championships, produced many great champions and witnessed many extraordinary events. Then suddenly, as a championship venue, it lost favour. It was dubbed 'old fashioned and unfair'; the lonely wilderness of a links was cast into the wilderness. Decades passed before it was agreed that it should receive minor surgical treatment. Officialdom placed St George's on parole. Initially the top players viewed it with a degree of suspicion, indeed, some reserved judgment right up to the beginning of that glorious week in July 1993.

The links was 'found' in the mid-1880s by two Scottish gentlemen, Dr Laidlaw Purves and Henry Lamb. With the avowed intention of unearthing a St Andrews in the south of England, the two travelled to Bournemouth from where, heading in an easterly direction, they set off along the coast in search of suitable linksland. Having had no luck by the time they approached the east side of Kent, they must have been feeling a little dejected. Then, from the tower of St Clement's Church in Sandwich, Dr Laidlaw Purves glimpsed something that warmed his heart: vast tumbling sandhills – lots of them. This was the ideal site.

A golf club was quickly formed and St George's – the name seemed appropriate – was ready for play in 1887. The new course met with instant and universal approval. The original layout actually had more in common with Prestwick than St Andrews. In particular, it included several blind carries over large sand dunes. In 1887 this was extremely fashionable, if not de rigueur. Moreover, there is a wonderful feeling of spaciousness and solitude about St George's. Overlooking Pegwell Bay, with views of the famous white cliffs, it has a stark and silent beauty.

Five years after it opened, St George's hosted the British Amateur Championship and, just two years later, the Open Championship – the first time the event had been held outside Scotland. John H. Taylor's victory ushered in the era of the

Opposite: Royal St George's possesses a wild and rugged beauty; it was the Open Championship's first English venue.

1	Championship	441 yards	Par 4
	Medal	413	Par 4
	Ladies'		

2	376 yards	Par 4
	339	Par 4

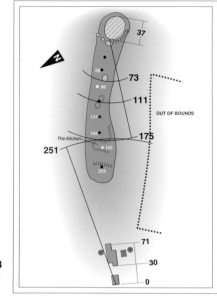

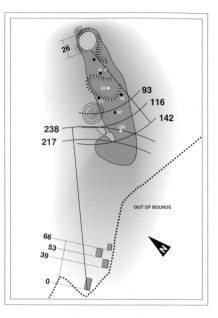

168

3	Championship	210 yards	Par 34
	Medal	198	Par 3
	Ladies'		

4	468 yards	Par 4
	417	Par 4

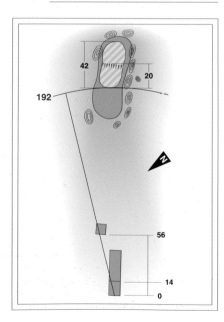

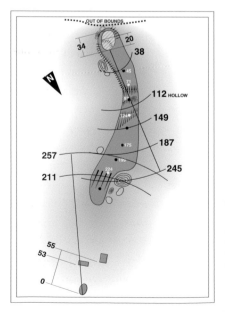

Great Triumvirate. When the Open Championship returned to St George's in 1899, it was Harry Vardon's turn to win. In 1902 St George's became Royal St George's, and it staged two more Opens before the outbreak of the First World War.

The glory years resumed in the 1920s and 1930s. True, there were the odd mumblings of discontent about the sheer number of blind shots and the frequency with which golfers found themselves playing a fairway shot from an uneven lie. But if it was good enough for the likes of Walter Hagen (who won the first two post-war Sandwich Opens), Bobby Jones and Gene Sarazen, it was good enough for anyone. Besides, St George's (unlike everywhere else it seemed) was still able to produce home-grown Open champions. In 1934 Henry Cotton stemmed the tide of American dominance, thanks mainly to a brilliant 67–65 start.

Things were very different after the Second World War. Bobby Locke won the ninth St George's Open in 1949, but this was the last to be played over the links for more than three decades. Quaint old Sandwich and the surrounding area's inability to cope with an increase in road traffic was one cause, but a more fundamental reason was that St George's was no longer considered an appropriate test for the modern professional. Blind shots and funny stances were no longer in vogue. In the 1950s and 1960s, Royal Birkdale came to be regarded as England's premier links: 'a much fairer test'.

In the early 1970s a decision was made

to modernize St George's – nothing too radical, but it was felt that if much of the overt blindness could be eradicated without disturbing the essential character of the links, St George's might once again be considered a worthy venue for the game's greatest championship. Architect Frank Pennink directed affairs and the changes were completed by 1975. Effectively three new holes were created, namely the 3rd, 8th and 11th, and on two other holes, at the 4th and 14th, the fairway was made more visible from the tee. All but the most die-hard traditionalists agreed that the changes improved the layout.

With knowledge of the impending alterations, the European Tour decided to bring the PGA Championship to Sandwich in the mid-1970s. This was encouraging; so, too, was the decision of the Ministry of Transport to build a new by-pass, thus helping to alleviate the problem of traffic congestion. The revised links was given a guarded thumbs-up by the Tour players (a few still found the experience bewildering, St George's being so far removed from the type of course they were used to playing), and the R & A's decision to bring the

169

Royal St George's has a stark and silent beauty: in the opinion of Bernard Darwin, 'as nearly my idea of heaven as is to be attained on an earthly links'.

5	Championship	421 yards	Par 4
	Medal	421	Par 4
	Ladies'		

6	155 yards	Par 3
	155	Par 3

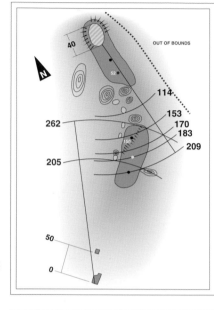

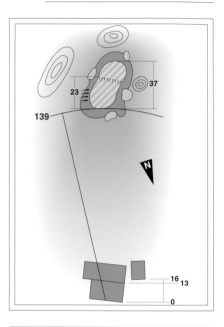

7	Championship	530 yards	Par 4
	Medal	487	Par 4
	Ladies'		

8	418 yards	Par 4
	410	Par 4

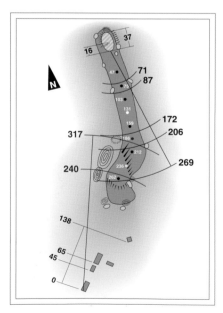

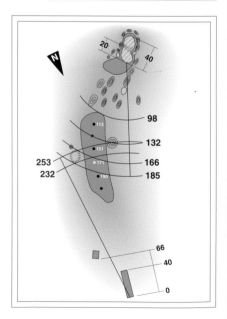

170

9	Championship	389 yards	Par 4
	Medal	376	Par 4
	Ladies'		

10		399 yards	Par 4
		378	Par 4

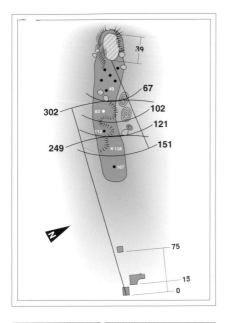

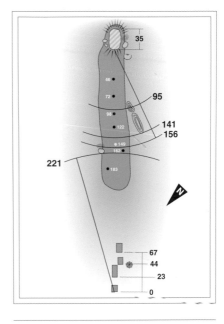

171

11	Championship	216 yards	Par 3
	Medal	216	Par 3
	Ladies'		

12		365 yards	Par 4
		347	Par 4

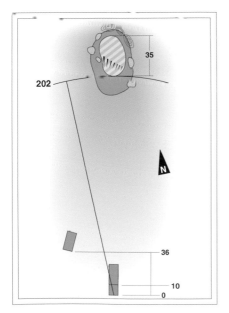

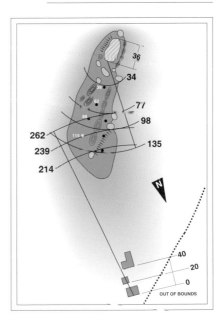

13	Championship	443 yards	Par 4
	Medal	438	Par 4
	Ladies'		

14	507 yards	Par 5
	497	Par 5

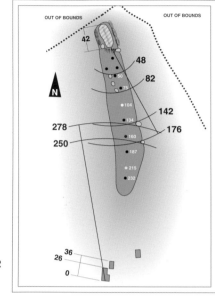

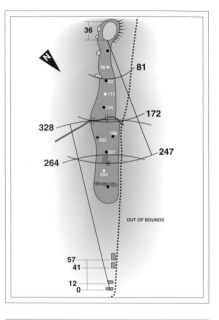

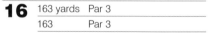

172

15	Championship	466 yards	Par 4
	Medal	437	Par 4
	Ladies'		

16	163 yards	Par 3
	163	Par 3

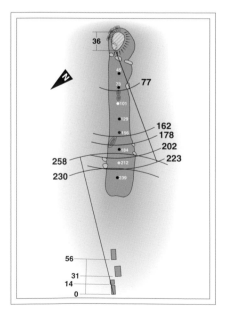

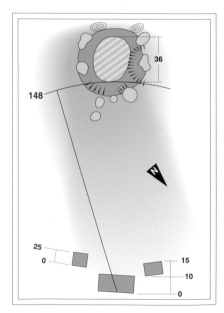

17

Championship	425 yards	Par 4
Medal	413	Par 4
Ladies'		

18

	468 yards	Par 4
	455	Par 4

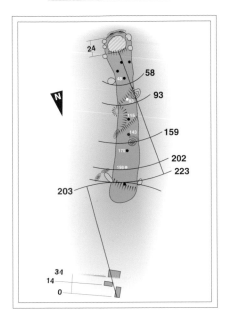

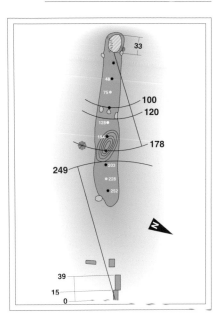

173

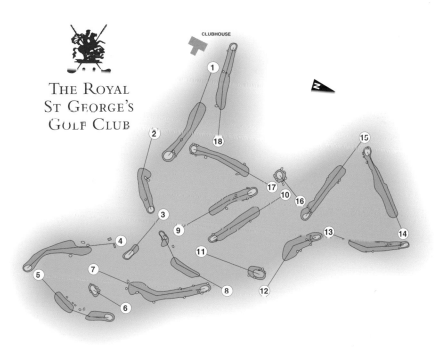

CLUBHOUSE

THE ROYAL
ST GEORGE'S
GOLF CLUB

Open Championship back to Sandwich in 1981 was widely applauded.

The 'Renaissance Open' was won by the American Bill Rogers. The event was deemed a success and St George's was awarded the Open again in 1985. This was Sandy Lyle's year, and the first British victory in the championship for sixteen years. With hindsight, however, neither the 1981 nor 1985 Open was especially memorable for the quality of the golf, and neither particularly advanced the cause of Sandwich as a great 'modern' as well as classic links.

The Open of 1993 was very different. A lengthy dry spell in the month leading up to the Championship had caused many players to fret about the extreme firmness of the fairways, but then came an overnight soaking and St George's turned from yellow-white to yellow-green. If the ultimate test of a great links is its ability to sift potential champions from the supporting cast, then St George's was about to pass with flying colours. After three rounds the leaderboard boasted a galaxy of international stars. Nick Faldo, the defending champion, and Corey Pavin led on 202; Norman and Langer were on 203, while hard on their heels were Nick Price, Ernie Els and Fred Couples: seven of the world's best were in contention. And it got better. The final round turned into an incredible golfing showdown between the top three ranked players in the world, Faldo, Norman and Langer.

The birdies came thick and fast. Playing immediately ahead of Faldo, both Norman and Langer birdied the 1st; Faldo responded with a birdie at the 2nd and Norman birdied the 3rd. The 4th, 5th and 6th comprise the most celebrated run of holes at St George's. To the right of the 4th fairway is the 'tallest and deepest bunker in the United Kingdom' – a good drive must sail pretty close to it; the second shot is then played to a magnificently sited, severely sloping plateau green. The 5th features an exhilarating downhill drive and a sharp dog-leg through a gap in the dunes and the short 6th, the storied 'Maiden', is superbly framed by dunes and encircled by large cavernous pot bunkers. Faldo and Langer each played the stretch in level par, while Norman had two pars and a birdie at the 6th to move one ahead of Faldo and two ahead of Langer. The par five 7th, with its drive across sand-hills, yielded a birdie to Langer. All three parred the 'new' 8th hole, a beautiful two-shotter to a punchbowl green, and Norman gained his fourth birdie at the 9th.

174

The 4th hole at Royal St George's features 'the tallest and deepest bunker in the United Kingdom'; it is also one of the greatest two-shot holes in golf.

As they entered the back nine, Faldo and Langer were having to play 'catch-up golf'. Faldo struck an astonishing tee-shot at the long par three 11th – his ball actually hit the hole; it didn't drop in for an ace (how sensational that would have been!), but he sunk the putt for a two. Langer birdied the 12th and 13th, but Norman continued to play sparkling golf. His approach to the 9th had finished six inches from the flag and at the 12th he hit his second to within four feet. At the par five 14th he got down in two from the edge of the green for his sixth birdie of the round. This hole, the notorious 'Suez', effectively ended Langer's challenge. An out-of-bounds fence runs all the way up the right side of the fairway – and the German's ball drifted too far to the right.

Faldo, like Norman, managed to birdie 'Suez'. It was building to an incredible climax. Up ahead Norman faced a six-footer to save his par at the 15th. Courageously, he holed it. Faldo's approach to the 15th, a searching shot over cross bunkers and dead ground, finished 15 feet from the flag. Meanwhile, Norman had played another marvellous tee-shot to the stage-like green at the short 16th. Faldo's putt shaved the cup, and Norman holed from three feet. It was the decisive birdie. Faldo couldn't repeat his 'best four holes of my life' finish that had swept him to victory at Muirfield and, though Norman missed a very short putt at the 17th, a rifled four iron to the heart of the 18th green and two putts secured him the title. Norman had scored a 64 to eclipse the 67s of Faldo and Langer. His four-round total of 267 was a new championship record.

Special guest at the prize-giving ceremony was the 1932 open champion, Gene Sarazen. 'Are they football scores or golf scores?' asked the sprightly 91-year-old, as he presented Norman with the famous claret jug. Then, endorsing the comments Langer had made on the 18th fairway, he declared, 'That was the most awesome display and the greatest championship I have seen in my seventy years in golf.'

The classic links of Royal St George's had produced the greatest championship of modern times.

Hole	Championship	Medal	Par	Stroke Index	Ladies'	Par	Stroke Index
1	441	413	4	5			
2	376	339	4	14			
3	210	198	3	11			
4	468	417	4	2			
5	421	421	4	9			
6	155	155	3	17			
7	530	487	5	8			
8	418	410	4	3			
9	389	376	4	16			
Out	3408	3216	35				
10	399	378	4	6			
11	216	216	3	15			
12	365	347	4	13			
13	443	438	4	1			
14	507	497	5	12			
15	466	437	4	7			
16	163	163	3	18			
17	425	413	4	4			
18	468	455	4	10			
In	3452	3344	35				
Out	3408	3216	35				
Total	6860	6560	70				

ROYAL BIRKDALE

MERSEYSIDE WAS A GOOD PLACE TO BE IN THE 1960s, FOR THE
GOLFERS AT BIRKDALE, AS WELL AS THE BEATLES IN LIVERPOOL.
BETWEEN 1961 AND 1971 – GOLF'S 'SWINGING SIXTIES' – ROYAL BIRKDALE
STAGED THREE OPEN CHAMPIONSHIPS AND TWO RYDER CUPS.

The halcyon days began with Arnold Palmer slashing his way though strong winds and rain to win a first British Open title, and ended with Lee Trevino ('you can talk to a fade, but a hook won't listen') wisecracking all the way to his first Open Championship success. In between, Jack Nicklaus conceded Tony Jacklin's 'very missable putt' and the two shook hands on a Ryder Cup tie. It all happened amidst the dunes at Birkdale, near Southport in Merseyside.

Royal Birkdale's early history contrasts markedly with its post-war rise to prominence and current status as one of the world's premier championship venues. The club was founded in 1889. Golf was played over a simple nine-hole course on land leased from the local council at a rental of £5 per year. Forced eviction in 1897 led to the club relocating to its present position, where eighteen holes were laid out by George Low.

Even on this excellent new site, things began unpropitiously when the members' first clubhouse had to be unceremoniously pulled down after it was discovered that it had been constructed on land owned by somebody else. The links itself was considered good enough to host a British Ladies' Championship in 1909, but the present course didn't really take shape until it was substantially revised in the mid-1930s by Fred Hawtree (senior) and John H. Taylor. It was also in the 1930s that the club's striking art deco style clubhouse was built. Birkdale was scheduled to stage the 1940 Open Championship, until the outbreak of war forced its cancellation. The Amateur Championship, however, was held on the links in 1946 and Birkdale was duly awarded the 1954 Open: the Australian Peter Thomson won in fine style, and Birkdale had arrived at last.

From a distance Birkdale looks the wildest, most rugged links imaginable. The sand-hills are the largest and most extensive in England. In fact, in the entire British Isles, their size is probably only exceeded by those at Ballybunion. And yet, for all the impressive ruggedness of these dunes, the fairways at Royal Birkdale are among the flattest you are ever likely to experience on a links. It should be emphasized that this flatness does not encompass changes in elevation, for Birkdale has several of these, rather it is the rippling undulations that are absent – or have been eliminated – from the fairways. As a consequence, awkward stances and unfortunate bounces have no place at Birkdale.

The fairways run along valleys

Opposite: The par five 17th at Royal Birkdale is where Tony Jacklin drew level with Jack Nicklaus during their epic Ryder Cup match in 1969.

ROYAL BIRKDALE

1

Championship	452 yards	Par 4
Medal	450	Par 4
Ladies'	418	Par 5

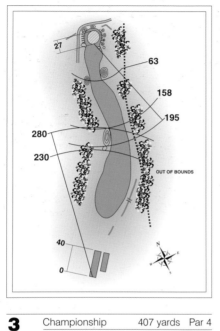

27
63
158
195
280
230
OUT OF BOUNDS
40
0

2

	420 yards	Par 4
	418	Par 4
	391	Par 5

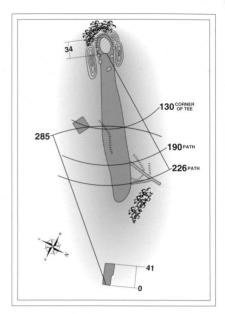

34
130 CORNER OF TEE
285
190 PATH
226 PATH
41
0

3

Championship	407 yards	Par 4
Medal	406	Par 4
Ladies'	327	Par 4

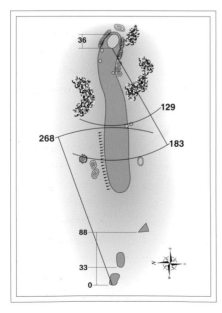

36
129
268
183
88
33
0

4

	202 yards	Par 3
	200	Par 3
	164	Par 3

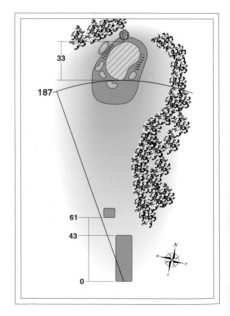

33
187
61
43
0

Royal Birkdale is immensely popular with modern tour players and spectators alike.

beneath the avenues of towering sand-hills; what they don't do is clamber over the top of the dunes, as happens at Royal St George's. Nearly every fairway at Birkdale (and every green for that matter) is impressively framed, therefore the golfer receives a little more protection from the wind than he would on a more open links, such as Hoylake.

The evenness of the lies is one reason why modern professionals hold Royal Birkdale in such high regard, another is that the greens are all very visible targets, with blind and even semi-blind approaches non-existent – provided, of course, you guide your tee-shots into the correct position in the fairway. This is not the place to discuss whether golf is or is not meant to be a 'fair' game, but if it is, then Birkdale must be the nearest thing to a perfect links.

You will not think Birkdale at all

perfect or fair if you frequently stray from the fairways. The rough is extremely punishing and laced with a profusion of willow scrub and buckthorn, which is all very colourful but, unless you have hands like Arnold Palmer, can be devilish to play out of. It also begins with three test-ing par fours, all more than 400 yards long, followed by a par three of over 200 yards. Each of the two-shot holes runs in a different direction, so if there is any amount of wind, you will not have to wait long to confront it.

The 5th, 6th and 7th comprise the best sequence of holes on the front nine. The 5th is a short, curving par four which, if the wind is favourable, can tempt very big hitters to go for the green. It requires a long and risky carry over a pond sited 40 yards short of the green, and with seven bunkers guarding the entrance, the chances of finding the

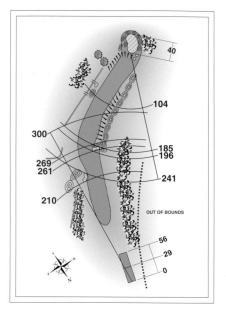

ROYAL BIRKDALE

5	Championship	343 yards	Par 4
	Medal	338	Par 4
	Ladies'	304	Par 4

6	485 yards	Par 5
	484	Par 5
	440	Par 5

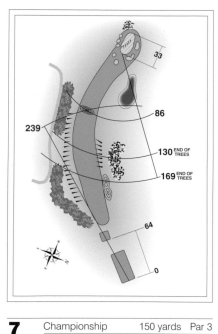

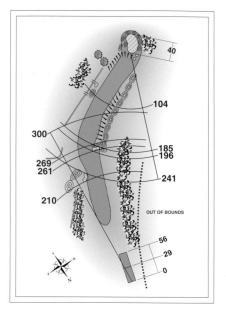

180

7	Championship	150 yards	Par 3
	Medal	150	Par 3
	Ladies'	114	Par 3

8	458 yards	Par 4
	410	Par 4
	352	Par 4

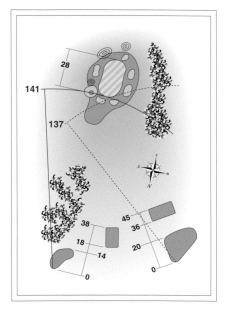

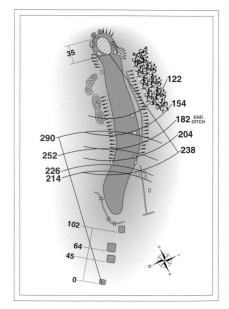

9	Championship	408 yards	Par 4
	Medal	407	Par 4
	Ladies'	354	Par 4

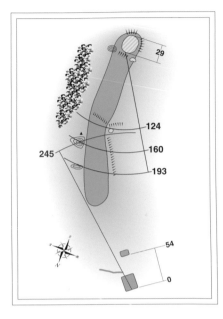

10	403 yards	Par 4
	384	Par 4
	337	Par 4

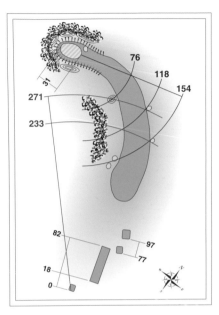

181

11	Championship	407 yards	Par 4
	Medal	374	Par 4
	Ladies'	317	Par 4

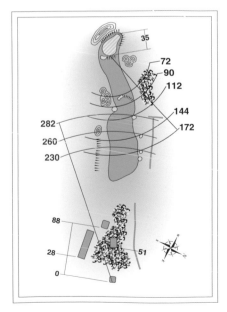

12	183 yards	Par 3
	181	Par 3
	145	Par 3

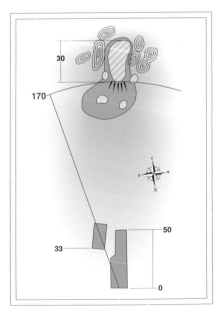

13	Championship	474 yards	Par 4
	Medal	433	Par 4
	Ladies'	422	Par 5

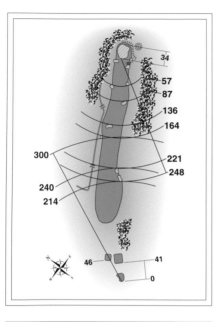

34
57
87
136
164
300
221
248
240
214
46
41
0

14	198 yards	Par 4
	197	Par 4
	137	Par 5

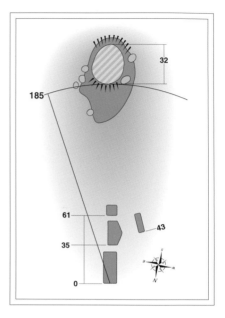

32
185
61
43
35
0

15	Championship	544 yards	Par 5
	Medal	542	Par 5
	Ladies'	392	Par 5

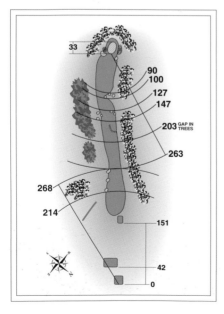

33
90
100
127
147
203 GAP IN TREES
263
268
214
151
42
0

16	417 yards	Par 4
	347	Par 4
	293	Par 4

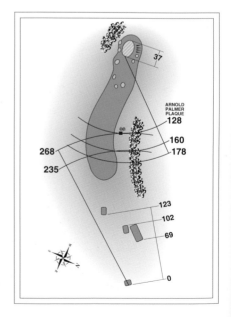

37
ARNOLD PALMER PLAQUE
128
160
178
268
235
123
102
69
0

17	Championship	518 yards	Par 5
	Medal	497	Par 5
	Ladies'	425	Par 5

18	472 yards	Par 4
	476	Par 5
	441	Par 5

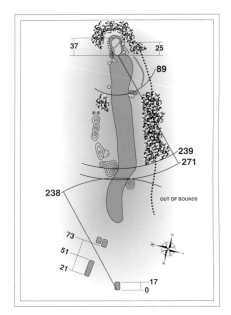

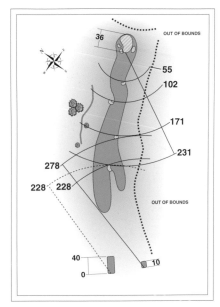

183

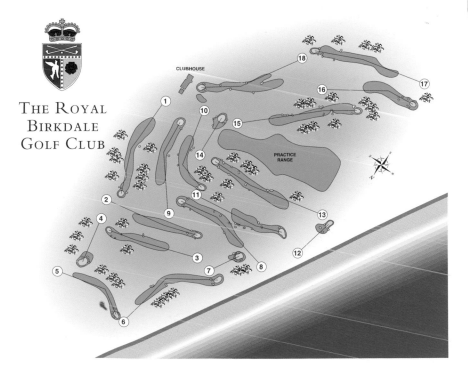

THE ROYAL BIRKDALE GOLF CLUB

putting surface are remote. The 6th has scuppered the hopes of many a would-be Open champion. From the championship tee, it is probably the toughest par four on the course, although from the medal and forward tees it does become a par five. The hole sweeps to the right and a bunker eats into the angle of the dogleg. At one time the sand completely traversed the fairway, but it is now possible to squeeze a long drive through a gap on the left. This still leaves a long and searching second to a large sloping green. It is followed by the shortest hole on the course. The 7th has an elevated tee and its green is almost encircled by bunkers – a real target golf hole. You may leave this green scratching your head and wondering how Ian Baker-Finch could possibly have been five under par at this stage of his final round in the 1991 Open Championship.

The 8th features another high tee and

184

a green 'blessed' by Trevino after he holed a 35-foot putt on the final day of the 1971 Open: it was his seventh single putt in eight holes. The 9th is a better golf hole, however; its superb approach to a raised green brings you back to the clubhouse. Not wishing to leave Baker-Finch stranded on the 7th green, it should be recorded that he completed his front nine holes in 29 strokes, the lowest-ever by an Open champion.

The longer back nine starts with a strong dog-leg left to a green tucked neatly into the hills. The 11th is a slightly longer and straighter par four, then there is an outstanding short hole. Birkdale's 12th has been carved out of the most rugged part of the links. It is a relatively new hole, constructed by Fred Hawtree (junior), but originally planned by his father. Tom Watson regards it as one of the world's greatest par threes. The tee is situated in the dunes, as, most handsomely, is the green, and to get from one to the other you must hit across a shallow valley and try to avoid a quartet of pot bunkers.

The 13th and 14th have witnessed the very best and worst of Open Championship drama. Nowadays the 13th is a long par four, but in the 1976 'year of the drought' Open it was played as a par five. Johnny Miller, the mercurial American,

Soon after the Second World War, Royal Birkdale emerged as 'the fairest links in England'; between 1961 and 1971 it staged three Open Championships and two Ryder Cups.

sealed his victory at the 13th when he chipped in for an eagle three. In 1983 Hale Irwin tried to backhand a two-inch putt on the short 14th, but completely missed his ball: of course the 'shot' counted, and Irwin eventually missed out on a play-off by a single stroke.

The 15th is a giant of a hole. It measures 543 yards from the back tee and has no fewer than thirteen bunkers, many of which are placed to snare errant second shots. If you visit one of these fairway traps, you could be staring a seven or an eight in the face. The 16th belongs to Arnold Palmer. A plaque marks the spot in the rough from where he played a miraculous recovery stroke in the 1961 Open. The hole was then the 15th (this was before Hawtree had built the celebrated 12th). Palmer's ball was buried beneath thick scrub, yet he somehow smashed it out with a six iron and it landed on the green, finishing 15 feet from the flag. The green is not overly large and is plateaued, which makes Palmer's stroke even more remarkable.

Scylla and Charybdis await at the par five 17th. You must drive between these twin sentinel dunes to reach the fairway from a platform tee. A birdie opportunity beckons if you can get a good drive away. Jacklin did even better than this when he sank a putt of 60 feet for an eagle three to draw level in his epic duel with Nicklaus in the final singles of the 1969 Ryder Cup.

If the 16th belongs to Palmer and the 17th to Jacklin, the long par four 18th has two principal claimants. In 1976 there was 'the shot that gave birth to a legend': nineteen-year-old Severiano Ballesteros (whose name no one could pronounce) executed the most audacious bump-and-run shot between two greenside bunkers – a stroke that enabled him to share second place with Nicklaus behind Miller. And in 1983, Watson, needing a four to secure a one stroke triumph and his fifth Open crown in nine years, drilled a 200-yard-plus two iron into the heart of the green, then two-putted for victory – the perfect shot when he needed it most. 'I'll take that shot to the grave,' said Watson. Clearly, a 'life' and 'death' hole.

Hole	Championship	Medal	Par	Stroke Index	Ladies'	Par	Stroke Index
1	448	447	4	11	418	5	11
2	417	416	4	3	391	5	3
3	409	407	4	7	327	4	7
4	203	202	3	15	164	3	15
5	346	341	4	13	304	4	13
6	473	488	4/5	1	440	5	1
7	156	150	3	17	114	3	17
8	458	414	4	9	352	4	9
9	414	413	4	5	354	4	5
Out	3324	3278	34/35		2864	37	
10	395	372	4	14	337	4	14
11	409	374	4	8	317	4	8
12	184	181	3	18	145	3	18
13	475	436	4	4	422	5	4
14	199	198	3	16	137	5	16
15	543	542	5	2	392	5	2
16	414	344	4	12	293	4	12
17	525	502	5	6	425	5	6
18	472	476	4/5	10	441	5	10
In	3616	3425	36/37		2909	40	
Out	3324	3278	34/35		2864	37	
Total	6940	6703	70/72		5773	77	

ROYAL LYTHAM & ST ANNES

IMAGINE TRAVELLING FROM TURNBERRY IN AYRSHIRE TO ROYAL LYTHAM & ST ANNES IN LANCASHIRE; IMAGINE TRADING THE LAND OF ROBBIE BURNS FOR THE LAND OF L. S. LOWRY.

Goodbye Ailsa Craig, the Isle of Arran and Bruce's Castle; hello red brick suburbia, a railway line and Blackpool Tower.

Lytham is not easy to love. If Cypress Point is the 'Sistine Chapel of Golf' Royal Lytham & St Annes could be its 'Dark Satanic Mill'. After all, American writer Art Spander once described the Victorian clubhouse as 'an ominous gabled structure of brick and wood, undoubtedly the former residence of Count Dracula.' He then added, 'But you don't get really frightened until you see the golf course.'

So why would you be travelling to Royal Lytham & St Annes? Maybe it doesn't bother you that the links is situated a full mile inland or that you may get the occasional whiff of the Irish Sea, but you will never see nor hear it. Golf, you might point out, especially golf in the North of England, is not a beauty contest: it is about challenge and character. How many golf courses on Earth can provide as great a challenge and exude as much character as Royal Lytham?

Or perhaps you are on a pilgrimage. The wealth of history and tradition at Royal Lytham is almost tangible, and to play the course is to walk on hallowed ground. This is the links immortalized by Bobby Jones and twice conquered by Seve Ballesteros. It has staged the Open Championship on no fewer than nine occasions, most recently (and so memorably for Tom Lehman), in 1996.

Art Spander was guilty of exaggeration. Lytham's clubhouse can appear somewhat imposing from the outside, but Bram Stoker's creation never set foot inside. In fact, the atmosphere within is certainly more relaxed than at many 'Royal' clubs. Nor should first-timers expect to be terrified by the prospect of the opening hole. Although expertly bunkered, the 1st at Lytham is fairly straightforward. It is also a par three, which is unique for an Open Championship venue, but by Lytham standards such an anomaly is par for the course. The entire layout has maverick tendencies. In addition to beginning with a short hole, it contains successive par fives on the front nine and, owing to greater yardage and the prevailing north-westerly wind, has a much tougher back nine. Lytham is frankly lopsided. It is the type of course on which a scratch player can scorch to the turn in 32 or 33, only to limp home in 40.

The land is equally nonconformist. The turf is excellent – true links terrain with firm, fast greens – but while some of the holes appear to have been plucked from Carnoustie, others are fashioned in the spirit of Birkdale and a couple invoke

Opposite: Seve Ballesteros plays his second to the 18th in the final round of the 1988 Open Championship. Despite hitting through the green, the Spaniard parred the hole and held off the spirited challenge of Nick Price.

1	Championship	206 yards	Par 3
	Medal	206	Par 3
	Ladies'	172	Par 3

2	437 yards	Par 4
	420	Par 4
	370	Par 4

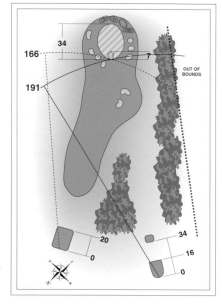

OUT OF BOUNDS

34

166

191

7

20

0

34

16

0

188

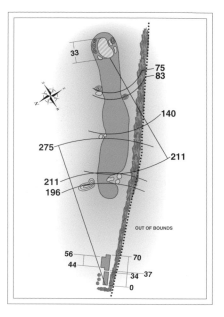

33

75
83

140

275

211

211
196

OUT OF BOUNDS

56
44

70

34 37

0

3	Championship	457 yards	Par 4
	Medal	457	Par 4
	Ladies'	418	Par 5

4	393 yards	Par 4
	393	Par 4
	357	Par 4

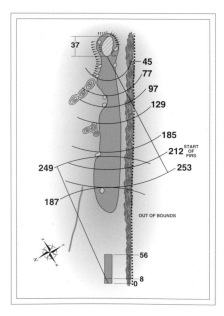

37

45
77

97

129

185

212 START OF FIRS

253

249

187

OUT OF BOUNDS

56

8
0

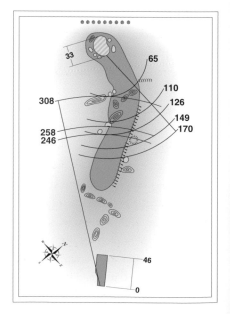

33

65

110

126

149
170

308

258
246

46

0

memories of Sandwich and Prestwick. It is an extraordinary mix. One tree-lined fairway (at the 11th) wouldn't look out of place at Royal Blackheath, an historic London parkland course. Inconsistent topography partly explains the constant changes in form and mood, but another reason is that over the years various course architects, including such master craftsmen as Tom Simpson, Herbert Fowler and Harry Colt, have all contributed to the design.

A plaque in the rough on the left of the 17th fairway marks the spot where Bobby Jones played a sensational recovery shot in the 1926 Open.

Anyone requiring proof as to the angle of the prevailing wind need only peer down the 2nd and 3rd fairways. The Preston to Blackpool railway line runs parallel to these holes all along their right-hand side and serves as a slicer's graveyard. Some willow trees have taken root amidst the rough on a thin strip of land between the fairway and the railway line, and these trees stoop and bow in deference to the wind. At Royal Lytham, the wind is always king.

The 2nd and 3rd are formidable two-shotters. At first glance they appear similar, yet they play quite differently. The 2nd rewards a brave drive directly over a giant nest of bunkers to the right of the fairway, whereas on the 3rd the left side should be favoured from the tee, and followed by a very precise approach to a green guarded by deep pot bunkers and a menacing bank of rough. Pitching and chipping is rarely easy at Lytham, for not only are the greens jealously protected, but many also sit on natural plateaux with swales and hollows characterizing the surrounding ground.

The 4th and 5th are the only holes on the outward nine that do not head away from the clubhouse. Blackpool Tower, as well as three church spires, can be glimpsed from the tee of the 4th, but there is little to catch the eye at the short 5th which, as it turns out, is a 'wolf in sheep's cloth-ing' since the green is almost encircled by six traps of varying size and depth.

A fine sequence of holes begins at the 6th, the first of the back-to-back par fives. Whether your preference is for the 6th or 7th depends on whether you favour the Royal St George's (crumpled fairway – awkward stance) type of links hole or the Royal Birkdale (level fairway – even stance) approach. The St George's-like 6th has the more interesting collection of fairway bunkers to negoti-ate, while the 7th has the more attractively sited green, nestling in a bowl amid the dunes.

The 8th pays homage to no other links. It is a truly heroic hole and, though it may not be the most famous at Lytham, surely rivals the 18th as the great-est hole. The view from the elevated tee is positively inspiring. Measuring in excess of 400 yards from the championship markers, it features some vast sand-hills

5	Championship	212 yards	Par 3
	Medal	188	Par 3
	Ladies'	148	Par 3

6	490 yards	Par 5
	486	Par 5
	400	Par 5

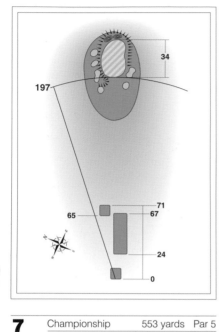

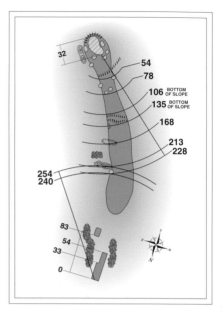

7	Championship	553 yards	Par 5
	Medal	551	Par 5
	Ladies'	506	Par 5

8	418 yards	Par 4
	406	Par 4
	311	Par 4

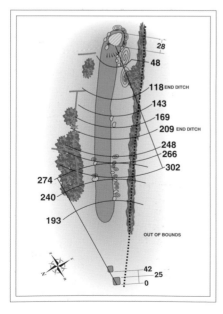

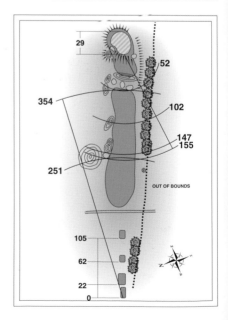

9	Championship	164 yards	Par 3
	Medal	162	Par 3
	Ladies'	137	Par 3

10	334 yards	Par 4
	334	Par 4
	305	Par 4

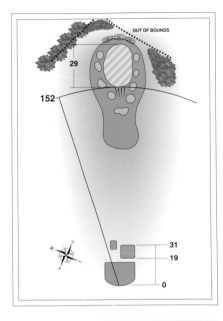

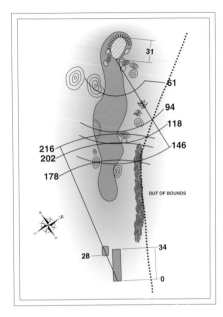

191

11	Championship	542 yards	Par 5
	Medal	485	Par 5
	Ladies'	381	Par 5

12	196 yards	Par 3
	189	Par 3
	151	Par 3

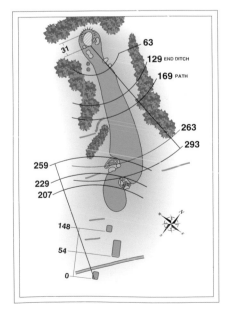

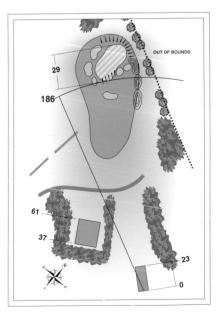

13	Championship	342 yards	Par 4
	Medal	339	Par 4
	Ladies'	275	Par 4

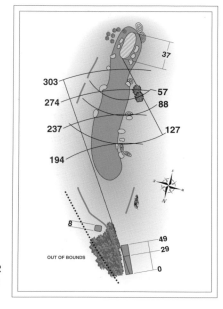

14	445 yards	Par 4
	445	Par 4
	418	Par 5

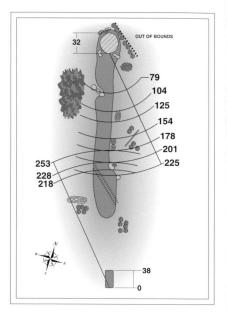

15	Championship	463 yards	Par 4
	Medal	463	Par 4
	Ladies'	433	Par 5

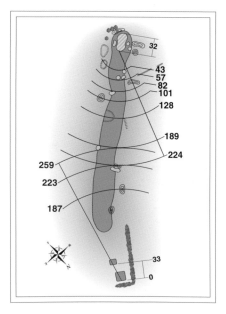

16	357 yards	Par 4
	356	Par 4
	331	Par 4

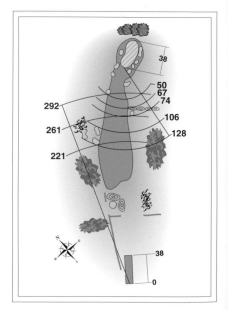

192

17			
	Championship	467 yards	Par 4
	Medal	413	Par 4
	Ladies'	386	Par 5

18		
	414 yards	Par 4
	386	Par 4
	315	Par 4

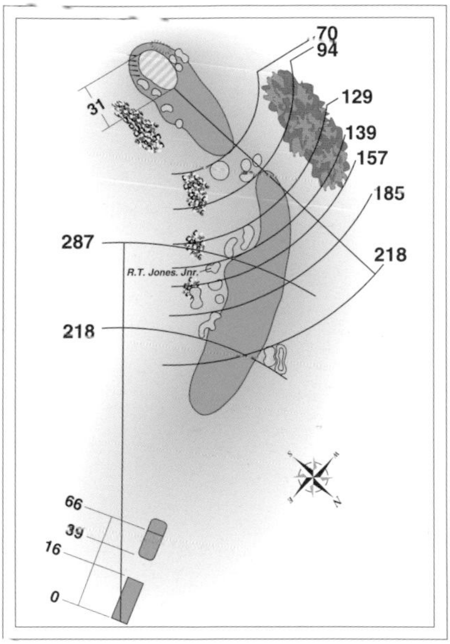

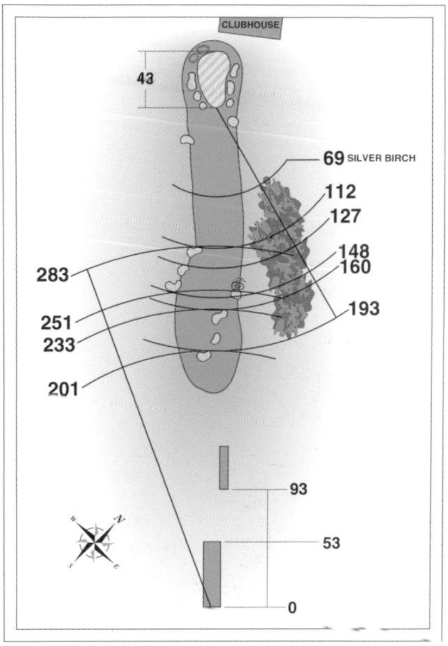

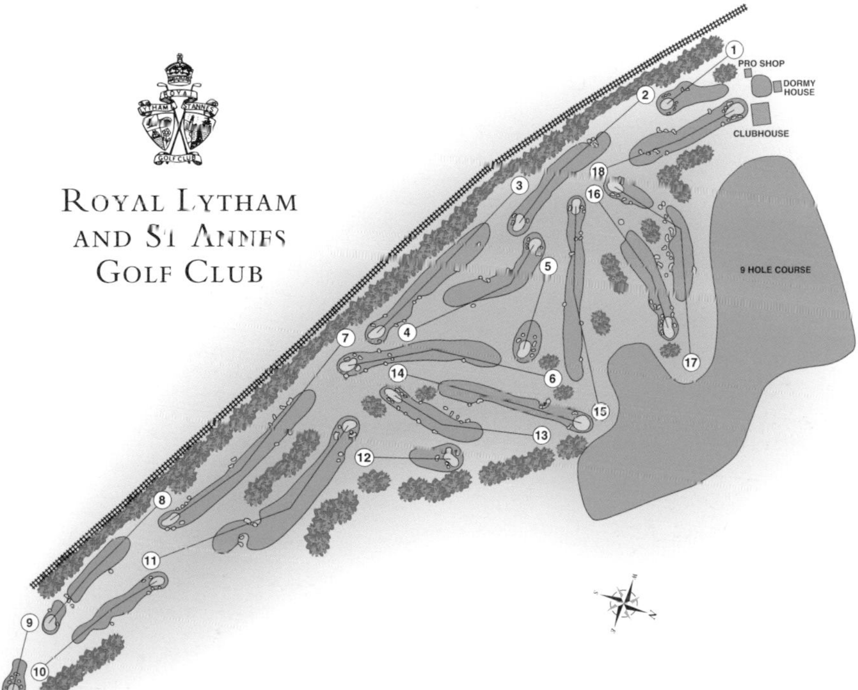

70
94
31
129
139
157
185
287
218
R.T. Jones. Jnr.
218
66
39
16
0

CLUBHOUSE
43
69 SILVER BIRCH
112
127
283
148
160
251
233
193
201
93
53
0

PRO SHOP
DORMY HOUSE
CLUBHOUSE
9 HOLE COURSE
1
2
3
4
5
6
7
8
9
10
11
12
13
14
15
16
17
18

ROYAL LYTHAM AND ST ANNES GOLF CLUB

The green (as well as the fairway) at the par five 6th is defended by a series of cavernous pot bunkers.

and a cavernous fairway bunker to the left (visit here and a sand-iron might just get you back out on to the fairway); the railway line and trees form a continuous boundary to the right and, straight ahead as you drive, a trio of cross bunkers are set into a rise in the fairway 50 yards short of the green. As for the green, it is perched, in crown-like fashion, beyond an area of dead ground at the top of the hill. It is also defended by a pair of gaping pot bunkers. If you miss the putting surface and the greenside traps, chances are that you will be playing your next from deep gorse or from rough 30 feet below the level of the green.

The 9th is located at the far end of the links and is a gem of a par three. Then – 'All change!' – time to turn and face the wind. Should one start to tremble? Not yet. The 10th twists and tumbles, but it is only a short par four; the 11th, the 'parkland hole', has a difficult tee-shot but is a par five nonetheless. Although the next is a fairly long and fiendishly bunkered par three, the 13th offers another birdie opportunity.

It is now, with five holes to play, that Royal Lytham throws down the gauntlet. You stand on the 14th tee at Lytham, hoping your knuckles don't turn white. For optimists, it is the hour of reckoning; for pessimists, the wrecking hour. Champions, of course, rise to the challenge. In the second round of the 1979 Open, Ballesteros played the fearsome finishing stretch in four under par and, in his final round, he missed all but two fairways, including each of the last five (who can forget his famous car-park escapade at the 16th?), yet played these closing holes in level par.

The 14th, 15th and 17th are all prodigiously long par fours. The 15th is possibly the most difficult of the trio: a slightly uphill drive paves the way for a long and semi-blind approach; the fairway undulates more than most and is strewn with a sea of seemingly magnetic pot bunkers … the Killing Fields of Royal Lytham.

History envelops the 17th and 18th. The former dog-legs sharply to the left and is almost as long and as difficult as the 15th. It is on this hole that Bobby Jones effectively won the 1926 Open. Sharing the lead in the final round with his playing partner, Al Watrous, whose ball was lying safely on the green in two, Jones had hooked his tee-shot wildly into an area of sand and scrub. He was 175 yards from the flag and faced a blind shot across a wilderness of dunes and rough. Jones selected his hickory-shafted mashie iron and proceeded to play the greatest shot of his life. This outrageous stroke – Jones's ball finished inside his partner's knocked the stuffing out of Watrous. 'There goes a hundred thousand bucks,' he allegedly cried, and duly three-putted the 17th (or 71st) green. Watrous then dropped another stroke at the last.

The 18th owes its reputation as one of the world's most celebrated finishing holes to some magnificent fairway and greenside bunkering. Like the 17th, it has witnessed more than its fair share of drama. British commentators wax lyrical whenever they recall Tony Jacklin's arrow-straight drive that split the final fairway and secured his triumph in 1969. Five years later South African Gary Player was forced to putt left-handed from up against the clubhouse wall, yet held on to win his third Open Championship. Ballesteros also claimed a hat trick of victories when he all but holed his pitch shot from behind the green to defeat Nick Price after a titanic duel in 1988.

Hole	Championship	Medal	Par	Stroke index	Ladies'	Par	Stroke Index
1	206	206	3	13	172	3	13
2	437	420	4	5	370	4	5
3	457	457	4	1	418	5	1
4	393	393	4	9	357	4	9
5	212	188	3	15	148	3	15
6	490	486	5	7	400	5	7
7	553	551	5	3	506	5	3
8	418	406	4	11	311	4	11
9	164	162	3	17	137	3	17
Out	3330	3269	35		2819	36	
10	334	334	4	10	305	4	10
11	542	485	5	4	381	5	4
12	198	189	3	14	151	3	14
13	342	339	4	18	275	4	18
14	445	445	4	6	418	5	6
15	463	463	4	2	433	5	2
16	357	356	4	16	331	4	16
17	467	413	4	8	386	5	8
18	414	386	4	12	315	4	12
In	3562	3410	36		2995	39	
Out	3330	3269	35		2819	36	
Total	6892	6679	71		5814	75	

GANTON

Is this the WALTON HEATH OF THE NORTH OR THE MUIRFIELD OF THE SOUTH? IS IT AN 'INLAND LINKS' OR A 'LINKS INLAND'? SITUATED NINE MILES FROM THE COAST, YET POSSESSING MANY OF THE CHARACTERISTICS OF SEASIDE GOLF, GANTON IS A COURSE APART.

The North Yorkshire club was formed in 1891. Originally it was called the Scarborough Golf Club, although its quiet location on the edge of the Vale of Pickering has never changed. Good fortune and fame came early to Ganton, for just five years after its foundation the club appointed Harry Vardon as its professional and within a few weeks of the appointment Vardon claimed the first of his record six Open Championship victories.

Whilst it is pretty much surrounded by trees, the course itself occupies open heathland, similar to Walton Heath, and lies on a substratum of rich sand, hence its seaside nature. Unlike many of the best heathland layouts in the south of England, trees have never really been encouraged to grow on the course. There is, however, a profusion of gorse, as well as a fair smattering of broom and heather. Bernard Darwin did Ganton a bit of a disservice when he described it as 'charmingly pretty in a way that is comparatively ordinary to anyone who has seen Surrey and Berkshire.' On a fine sunny day when the gorse is in full bloom, Ganton becomes a riot of blue, green and gold. (Moreover, as every Yorkshireman will point out, at Ganton you cannot hear the roar of the M25).

The eighteen holes were originally laid out by Tom Chisholm of St Andrews. Chisholm's design was revised on several occasions, but never substantially. With architectural input from, among others, Vardon, James Braid, Herbert Fowler, Harry Colt and Alister Mackenzie, Ganton gradually evolved into a great course.

If the exposed, windswept nature of the heath causes Ganton to resemble Walton Heath, it is the style and extent of the bunkering which likens it to a links course. No inland course, in Surrey or elsewhere, has bunkers remotely similar to those at Ganton. Here they are far larger, much deeper and more prolific – as any player straying to the right at either of the first two holes quickly discovers. With their steep revetted faces, they are, of course, links-type bunkers and Ganton has more than a hundred of them. Whenever new ones are cut, seashells are discovered beneath the surface: apparently Ganton and the surrounding area were once an arm of the sea.

The placement of the bunkers is also superb: it is very strategic, indeed more so than on a typical links course, where nature tends to make the bunkering somewhat haphazard. In this regard

197

GANTON

1

Championship	373 yards	Par 4
Medal	373	Par 4
Ladies'	357	Par 4

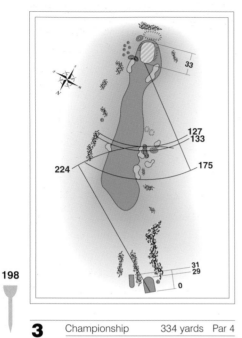

2

418 yards	Par 4
418	Par 4
371	Par 4

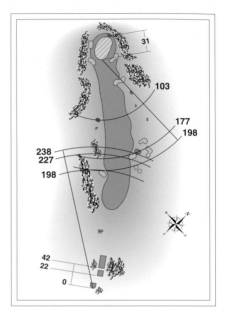

3

Championship	334 yards	Par 4
Medal	334	Par 4
Ladies'	275	Par 4

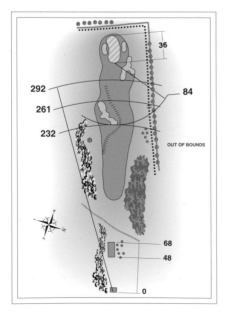

4

406 yards	Par 4
406	Par 4
349	Par 4

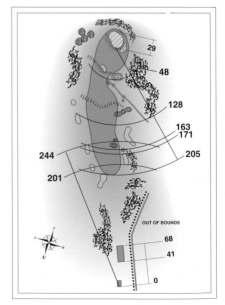

With a pond to the left and gorse and bunkers all around, the only place to be is on the green; the 5th is one of only two par threes at Ganton.

Ganton resembles Muirfield, and it is difficult to pay it a higher compliment than that. Patric Dickinson had his finger on the pulse when he wrote, 'The secret of Ganton lies in its subtle use of ground and its brilliant, suggestive bunkering.'

The course has no major climbs to negotiate and the fairways have only a few significant undulations. Considering that Alister Mackenzie had a hand in fashioning many of the greens, they, too, seem surprisingly flat – that is, at first glance. In fact, subtlety, as Patric Dickinson observed, and understatement reign supreme at Ganton. It is not an overly long course, but the routing ensures that if there is any wind about, it will both assist and confront the player at regular intervals throughout the round.

If Ganton has a weakness, it is that there are only two par threes. However, the two-shot holes more than compen-sate, and provide enormous variety. Most modern courses – or most modern archi-tects – seem to spurn the short par four, even though many golfers relish playing a hole where they can weigh up the risks and rewards of 'going for the green' with their drive; Ganton has two, if not three of these holes.

The diversity among the par fours is experienced in the first four holes. Provided those cavernous bunkers to the right of the fairway are avoided, the 1st is a fairly gentle opening hole. On the 2nd you must drive over a crest, then hit down to a green that slopes sharply away from you – a much tougher proposition. The 3rd is just about drivable from the front tee, though you must somehow thread your tee-shot along an hourglass-shaped fairway. The 4th is an absolute gem. Many rate it as the best hole on the course. You can afford to open your

5

Championship	157 yards	Par 3
Medal	157	Par 3
Ladies'	144	Par 3

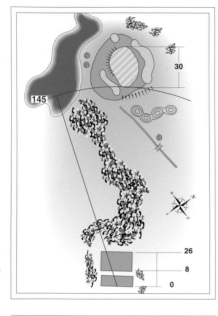

6

449 yards	Par 4
449	Par 4
435	Par 5

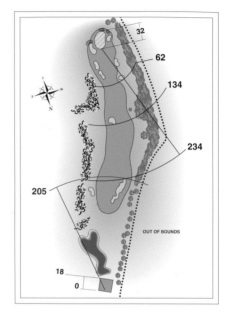

200

7

Championship	435 yards	Par 4
Medal	435	Par 4
Ladies'	405	Par 4

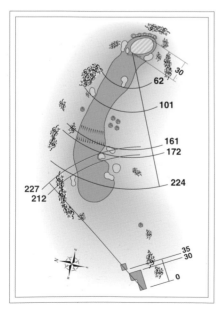

8

414 yards	Par 4
392	Par 4
359	Par 4

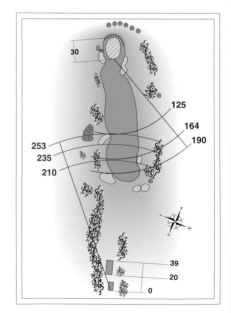

9	Championship	506 yards	Par 5
	Medal	504	Par 5
	Ladies'	431	Par 5

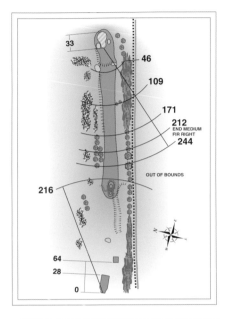

10	168 yards	Par 3
	164	Par 3
	133	Par 3

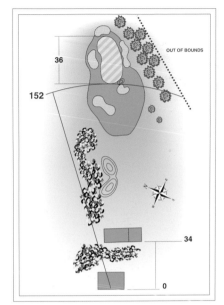

201

11	Championship	417 yards	Par 4
	Medal	390	Par 4
	Ladies'	381	Par 4

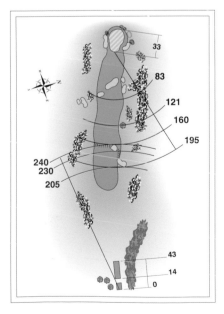

12	363 yards	Par 4
	344	Par 4
	321	Par 4

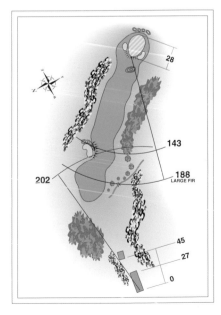

13	Championship	524 yards	Par 5
	Medal	499	Par 5
	Ladies'	468	Par 5

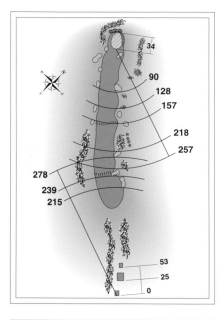

14	282 yards	Par 4
	282	Par 4
	279	Par 4

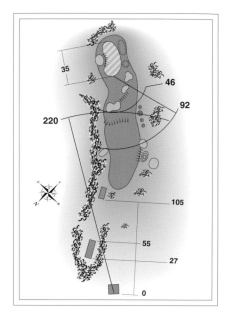

15	Championship	461 yards	Par 4
	Medal	437	Par 4
	Ladies'	421	Par 5

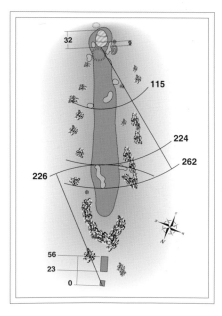

16	448 yards	Par 4
	448	Par 4
	391	Par 4

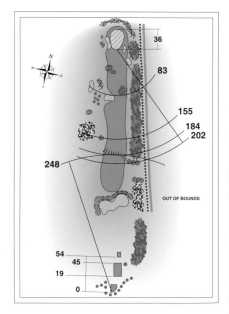

GANTON

17	Championship	249 yards	Par 4
	Medal	252	Par 3
	Ladies'	169	Par 3

18	434 yards	Par 4
	400	Par 4
	363	Par 5

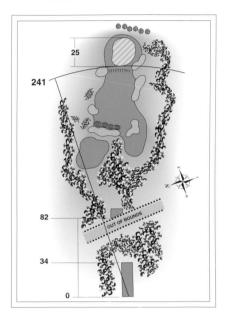

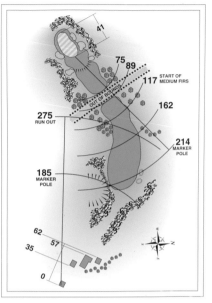

GANTON GOLF CLUB

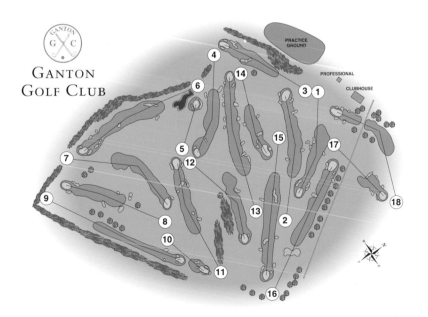

shoulders a little as you drive, but it is the exciting second shot that really makes the hole: it is fired across a watery gully to an attractive plateau green; there is a steepish fall-away to the left and a bunker eats into the right side of the green.

Sand and gorse are about all you see when you arrive at the tee of the short 5th. You have no option but to carry the gorse, and if you pull your shot badly and miss both the green and the sand, your ball could finish in a large pond. Most people are happy with a par at this hole! Three strong fours now follow, the best of these being the classic 7th.

For all the comparisons with Walton Heath and Muirfield, Ganton's 7th hole **204** looks as if it could have been plucked from one of the great sand-belt courses of Melbourne. It is a beautiful, swinging dog-leg to the right and features a nest of Mackenzie-style bunkers lurking just

beyond the fairway at the corner of the dog-leg. The approach is struck very slightly uphill to a raised green defended by twin bunkers to the left and another to the right. Approximately 60 yards short of the green, a large fairway bunker serves to confuse distance perception.

The front nine concludes with a genuine par five. It is possible to reach the green at the 9th with two good blows, but it requires an accurate drive along a gathering valley and a long, straight second to a small, sloping green.

The 10th is the second short hole and, like the 5th, the only place to be is on the green – the putting surface is virtually encircled by five bunkers. Then come two very contrasting par fours. The 11th is an undulating but fairly straight hole with a second that must carry a vast cross bunker, and the 12th a severe dog-leg played from an elevated tee, where you are tempted to drive over the top of some tall pines to leave yourself a simple pitch to the green. The 13th is a par five with thirteen bunkers, but Ganton's acclaimed finish doesn't properly begin until you reach the 14th tee. The 14th is the second of Ganton's drivable par fours. Unless there is a strong helping wind, it takes a brave man to attempt the shot, for the direct route to the

The 'home hole: the 18th at Ganton dog-legs sharply from right to left. The approach must be threaded between trees to find a green protected by five bunkers.

flag requires a 240-yard carry over a huge crater-like bunker. The green itself is defended by sand to the left and swales to the right, with yet more gorse over the back.

The 15th and 16th are both big par fours, comparable in quality to the 4th and 7th, and running in opposite directions. The 15th has an elevated tee and some very interesting bunkering, including a 40-yard-long bunker that snakes its way up the left side of the fairway. It also has a depression in front of the green and another in the central portion of the green. At the 16th you must drive over a huge cross bunker, the biggest on the entire course. There is quite a lot of movement in the fairway and the approach is downhill to a green fringed by gorse and sand and overlooked by a number of sentinel pines.

Ganton's penultimate challenge is the third 'risk and reward' hole. It only just qualifies as a par four, although with the green perched at the top of a steep rise and defended by typically deep traps, it requires a very solid stroke if it is to be reached from the tee. Careful positioning of the drive is the key to mastering the dog-legged 18th; if you fail to find the centre of the fairway, your view of the green may be restricted by trees. . . So hit a good tee-shot, avoid the five greenside traps with your approach and roll the putt in for a birdie three!

In the pleasantly intimate clubhouse you will assuredly sample the famous Ganton Cake and be reminded of the club's illustrious history. Ganton's name

will always be linked with Vardon's, but another great player also developed his talents on the Yorkshire course – Ted Ray, the famed long hitter who, like Vardon, won the Open on both sides of the Atlantic. Over the years, the club has staged numerous major amateur events including, on three occasions, the British Amateur Championship. In 1949 Ganton hosted the Ryder Cup: the home side led by three matches to one at the end of the first day only to lose eventually by seven matches to five. Ben Hogan, convalescing from his near-fatal accident, led the victorious American side as non-playing captain.

Hole	Championship	Medal	Par	Stroke Index	Ladies'	Par	Stroke Index
1	373	373	4	15	357	4	15
2	418	418	4	7	371	4	7
3	334	334	4	13	275	4	13
4	406	406	4	5	349	4	5
5	157	157	3	17	144	3	17
6	449	449	4	9	435	5	1
7	435	435	4	91	406	5	9
8	414	392	4	11	359	4	11
9	506	504	5	3	431	5	3
Out	3492	3468	36		3126	38	
10	168	168	3	18	133	3	18
11	417	417	4	6	381	4	6
12	363	363	4	10	321	4	10
13	524	499	5	2	468	5	2
14	282	282	4	14	279	4	14
15	461	437	4	4	421	5	4
16	448	448	4	8	391	4	8
17	249	252	4/3	16	169	3	16
18	434	400	4	12	363	5	12
In	3346	3266	36/35		2926	37	
Out	3492	3468	36		3126	38	
Total	6838	6734	72/71		6052	75	

SUNNINGDALE (OLD)

THE AVERAGE LONDONER LIVING IN LATE VICTORIAN ENGLAND MUST HAVE WONDERED WHAT THE SCOTS SAW IN A GAME OF GOLF — CERTAINLY IF WHAT THEY WITNESSED IN AND AROUND THE CAPITAL WAS ANYTHING TO GO BY.

There were two types of golf and golf course in late 19th-century London: the unimaginative, muddy parkland sort, where flat square-shaped greens were the order of the day, and the anything-but-dull game that was played on the famous commons such as Blackheath, Tooting Bec and Wimbledon. Lord Newton, a keen Victorian golfer, provided this evocative description of the 'golf course' on Tooting Bec Common: 'A confined area intersected by numerous roads, frequented by perambulator-wheeling nursemaids and also by loafers and tramps. The hazards consist largely of street lamps and forbidding gorse clumps whose recesses, for various reasons, are best left unexplored.'

And yet, waiting to be discovered only a few miles to the south-west of London lay some of the finest natural golfing terrain in the world. Woking Golf Club, founded in 1893, was the first course to be built over the glorious heathland of Surrey and Berkshire, while the one widely acknowledged as the finest was started seven years later when Willie Park, jun., son of the first Open champion, was commissioned to design eighteen holes at Sunningdale.

The great heathland courses didn't need discovering so much as uncovering.

The soft, quickly draining sandy terrain – very similar to that found on a links – was largely concealed by a conspiracy of heather, bracken, gorse and often (though not at Sunningdale despite its present appearance) forests of pine and silver birch. The land at Sunningdale was especially sandy, and it was a gracefully – and sometimes dramatically – undulating site that was presented to Willie Park.

Naturally blessed, Sunningdale was fortunate to receive the skilful attention of Park, and perhaps even more fortunate in its choice of a first golf club secretary. That man was Harry Colt, a young lawyer in 1901 and, as he would later prove at Sunningdale and elsewhere, a budding golf architect of the highest calibre. It was Colt who made minor adjustments and improvements to Park's design (the introduction of the revolutionary rubber-cored Haskell golf ball soon after the course's opening required it to be lengthened) and was responsible for an extensive tree planting programme, the spectacular results of which are so visible today.

Colt remained Secretary at Sunningdale for twelve years. His link with the club continued when he was invited to construct a second eighteen holes, the Sunningdale New Course in 1922. The

---

Opposite: Golf beneath a splendid Sunningdale sky. Designed by Willie Park, jun., around the turn of the century, the Old Course remains the premier heathland course in the British Isles.

1	Championship	494 yards	Par 5
	Medal	494	Par 5
	Ladies'	449	Par 5

2	484 yards	Par 5
	456	Par 4
	436	Par 5

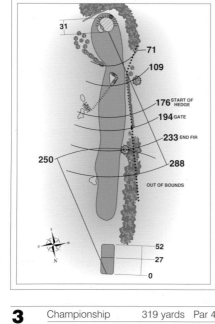

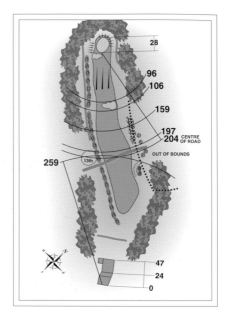

3	Championship	319 yards	Par 4
	Medal	296	Par 4
	Ladies'	268	Par 4

4	161 yards	Par 3
	161	Par 3
	138	Par 3

208

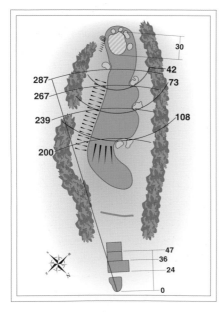

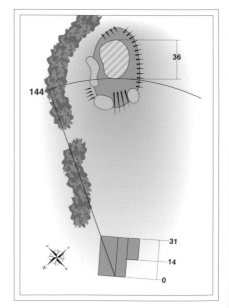

two courses compare and contrast sufficiently to cause many heated debates as to which is superior. The majority view is that the Old Course is the jewel in Sunningdale's crown; however, there is a general consensus that together they provide the best thirty-six holes of inland golf in the British Isles.

The Old Course is relatively short for a championship layout by present-day standards. But then, length has never been a significant weapon in Sunningdale's armoury. The Old Course charms rather than intimidates. The bunkering is striking – brilliant splashes of silver sand – yet not overdone. The fairways are quite generous. The heather is nowhere near as

A glimpse of Sunningdale (New) from behind the 18th green on Sunningdale (Old).

vicious as it is at Walton Heath, for instance, but it does border every fairway, and beyond the heather are the pines and silver birch trees. There is diversity, notably in direction, among the par threes, but the real strength of Sunningdale lies in the range and quality of the second shots to the par four holes.

You are encouraged to play well from the outset, the 1st being one of just two par fives and running downhill. Provided you don't slice out of bounds, it offers the prospect of an opening birdie.

Unfortunately, the 2nd dashes a lot of hopes. Once a par five, it is now a long par four where both the drive – up and over a crest – and the approach – down to a hidden shelf green – are blind. Next you play the first of three inviting short par fours. From an elevated perch, the shape of the 3rd dares the big hitter to go for the green, even though the direct route to the flag is paved with bunkers. The 4th is a deceptively difficult uphill par three. A false front to the green gives the impression that the flag is much nearer than you think. Also the wind has a tendency to swirl, adding to the confusion.

The full splendour of Sunningdale is encapsulated by the view from the 4th green and the 5th tee. Stretching out below, in the midst of two dark green wooded oceans, are the emerald fairways of the 5th and 6th. Heather, which can appear rusty brown or purple depending on the season, a fair sprinkling of those silver sand bunkers and a famous pond complete the picture. Although the 5th is properly a right-to-left dog-leg, a good drive can flirt with the trees on the left. The pond to the right of the fairway shouldn't really come into play, but is of great historical interest in that it is

209

5	Championship	410 yards	Par 4
	Medal	400	Par 4
	Ladies'	371	Par 4

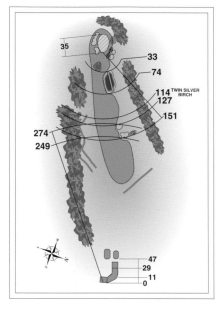

6	415 yards	Par 4
	388	Par 4
	344	Par 4

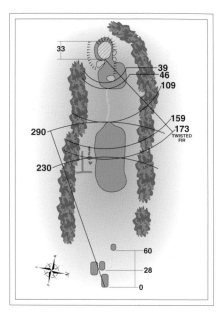

7	Championship	402 yards	Par 4
	Medal	383	Par 4
	Ladies'	375	Par 4

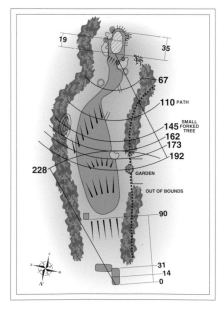

8	184 yards	Par 3
	172	Par 3
	139	Par 3

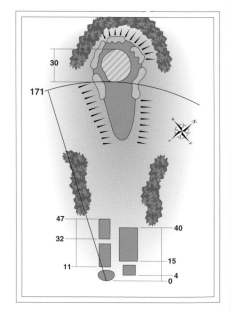

9	Championship	267 yards	Par 4
	Medal	267	Par 4
	Ladies'	243	Par 4

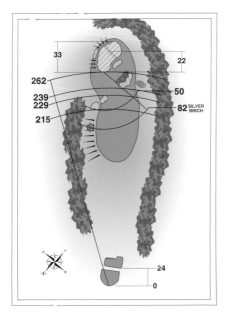

10		478 yards	Par 5
		463	Par 4
		441	Par 5

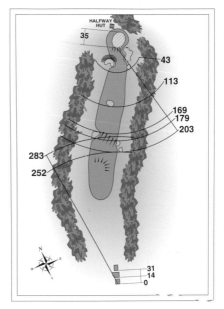

11	Championship	325 yards	Par 4
	Medal	299	Par 4
	Ladies'	245	Par 4

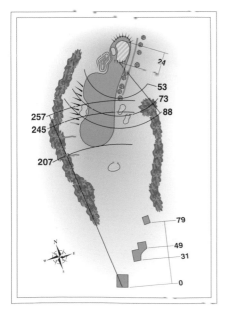

12		451 yards	Par 4
		423	Par 4
		397	Par 5

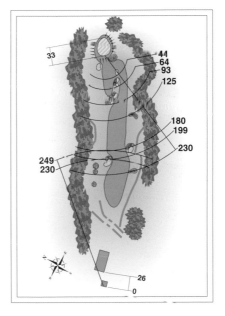

13	Championship	185 yards	Par 3
	Medal	178	Par 3
	Ladies'	162	Par 3

14	509 yards	Par 5
	477	Par 5
	469	Par 5

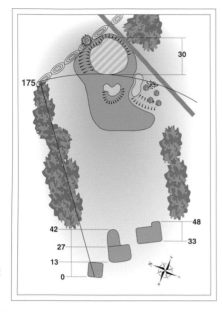

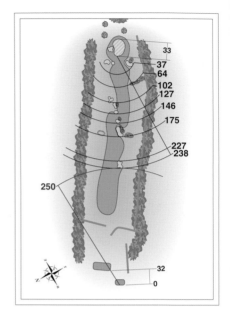

15	Championship	226 yards	Par 3
	Medal	226	Par 3
	Ladies'	205	Par 3

16	438 yards	Par 4
	423	Par 4
	365	Par 4

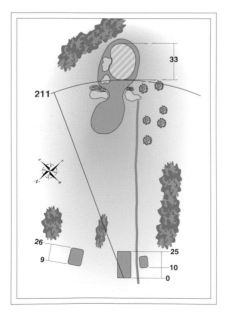

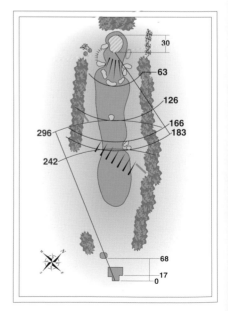

17	Championship	421 yards	Par 4
	Medal	421	Par 4
	Ladies'	385	Par 5

18	432 yards	Par 4
	414	Par 4
	393	Par 5

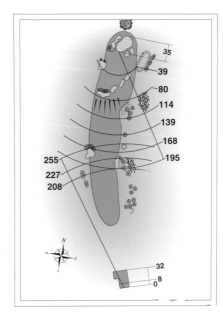

33
42
69
124
158
197
238
200
31
6
0

35
39
80
114
139
168
195
255
227
208
32
8
0

213

SUNNINGDALE
GOLF CLUB

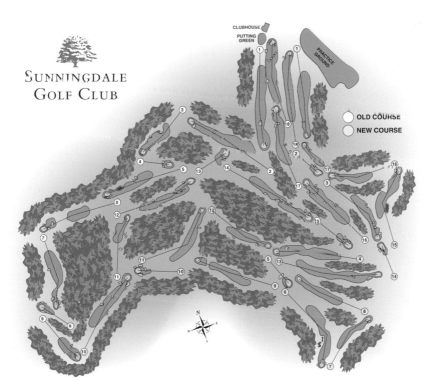

CLUBHOUSE
PUTTING
GREEN
PRACTICE
GROUND

OLD COURSE
NEW COURSE

Where landscape merges with golfscape: a glorious view of the 5th and 6th holes
from beside the 4th green.

thought to be golf's first man-made water hazard.

The 6th is a marvellous two-shotter, a Pine Valley-like hole where you drive from an elevated tee to an island fairway surrounded by heather, then hit over sand to a slightly raised green. Providing a nice contrast, the 7th is a thoroughly old fashioned golf hole: it calls for a high tee-shot over a hill to find a beautiful S-shaped valley fairway. The approach is played to a narrow plateau green defended by a combination of bunkers and mounds. Five bunkers almost encircle the green at the short 8th – beware of crosswinds at this hole – while a two-tiered green is the feature of the drivable par four 9th.

The view from the 10th tee is almost as famous as the one at the 5th. On this occasion there is only one hole that demands your open-mouthed attention. According to Peter Dobereiner, 'If all the

other holes were undistinguished, Sunningdale would still justify a pilgrimage by enthusiasts for the glory of the 10th, one of the most magnificent holes in Britain, or indeed the world.' From the highest point on the course, you drive spectacularly downhill to a fairway that looks far narrower than it really is. The second shot is fired uphill, invariably with a long iron to another plateau green.

The 11th is the third of the Old Course's trio of short two-shot holes. Like the 3rd and 9th, it can be driven in favourable conditions, although it is a very risky shot. The green is invisible from the tee and the fairway is crowned, while a bunker to the left, a ditch to the right and a rise at the front ensure that chipping on to the green is anything but straightforward. The 12th hole runs parallel to the 5th – not that you would realize, so dense is that 'dark wooded ocean' in

between. A drive to a narrow landing area is followed by a very searching second to find a green cut into the side of a hill with steep slopes all around.

After a downhill par three, with a slippery green, comes an attractive par five. The 14th climbs steadily uphill with a diagonal line of bunkers dividing the fairway. This could be the last chance to register a birdie, because the finishing four holes on the Old Course comprise a 226-yard par three and three par fours all measuring in excess of 420 yards.

The 15th is not only the longest but also possibly the best of the short holes. The green is large and diligently patrolled by four bunkers. A necklace of cross bunkers adds to the excitement and challenge of the down-and-up 16th; a potentially hanging lie and a cleverly angled green pose the problems at the dog-legging 17th. A legion of bunkers at the 18th — one on either side of the fairway to pinch the drive, four cross bunkers and another quartet around the green — threaten a sandy conclusion to a memorable round.

Standing immediately behind the 18th green is a majestic spreading oak tree, the proud emblem of Sunningdale, so perfectly symbolic of the club's quintessentially English ambience. The wise old oak has seen many great happenings: the first and only Walker Cup match to have been held on an inland course on this side of the Atlantic; numerous European Open Championships (both men's and women's) and perhaps the greatest-ever single round of golf. On 16 June 1926, the great Bobby Jones, playing in an Open Championship qualifying event and using equipment vastly inferior to that employed by today's stars, went around the Old Course in 66 strokes. He took 33 for the front nine and 33 for the back nine; Jones played 33 shots from tee to green and took 33 putts. It was a near-perfect round by a near-perfect golfer. 'After a reverential cheer at the final green,' Bernard Darwin wrote, 'the crowd dispersed awe-struck, realizing that they had witnessed something they had never seen before and would never see again.'

Hole	Championship	Medal	Par	Stroke Index	Ladies'	Par	Stroke Index
1	494	494	5	8	449	5	9
2	484	456	5/4	4	436	5	4
3	319	296	4	12	268	4	14
4	161	161	3	16	138	3	16
5	410	400	4	2	371	4	2
6	415	388	4	10	344	4	11
7	402	383	4	6	375	4	6
8	184	172	3	18	139	3	18
9	267	267	4	14	243	4	8
Out	3136	3017	36/35		2763	36	
10	478	463	5/4	5	441	5	7
11	325	299	4	15	245	4	15
12	451	423	4	1	397	5	1
13	185	178	3	17	162	3	17
14	509	477	5	7	469	5	3
15	226	226	3	11	205	3	12
16	438	423	4	3	365	4	10
17	421	421	4	13	385	4	5
18	432	414	4	9	393	5	13
In	3465	3324	36/35		3062	38	
Out	3136	3017	36/35		2763	36	
Total	6601	6341	72/70		5825	74	

WENTWORTH (WEST)

'HOLE HALVED IN THREE, BALLESTEROS REMAINS TWO UP.' ...
IF KEATS WERE ALIVE TODAY, HE WOULD SURELY WRITE AN ODE
TO WENTWORTH. FOR GOLFERS, THOSE IN GREAT BRITAIN AT LEAST,
WENTWORTH AND AUTUMN ARE INEXTRICABLY LINKED.

Autumn: season of mists, mellow fruitfulness and the World Match Play Championship.

Wentworth is probably the most famous golf club in England and, thanks to television and the World Match Play Championship, the West Course at Wentworth is probably the nation's best known golf course.

The club is located approximately 20 miles south-west of London near Ascot and it is linked to the capital (and reality) by the A30. This is the heart of heath country – Sunningdale and The Berkshire are neighbours – and yet the golf at Wentworth could be described as a mixture of woodland and heathland. Here the pines and silver birch trees mingle with stately oaks; the subsoil is decidedly sandy in nature; there is plenty of heather at Wentworth, but in late spring and early summer it is a mass of rhododendrons that dazzle and grab the attention.

Wentworth is both classy and classic. You realize as much the instant you turn off the A30 and enter the opulent estate. Wentworth's origins were not exactly humble. At one time Wentworth House was owned by the Duke of Wellington's sister and it was later acquired by a Spanish count. In 1920 the 1,750-acre site

was purchased by a property developer with big ideas. Walter Tarrant, the man in question, had the very American dream of creating a golf and country club complex and combining it with a luxury housing estate.

Perhaps the greatest decision Tarrant made was to appoint Harry Colt as his golf architect. Colt ranks alongside Alister Mackenzie and Donald Ross as one of the finest golf course architects who ever lived. Several of the best links courses in the British Isles, notably Royal Portrush and Muirfield, were fashioned by Colt, although he is better known as the great heathland course designer. It was Colt who produced the likes of Swinley Forest, St George's Hill, Sunningdale (New) and, by 1924, the East and West Courses at Wentworth. (Colt also played a prominent role in the design of Pine Valley near Philadelphia, widely regarded as the finest course in the world).

The East Course at Wentworth was the first to host important events. In 1926 it was the site of an unofficial match between British and American professionals, thus foreshadowing the Ryder Cup, which began in 1929, and in 1932 provided the stage for the inaugural Curtis Cup encounter. The West Course,

---

Opposite: A class apart. The 17th at Wentworth is among the best known, most loved and least liked par fives in golf. It has no bunkers, but features an awkward tee-shot, a blind approach and a punitive out of bounds.

1

Championship	471 yards	Par 5
Medal	462	Par 5
Ladies'	425	Par 5

2

155 yards	Par 3
137	Par 3
121	Par 3

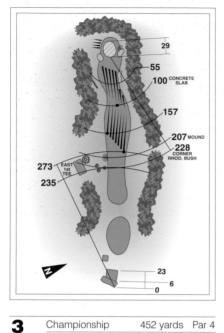

29
55
100 CONCRETE SLAB
157
207 MOUND
228 CORNER RHOD. BUSH
273 EAST 1st TEE
235

N

218

23
6
0

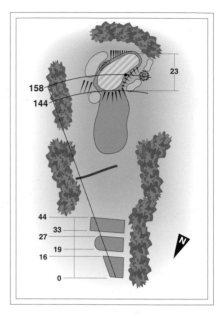

23
158
144
44
33
27
19
16
0

N

3

Championship	452 yards	Par 4
Medal	447	Par 4
Ladies'	376	Par 4

4

501 yards	Par 5
479	Par 5
421	Par 5

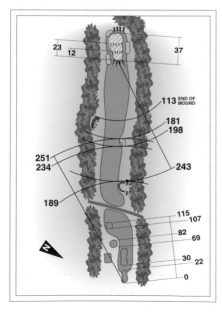

23
12
37
113 END OF MOUND
181
198
251
234
243
189
115
107
82
69
30
22
0

N

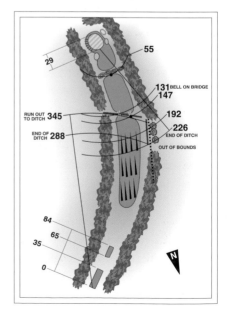

29
55
131 BELL ON BRIDGE
147
RUN OUT TO DITCH 345
192
226
END OF DITCH 288
END OF DITCH
OUT OF BOUNDS
84
65
35
0

N

The South African star, Ernie Els, drives at the 15th during the World Match Play Championship.
In 1996 Els became the first player to win the coveted title three years in succession.

which is also affectionately known as 'the Burma Road' on account of its toughness, established a pre-eminence in the 1950s, staging the Ryder Cup in 1953 and the Canada Cup (now the World Cup) in 1956. Arnold Palmer won the first World Match Play Championship in 1964, and it has been played on the West Course every year since. In the mid-1980s Volvo brought the British PGA Championship to the West Course and it, too, has become an annual fixture.

The West Course is a big course. From the back tees it measures a shade under 7,000 yards and, since it was built as a genuine championship course, it plays like one. The fairways are kept fairly narrow and the rough is encouraged to grow. There are a handful of very long par fours, namely the 1st (though this becomes a par five from the medal tees), 3rd, 9th, 13th and 15th, and yet accuracy

from the tee at these holes is just as important as length. In other words, you will need to use your driver and use it well.

For an inland course, the West Course has an unusual routing in that the front nine winds its way to the outer reaches of the estate and the back nine wanders all the way back. The opening three holes – the start of the Burma Road – can make or break your score. It is a formidable beginning. The 1st requires a long and precarious second across a deep gully – a stroke that may invoke memories of Ballesteros's majestic five iron shot in the 1991 PGA Championship play-off with Colin Montgomerie (he struck it to within two feet of the flag). The par three 2nd is one of many holes that look much easier on television: the giant Spanish oak tree that guards the right-hand entrance to the green encroaches more than you

5	Championship	191 yards	Par 3
	Medal	167	Par 3
	Ladies'	143	Par 3

6	356 yards	Par 4
	328	Par 4
	310	Par 4

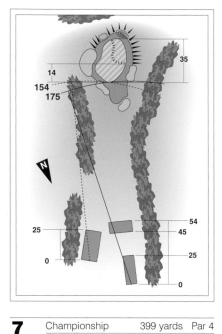

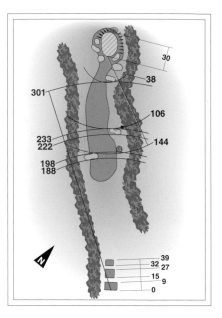

220

7	Championship	399 yards	Par 4
	Medal	362	Par 4
	Ladies'	310	Par 4

8	398 yards	Par 4
	389	Par 4
	346	Par 4

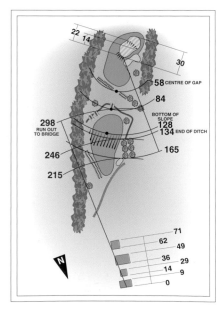

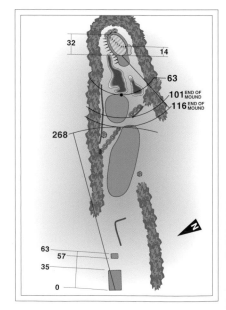

9	Championship	450 yards	Par 4
	Medal	435	Par 4
	Ladies'	423	Par 5

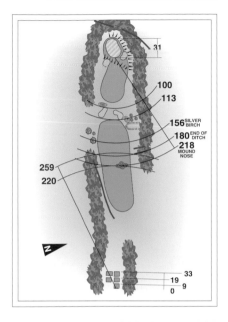

10	186 yards	Par 3
	177	Par 3
	174	Par 3

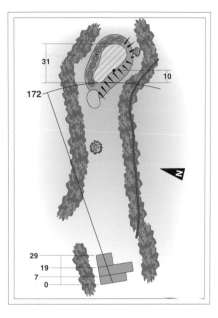

11	Championship	376 yards	Par 4
	Medal	371	Par 4
	Ladies'	318	Par 4

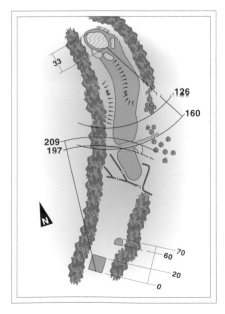

12	483 yards	Par 5
	468	Par 5
	448	Par 5

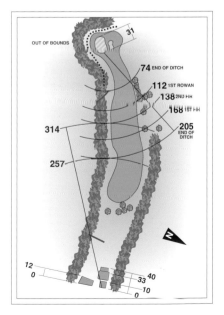

221

13	Championship	441 yards	Par 4
	Medal	423	Par 4
	Ladies'	400	Par 5

14	179 yards	Par 3
	179	Par 3
	117	Par 3

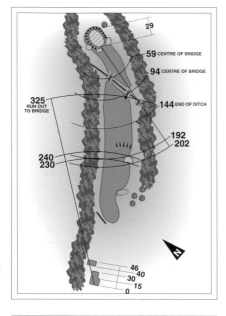

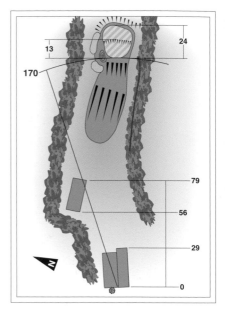

15	Championship	466 yards	Par 4
	Medal	458	Par 4
	Ladies'	405	Par 4

16	380 yards	Par 4
	369	Par 4
	352	Par 4

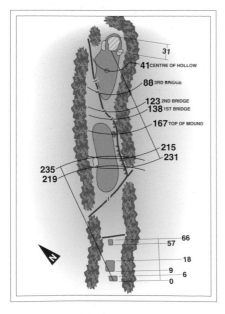

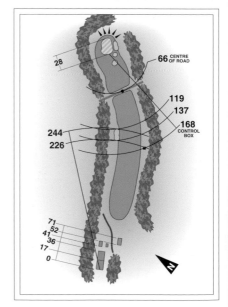

17	Championship	571 yards	Par 5
	Medal	538	Par 5
	Ladies'	474	Par 5

18	502 yards	Par 5
	486	Par 5
	458	Par 5

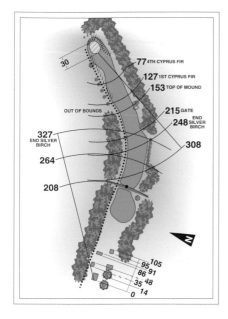

77 4TH CYPRUS FIR
127 1ST CYPRUS FIR
153 TOP OF MOUND
215 GATE
248 END SILVER BIRCH
308
327 END SILVER BIRCH
264
208
30
OUT OF BOUNDS
105
95 91
86 48
35 14
0

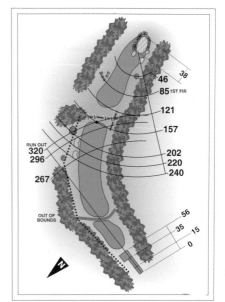

46
38
85 1ST FIR
121
157
202
220
240
RUN OUT
320
296
267
OUT OF BOUNDS
56
35 15
0

223

WENTWORTH

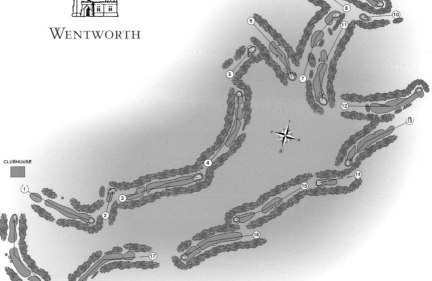

imagine and the green itself has little depth. The 3rd is a relentless, uphill par four of some 450 yards, with a vicious fairway bunker that restricts the drive and a vast three-tiered green. A three here is a considerable achievement.

Respite comes with the 4th, an attractive par five which sweeps gracefully downhill. The next is a tightly bunkered par three, and the 6th a short but semi-blind par four. By now you are truly 'out on the heath'. The middle part of the course, from the 7th to the 12th, is less well known. However, in the 7th, 8th and 11th it includes three classic two-shotters, none of which quite measures 400 yards. They are especially interesting, given that Wentworth is so famous for its par fives, notably the 17th and 18th.

224

The 7th starts by charging downhill; it then crosses a ditch, dog-legs to the right and climbs to a beautifully angled two-tiered green. A classic Colt bunker eats into the right side of the green. The 8th is very picturesque. Again the tee-shot is downhill, though this time to an island-style fairway, and the approach is played over a pond to a green that is raised and semi-circled by trees – a lovely and quiet corner. The long undulating 9th and the testing par three 10th are far from bad holes, but the 11th is a miniature masterpiece. The South African golfer Bobby Locke thought so highly of it, he included it in his 'world eclectic eighteen'. Bordered by a combination of trees, bracken and heather, the hole swings to the left and the second is played slightly uphill through a natural valley. The green is nicely contoured with three bunkers protecting its front entrance.

The par five 12th offers a definite birdie opportunity, so long as you clear the tall pines with your drive, while the 13th is in many ways a longer version of the 11th. The television cameras traditionally home in on the 14th, the last of the par threes. It is an exciting hole when viewed from the comfort of an armchair, but it is a brute to play. From tee to green, it climbs severely uphill all the way. The green also slopes dramatically from an upper to a lower level.

Not so long ago the 15th was rated a short par five and was considered a fairly easy hole; now that it is a par four, it seems suddenly to have

Classic golf: the raised green at the difficult par three 2nd.

grown horns. Whatever it says on the card, it is one of the best and most attractive holes at Wentworth. The 16th curves to the left. It has a reputation as a card-spoiler, but is only really difficult if you try to cut off too much of the dog-leg or if you take insufficient club for your second.

The 17th is the most celebrated – or notorious – hole on the West Course. It is a massive par five of 571 yards, which you either love or hate. The most neutral comment to make is that it must be one of the longest bunkerless holes in golf. Controversy centres around the fact that the fairway cambers sharply to the right in the area where you are attempting to land your drive, often propelling balls into the rough; this wouldn't be so harsh if the fairway didn't dog-leg sharply to the left at 300 yards. Also, as it begins to dog-leg, the fairway rises, making the second shot blind. All the way along the left there is an out-of-bounds fence, yet in order to get your approach anywhere close to the green, you must play to this side of the fairway.

The 18th is a less frightening proposition! Dog-legging to the right and skirting the trees, it is a much shorter par five, although for most of us it still requires two very good strokes if it is to be reached in two. For the professionals, it provides a good opportunity to finish with a flourish – perhaps, even, to win with an eagle.

The World Match Play has produced more than a few spectacular finishes. Indeed, the event has enjoyed an extraor-

dinary history. In its early years, in the 1960s and 1970s, Gary Player won five times, otherwise it was American golfers who dominated; then in the 1980s and early 1990s it was the turn of the Europeans to dominate, with Seve Ballesteros equalling Player's total of five victories. Recent years have seen Ernie Els create a new record by becoming the first player to win the World Match Play title three years in succession (1994–1995–1996). Who could possibly trump this achievement? Of course, there is only one man. And so the question every Wentworth member is asking: 'What will happen to the Burma Road if ever they let "the Tiger" loose?'

Hole	Championship	Medal	Par	Stroke Index	Ladies'	Par	Stroke Index
1	471	462	5	9	425	5	9
2	155	137	3	17	121	3	17
3	452	447	4	3	376	4	1
4	501	479	5	11	421	5	13
5	191	167	3	15	143	3	16
6	356	328	4	13	310	4	11
7	000	000	4	5	333	4	7
8	398	389	4	7	346	4	3
9	450	435	4	1	423	5	5
Out	3373	3206	36		2898	37	
10	186	177	3	10	174	3	14
11	376	371	4	6	318	4	4
12	483	468	5	14	448	5	10
13	441	423	4	2	400	5	15
14	179	179	3	18	117	3	18
15	466	468	4	4	405	4	2
16	380	369	4	16	352	4	12
17	571	538	5	8	474	5	6
18	502	486	5	12	458	5	8
In	3584	3469	37		3146	38	
Out	3373	3206	36		2898	37	
Total	6957	6675	73		6044	75	

THE BELFRY (BRABAZON)

At about four o'clock on 15 September 1985, Sam Torrance stood over a 20-foot putt on the 18th green at The Belfry. It was a curling, right-to-left putt and it was to win the Ryder Cup.

It is fair to say that at this precise moment European golf stood on the threshold of greatness. But consider how different things had been just a decade earlier. ...

In September 1975 the United States crushed Great Britain and Ireland (as the side then was) in the Ryder Cup at Laurel Valley in Pennsylvania. Jack Nicklaus was the best golfer in the world and, with the exception of Gary Player, the next ten best were also American. The leading player on the still fledgling European Tour that season was the South African, Dale Hayes. And The Belfry in 1975 was still being created.

Approximately 10 miles north of Birmingham, in an area where rich farmland meets rich suburbia, the British PGA had decided to build a new headquarters. The site was to include two eighteen-hole golf courses, one a championship layout on which, in due course, the Ryder Cup could be staged. The Belfry's two courses, the championship Brabazon and the shorter Derby Course, were opened in June 1977.

As the Brabazon Course matured in the late 1970s and early 1980s, European golf discovered some extraordinary talent. The first to emerge was Seve Ballesteros in the 1976 Open at Royal Birkdale. And it was Ballesteros who made The Belfry famous. In the 1978 Hennessy Cup, the first major professional event to be played on the Brabazon Course, the swashbuckling 21-year-old drove the green at the par four 10th. At the time the hole measured 310 yards, and it was considered such a remarkable shot that a plaque was placed on the tee to commemorate the feat. One year later, Greg Norman, a rising 24-year-old Australian star, emulated Seve's achievement. That was in the 1979 English Classic, a tournament won by Ballesteros. Within twelve months of his victory at The Belfry, the Spaniard had also captured the British Open and the Masters. By September 1985 Ballesteros was the best golfer in the world, the German player Bernhard Langer was the new Masters champion and Sandy Lyle had just won the British Open ... and, of course, Scotland's Sam Torrance holed that 20-footer.

The Brabazon Course was designed by Dave Thomas. His brief had been to produce an 'American-style' target golf course. (Tired of finishing second in the Ryder Cup, the PGA's philosophy was one of 'if you can't beat them, imitate them'). In particular, Thomas was asked to create a course that could be stretched to more than 7,000 yards with ultra-

Opposite: The 10th green at The Belfry is a perfect golfing stage. The hole was made famous by Seve Ballesteros when, as a swashbuckling 21-year-old, he drove the green in the 1978 Hennessy Cup.

1	Championship	411 yards	Par 4
	Medal	393	Par 4
	Ladies'	366	Par 4

2	379 yards	Par 4
	310	Par 4
	297	Par 5

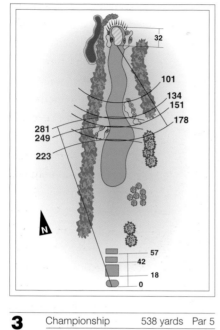

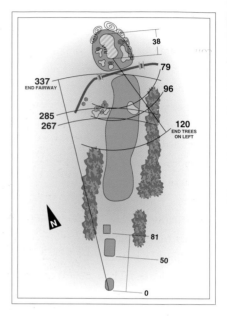

3	Championship	538 yards	Par 5
	Medal	512	Par 5
	Ladies'	424	Par 5

4	442 yards	Par 4
	407	Par 4
	465	Par 5

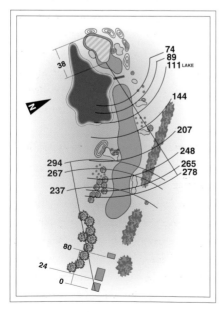

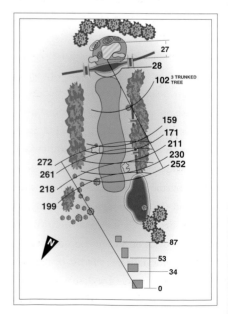

228

quick, severely contoured greens, with plenty of strategically positioned bunkers and an abundance of intimidating, do-or-die water hazards.

The land Thomas had to work with could hardly be described as natural golfing terrain: it included a small lake and a winding stream, yet it was very flat and many of the native trees had been cut down to make way for agriculture. But Thomas and his construction team worked wonders, and he fulfilled his brief to the letter. The Brabazon Course was a slice of Florida in the heart of England.

Sam Torrance celebrates after sinking a 20-foot putt to win the Ryder Cup for Europe.

Traditionalists were never going to like it, but the general golfing public took to it immediately; it made, and was made for, dramatic golf. Moreover, one rarely heard complaints from the professionals. Aesthetically, the course was lacking in natural beauty and charm when it opened, but over the years extensive landscaping, notably the planting of hundreds of trees, has gradually enhanced the look of the course. Adjustments have also been made to the layout itself, and on each occasion the Ryder Cup has been staged at The Belfry, Thomas has been invited back to advise on various improvements.

Following Europe's success in the 1985 Ryder Cup, it was inevitable that The Belfry would be awarded the match in 1989, and when this contest ended in a thrilling tie – Europe thus retaining the trophy – it was decided that it should host the event again in 1993. The Ryder Cup is scheduled to return to The Belfry for a fourth time in 2001.

There are two particularly memorable sequences on the Brabazon Course, the run of holes between the 6th and 10th, where water comes heavily into play, and the demanding finishing stretch which begins with the par five 15th. The beginning is relatively uneventful, with three straightaway par fours, the best of which is the 2nd, a classic lay-up hole with a pitch over a burn to a closely bunkered green. At the 4th comes the first of the Brabazon's three big par fives. The chances of getting up in two are fairly remote, because the burn that crossed in front of the 2nd green does so again here. On the 5th you must drive over the ubiquitous burn, but the approach is usually the more difficult shot with three bunkers barring the entrance to a shallow green.

The tempo clearly increases at the 6th, where you must confront a very demanding drive and risky approach. Water, now in the shape of a lake, threatens all the way down the left side of the fairway and practically laps the edge of the green. The

229

5	Championship	408 yards	Par 4
	Medal	388	Par 4
	Ladies'	350	Par 4

6	395 yards	Par 4
	387	Par 4
	284	Par 4

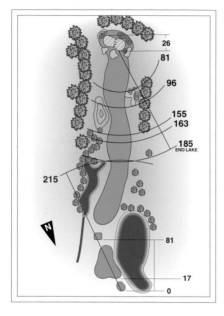

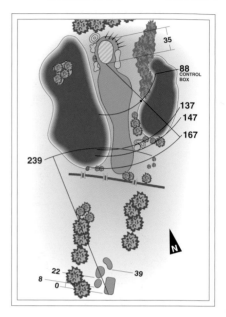

7	Championship	177 yards	Par 3
	Medal	177	Par 3
	Ladies'	150	Par 3

8	428 yards	Par 4
	409	Par 4
	400	Par 4

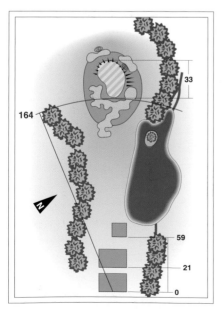

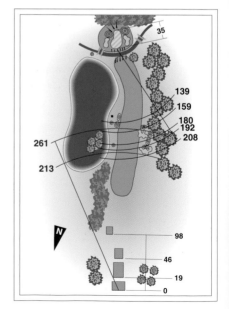

9	Championship	433 yards	Par 4
	Medal	402	Par 4
	Ladies'	340	Par 4

10	311 yards	Par 4
	301	Par 4
	252	Par 5

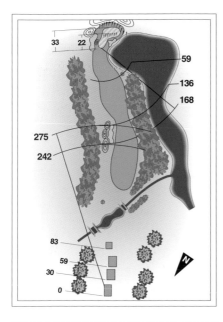

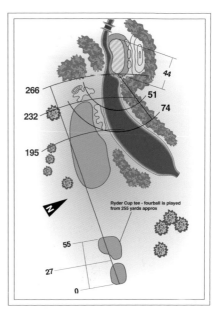

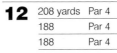

Ryder Cup tee - fourball is played from 255 yards approx

11	Championship	419 yards	Par 4
	Medal	399	Par 4
	Ladies'	336	Par 4

12	208 yards	Par 4
	188	Par 4
	188	Par 4

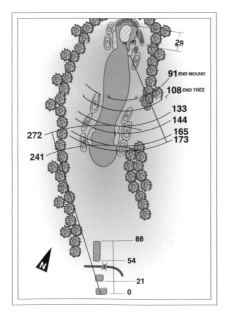

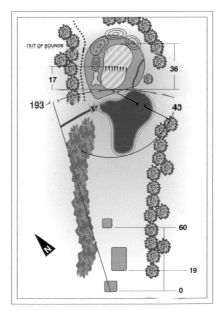

13	Championship	384 yards	Par 4
	Medal	363	Par 4
	Ladies'	335	Par 4

14	190 yards	Par 3
	183	Par 3
	158	Par 3

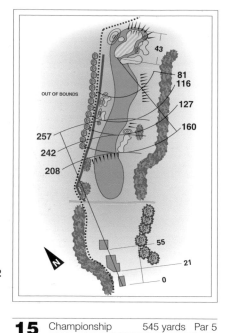

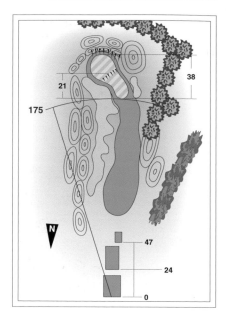

15	Championship	545 yards	Par 5
	Medal	500	Par 5
	Ladies'	458	Par 5

16	413 yards	Par 4
	405	Par 4
	346	Par 4

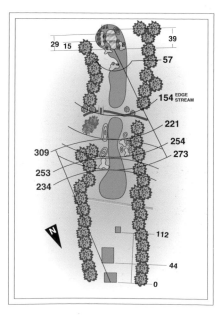

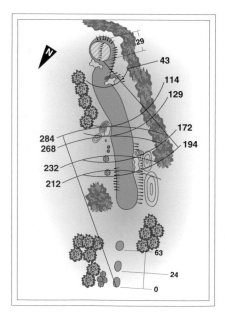

17	Championship	564 yards	Par 5
	Medal	545	Par 5
	Ladies'	527	Par 5

18	473 yards	Par 4
	441	Par 4
	382	Par 5

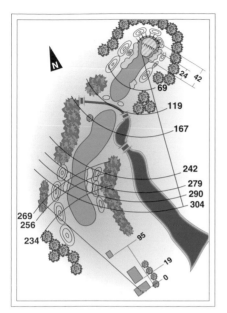

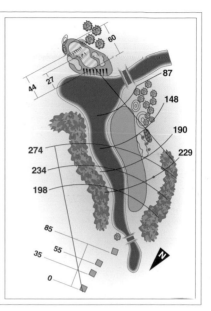

233

THE BELFRY

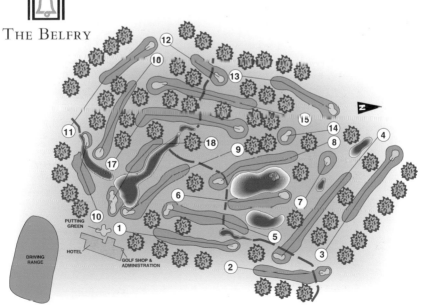

A golfing graveyard: there is as much water as fairway at the 18th. To find the sanctuary of the green, both the drive and the approach must be carefully executed.

234

fairway is no more than 30 yards wide and there is a bunker on the right. Another much larger trap defends the slightly raised green: nothing less than two good shots will suffice at this hole. A most unusual par three follows. The 7th green is very nearly encircled by sand. Two boomerang-shaped bunkers, one at the front and one at the back, almost join one another, allowing just sufficient room in between for you to walk onto the green; the aerial route is of course the only option from the tee.

The drive at the 8th is similar to the one at the 6th, although the fairway is a little wider. This is a long par four, and the second shot once again has to carry a burn. The par four 9th is possibly the best hole on the course. It may not be as visually spectacular as the 10th, yet it rewards intelligent as well as courageous play. The green is angled across a water hazard from front left to back right. There is a bunker to the left and another appears wedged between the edge of the water and the front centre of the green. The easier approach is from the left side of the fairway, but if you venture too far left from the tee, a tough fairway bunker awaits. If you decide not to challenge the water with your second, and instead lay up short, you will probably take no worse than five, but a par is unlikely due to a three-tiered green which complicates both chipping and putting. When the pin is positioned on the right half of the green, only a very brave and well executed stroke will finish close to the hole.

The 10th on the Brabazon Course is one of the best known holes in golf. For the conservative player, it is a long iron and pitch hole, the narrow green making the second shot anything but straightforward. For the devil-may-care golfer, the

10th presents a rare opportunity to follow in the footsteps of Ballesteros, Norman and Co. From the forward tee it is certainly possible, though the shot has to be very accurate as well as powerful. Surrounded by tall trees, the green enjoys an attractive stage-like setting which, in view of its history, is most appropriate.

The next four holes comprise two par fours and two short holes. Both the 11th and 13th dog-leg mildly to the right, and the 11th fairway is very tightly bunkered; the 12th is the longest of the par threes, while the 14th has a nicely angled, two-tiered green and is where Nick Faldo holed-in-one on the final day of the 1993 Ryder Cup.

The par five 15th is often played downwind. The professionals regularly reach the green in two, but for most players the principal obstacle is a cross bunker located approximately 50 yards short of the green. The approach to the 16th is one of the most adventurous of the round, as the green slopes sharply from right to left and is effectively on two levels. A deep bunker looms in front of the green.

The 17th is the best and most difficult of the par fives. The fairway swings sharply to the right, but trees and sand deter you from taking on the dog-leg. The second shot is played over a burn and should be kept away from a bunker on the left which, from 40 yards out, snakes all the way to the green. This will leave a simple pitch to the stadium-style green with its prominent spectator mounding.

The 18th provides an exciting climax to any round, never mind a Ryder Cup encounter. The question on the tee is always, 'how much of the corner can I – dare I – bite off with the drive?' The over-ambitious shot is destined for a watery conclusion. From the centre of the fairway, you face a second nerve-racking stroke over yet more water. This is where you hope to do better than Ballesteros managed (against Paul Azinger) in the 1989 Ryder Cup, and where you dream of emulating Christy O'Connor, jun., who, later that same incredible afternoon, struck a fabulous two iron to within three feet of the flag.

Hole	Championship	Medal	Par	Stroke Index	Ladies'	Par	Stroke Index
1	411	393	4	9	366	4	11
2	379	330	4	17	297	4	15
3	538	512	5	13	424	5	13
4	442	407	4	3	465	5	1
5	408	388	4	11	350	4	9
6	395	387	4	5	284	4	7
7	177	171	3	15	160	3	17
8	428	409	4	1	400	5	5
9	433	402	4	7	340	4	3
Out	3611	3600	36		3076	38	
10	311	284	4	8	252	4	16
11	419	365	4	16	336	4	6
12	208	179	3	6	188	3	14
13	384	350	4	18	335	4	1
14	190	166	3	14	158	3	18
15	545	488	5	2	458	5	10
16	413	388	4	12	346	4	4
17	564	530	5	10	527	5	2
18	473	418	4	4	382	5	8
In	3507	3168	36		2982	37	
Out	3611	3225	36		3076	38	
Total	7118	6393	72		6058	75	

CHART HILLS

'THERE IS ONLY ONE PLACE WHERE SUCCESS COMES BEFORE WORK, AND THAT IS IN THE DICTIONARY.' NICK FALDO DIDN'T COIN THE PHRASE, BUT HE MIGHT WELL HAVE DONE.

This is the man who headed the European Order of Merit in 1983, won the prestigious Heritage Classic on the US Tour in early 1984 and then turned to his manager, John Simpson, and said, 'I'm only kidding myself, my golf swing is not good enough to take me to the highest level.' It took Faldo more than two years to remodel his swing completely. During that period, he struck tens of thousands of practice balls and 99 per cent of the golfing public thought he had lost his marbles. Six Major Championship wins later (and counting), no one is questioning his sanity.

In recent years the three-time Masters and three-time Open champion has become extremely interested in golf course design. He has made special trips to several of the game's great architectural shrines, including Pine Valley, Royal Dornoch and Ballybunion. Moreover, he has let it be known that when his extraordinary resolve and desire to be recognized as one of the all-time greats is satisfied (when he is confident people will tell their grandchildren 'I saw Nick Faldo play'), golf course design will become his main occupation. The comparison with Jack Nicklaus is striking, and since it was a vision of Nicklaus playing at Augusta back in 1971 that ignited the golfing flame, it is also rather neat.

Faldo's ideas on course design are not merely being stored in the memory bank, he has started putting them into practice. In the early 1990s he teamed up with Steve Smyers to create Chart Hills, his first course in England.

Smyers is one of America's most talented and imaginative golf architects and in many ways is a kindred soul – he thinks along the same lines as Faldo. Above all, Smyers believes that you 'feel' a great golf course and that as far as possible its design should exude, even cultivate, the natural character of the landscape. Chart Hills opened in October 1993.

Imagine a setting in the heart of the Kent countryside, where ancient oak trees stand proud. Imagine a golf course that has clusters of fairway bunkers reminiscent of those at Royal Melbourne; where the fairways comprise a variety of sweeping tree-lined dog-legs and island sanctuaries; where holes twist and tumble downhill in an almost links-like fashion towards huge contoured greens; and where entry to the putting surfaces is protected by winding creeks and steep revetted pot bunkers similar to Carnoustie and Muirfield. This is Chart Hills.

But one shouldn't gain the impression that Chart Hills is purely a melting pot

237

Opposite: A hill of sand confronts the golfer at the spectacular uphill 9th.

CHART HILLS

1	Championship	599 yards	Par 5
	Medal	562	Par 5
	Ladies'	498	Par 5

2	459 yards	Par 4
	406	Par 4
	364	Par 4

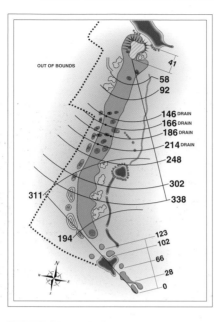

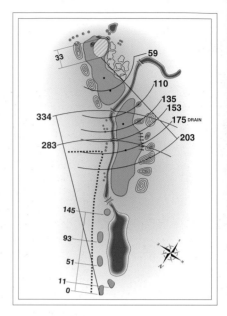

238

3	Championship	183 yards	Par 3
	Medal	155	Par 3
	Ladies'	111	Par 3

4	424 yards	Par 4
	391	Par 4
	329	Par 4

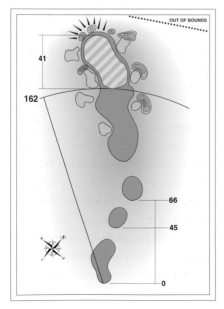

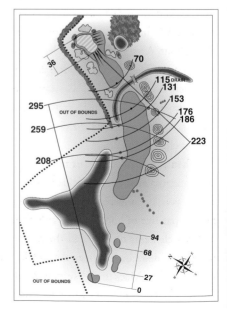

A view across the course from the green at the par five 12th

for design theories. There has been no crude imitation, rather it is the flavour of these great courses that has been incorporated and it has been done very subtly throughout. A very natural look has been achieved – indeed, the golf course doesn't so much occupy the land as seemingly melt into it. Young though it is, Chart Hills is developing its own special character and charm.

When you stand on the 1st tee, you are staring across at the green fields of Kent. Below you is an extraordinary opening hole, a par five of almost 600 yards that includes elements of nearly all the design influences described above. An intelligently angled Mackenzie-like spread of fairway bunkers must be confronted with

the drive; to the left of the fairway, the rough is savage and there is a creek off to the right, but the tee-shot is perhaps not quite so intimidating as it appears, for the landing area is quite generous. The hole then dog-legs sharply to the right, sweeping down towards the green as the fairway narrows and becomes heavily contoured – a genuine links feel has been created. Just short and left of the green there is another nest of traps, while guarding the front right entrance is a fairly cavernous pot bunker. The green itself is very large and full of wicked borrows.

And so the challenge continues, as dramatic holes are followed by more subtle ones with continual changes in direction and elevation. Among other

5	Championship	511 yards	Par 5
	Medal	474	Par 5
	Ladies'	369	Par 5

6	309 yards	Par 4
	289	Par 4
	264	Par 4

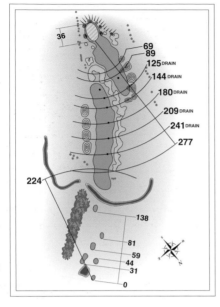

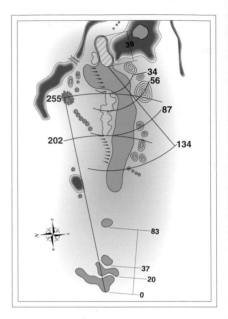

240

7	Championship	206 yards	Par 3
	Medal	185	Par 3
	Ladies'	147	Par 3

8	439 yards	Par 4
	399	Par 4
	358	Par 4

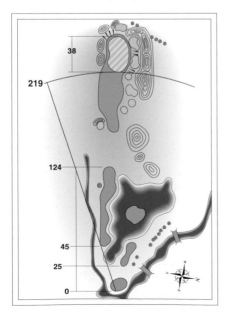

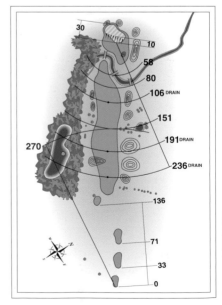

9	Championship	365 yards	Par 4
	Medal	327	Par 4
	Ladies'	276	Par 4

10	453 yards	Par 4
	405	Par 4
	391	Par 5

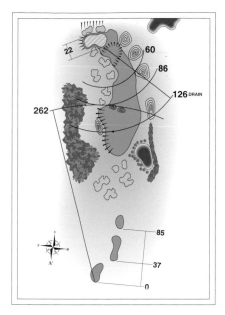

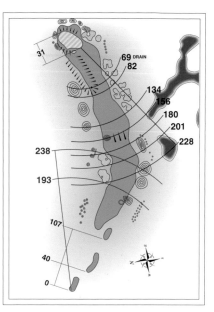

11	Championship	215 yards	Par 3
	Medal	165	Par 3
	Ladies'	127	Par 3

12	536 yards	Par 5
	487	Par 5
	412	Par 5

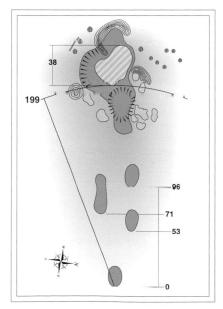

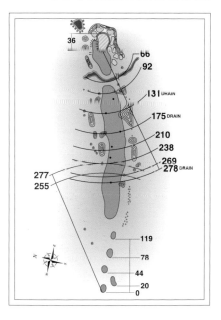

13	Championship	426 yards	Par 4
	Medal	412	Par 4
	Ladies'	347	Par 4

14	402 yards	Par 4
	362	Par 4
	305	Par 4

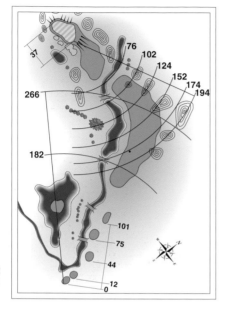

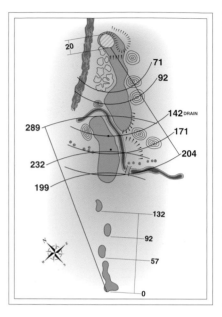

242

15	Championship	481 yards	Par 4
	Medal	409	Par 4
	Ladies'	363	Par 4

16	482 yards	Par 5
	457	Par 5
	402	Par 5

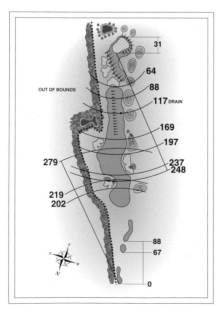

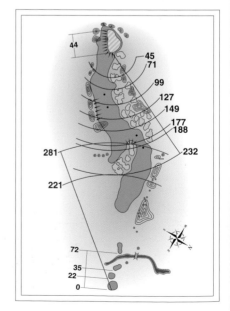

17	Championship	147 yards	Par 3		**18**	449 yards	Par 4
	Medal	126	Par 3			413	Par 4
	Ladies'	86	Par 3			375	Par 4

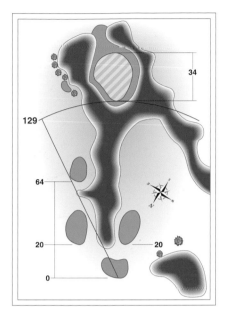

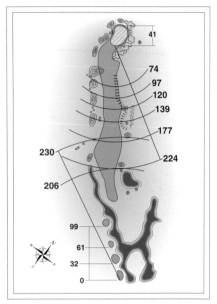

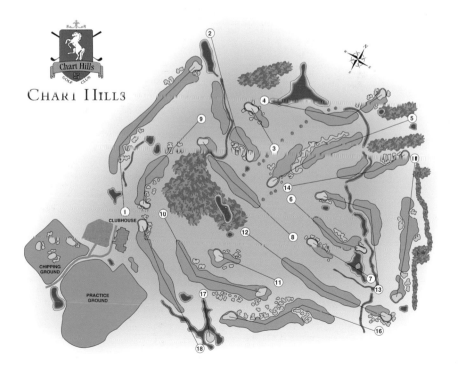

CHART HILLS

outstanding holes on the front nine are the short 3rd, with its 'Redan' fortress-style green; the 4th, a magnificent right-to-left dog-legging par four – a hole that would certainly grace Royal Melbourne; the teasingly short par four 6th; the 8th which features a natural valley fairway, wandering creek and plateaued green; and the spectacular uphill 9th where an island of green turf amid a sea of white bunkers provides a hint of Pine Valley.

The back nine commences with a long curving par four. After driving over a crest, the hole tumbles down towards an angled green, the contours of the fairway encouraging a low running approach. Defending the front left side of the green is a deep pot bunker, similar to the famous Road Hole bunker on the 17th at St. Andrews. The 11th is a par three of heroic proportions, and then comes possibly the finest sequence of all, the 12th, 13th and 14th. The 12th is an exhilarating par five with an approach played slightly uphill to a very handsome raised green; the 13th is a demanding right-to-left dog-leg, where the mischievous meanderings of a creek demand careful placement of the drive; and the thoroughly fascinating 14th dares you to attempt a brave carry over water – and of course rewards you with an easier second if you succeed. A vast sandy wilderness threatens players at the 's'-shaped par five 16th; the short 17th features an island green and the long par four 18th with its dramatic greenside bunkering presents a very testing finish.

According to Smyers, a great golf course should excite, thrill and sometimes frighten. Applying this test literally, the golfer walking off the 18th green at Chart Hills is likely to be emotionally disturbed.

As for Faldo, he is on record as saying that his twin ambitions in golf course design are to create the best inland course in the British Isles and the world's finest links course – Nick has never been one to set himself modest targets! Play a round at this golf course, though, and you may come to the conclusion that he's halfway there already. Chart Hills is nothing less than a golfing *tour de force*.

Hole	Championship	Medal	Par	Stroke Index	Ladies'	Par	Stroke Index
1	599	562	5	10	498	5	10
2	459	406	4	6	364	4	6
3	183	155	3	14	111	3	14
4	424	391	4	4	329	4	4
5	511	474	5	18	369	5	18
6	309	289	4	12	274	4	12
7	206	185	3	16	147	3	16
8	439	399	4	2	358	4	2
9	365	327	4	8	276	4	8
Out	3495	3188	36		2726	36	
10	453	405	4	5	391	5	5
11	215	165	3	11	127	3	11
12	536	487	5	17	412	5	17
13	426	412	4	1	347	4	1
14	402	362	4	3	305	4	3
15	481	409	4	13	363	4	13
16	482	457	5	7	402	5	7
17	147	126	3	15	86	3	15
18	449	413	4	9	375	4	9
In	3591	3236	36		2808	37	
Out	3495	3188	36		2726	36	
Total	7086	6424	72		5534	73	

A large nest of fairway bunkers threatens (and defines) the opening drive.

ROYAL PORTHCAWL

Lᴏᴄᴋ's Cᴏᴍᴍᴏɴ ᴄɪʀᴄᴀ 1893: 'A ᴄᴏw ᴋᴇᴇᴘs ᴍᴏᴏɪɴɢ ᴀᴛ ᴛʜᴇ ᴛᴏᴘ ᴏғ ᴍʏ ʙᴀᴄᴋsᴡɪɴɢ ᴀɴᴅ ᴀɴᴏᴛʜᴇʀ ɪs ғᴏʀᴇᴠᴇʀ ᴡᴀɴᴅᴇʀɪɴɢ ᴀᴄʀᴏss ᴛʜᴇ ғᴀɪʀᴡᴀʏ. Wʜᴀᴛ's ᴍᴏʀᴇ, ᴛʜᴇʀᴇ ɪs ᴀ ғᴀᴍɪʟʏ ᴏғ ᴇɪɢʜᴛ ᴘɪᴄɴɪᴄᴋɪɴɢ ɪɴ ᴀ ʙᴜɴᴋᴇʀ ʙᴇsɪᴅᴇ ᴛʜᴇ 5ᴛʜ ɢʀᴇᴇɴ. Hᴏᴡ ᴄᴀɴ I ᴘᴏssɪʙʟʏ ᴄᴏɴᴄᴇɴᴛʀᴀᴛᴇ ᴏɴ ᴍʏ ɢᴏʟғ?'

The next time you become stuck behind a laborious four-ball, spare a thought for the early golfers of Porthcawl. They formed a club in 1891, but the site chosen for their first golf course was hardly conducive to a peaceful round. As its name implies, Lock's Common belonged to every man (and beast). The golfers naturally grew frustrated and sought a more secluded home. Lady Luck was on their side, for an adjacent parcel of land that had been owned by Cistercian monks became available. Nine holes were laid out. For a short time it appears the members would play nine holes over this new ground and then 'cross the road' for a further nine holes on the common. This rather eccentric arrangement didn't last long, however, as the club was able to extend its newer nine to a full eighteen. The quest for privacy had inspired the move, but this second home really was – and is – a special place.

Situated on the Glamorgan coast between Cardiff and Swansea, the course spectacularly overlooks the Bristol Channel. The terrain is undulating and falls gently from high ground towards the sea. It is accurate to describe Porthcawl (or Royal Porthcawl as the club became in 1909) as a golf links, but only just. Bordering Lock's Common, the land not surprisingly has many heathland and moorland characteristics. For one thing, there is an abundance of gorse, more perhaps than on any other championship links with the exception of Royal County Down. Nor are there any significant sand-hills at Porthcawl, with the result that the links is very exposed, leaving the golfer at the mercy of the elements. And, as anyone who attended the 1995 Walker Cup will testify, Porthcawl is a wild place when the elements are stirred.

Over the years many architects have helped to shape the links, most notably Harry Colt in 1913 and Tom Simpson in 1933. It is not easy to find fault with their work. The routing of the course is excellent, first taking the player along the coast, then guiding him (or her) to the higher parts of the course where the views are magnificent; there then follows some interesting zigzagging across sandy ridges before the dramatic finale and a hole that plunges downhill directly towards the sea.

Thanks to the sloping terrain and the skill of the architects, the sea is visible from every hole on the course. There is plenty of variety in the bunkering, with a handful of cross bunkers adding an old-fashioned touch and complementing the other fairway traps and the numerous greenside pot bunkers.

Opposite: Royal Porthcawl is the jewel in the crown of Welsh golf. A rainbow illuminates the green at the par three 4th.

1	Championship	326 yards	Par 4
	Medal	326	Par 4
	Ladies'	328	Par 4

2	447 yards	Par 4
	416	Par 4
	370	Par 5

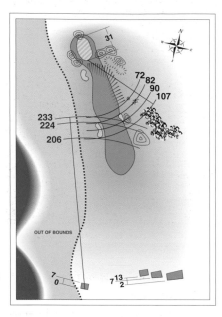

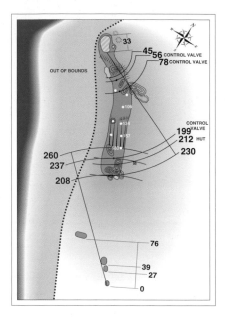

3	Championship	420 yards	Par 4
	Medal	377	Par 4
	Ladies'	332	Par 4

4	197 yards	Par 3
	193	Par 3
	143	Par 3

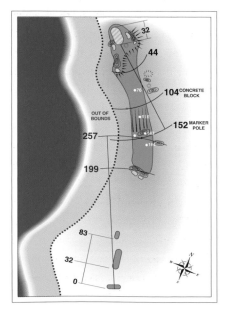

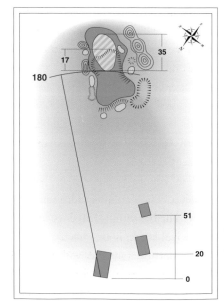

A stone wall out of bounds is a feature of the par five 5th, a hole which transports the golfer from sea-level to the higher parts of the course.

How good is Royal Porthcawl? Staunch supporters of Royal St. David's may beg to differ, but it is widely acknowledged as the greatest course in Wales. Ian Woosnam regards it as one of his three favourite links in the British Isles, while the late Tom Scott, a highly respected golf writer, once suggested it might be among the top dozen courses in the world.

Since the Second World War, the club has hosted many major events, both amateur and professional, including the British Amateur Championship and the Walker Cup.

The course begins, then, with a sequence of holes running adjacent to the shore. The 1st, with its raised tee in front of the clubhouse, is an attractive opener. It is a short par four and, with the wind behind, might even be drivable but for a rise in the fairway in front of the green.

The putting surface is small and considerably contoured.

The 2nd and 3rd holes are quite similar to one another. They are both beautiful two-shotters – strong par fours where the drive must carry sand and the approach must be fired slightly downhill to a green nestling close to the beach. This shingle beach probably threatens the green a little more at the 2nd, but makes the drive at the 3rd all the more intimidating.

Turning inland, you now face a handsome par three. Two factors distinguish the 4th: first, the large two-tiered green which sits in a slight bowl and, second, the severe nature of the greenside bunkering. Three-time Open champion Henry Cotton thought very highly of the par five 5th. This is the hole that transports players from near sea-level to the higher ground. Many fail to notice the climb,

5

Championship	513 yards	Par 5
Medal	476	Par 5
Ladies'	425	Par 5

6

443 yards	Par 4
413	Par 4
353	Par 4

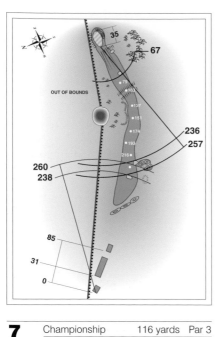

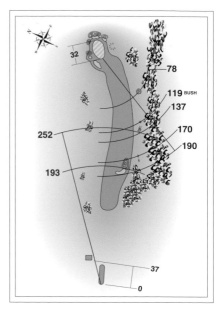

7

Championship	116 yards	Par 3
Medal	116	Par 3
Ladies'	113	Par 3

8

490 yards	Par 5
476	Par 5
418	Par 5

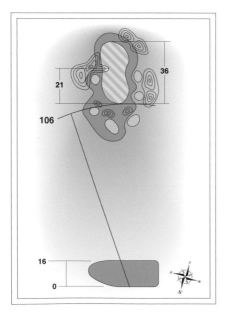

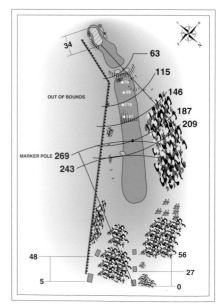

250

9	Championship	371 yards	Par 4
	Medal	368	Par 4
	Ladies'	311	Par 4

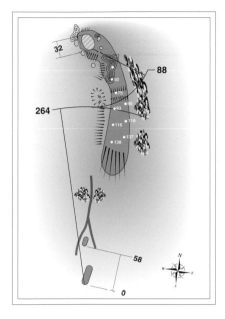

10	337yards	Par 4
	327	Par 4
	296	Par 4

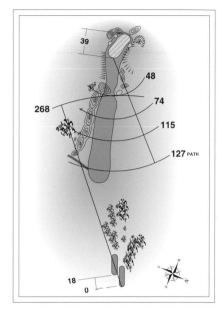

251

11	Championship	187 yards	Par 3
	Medal	187	Par 3
	Ladies'	143	Par 3

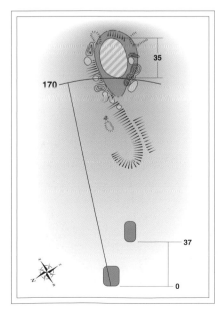

12	476 yards	Par 5
	476	Par 5
	427	Par 5

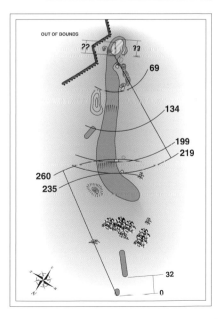

13	Championship	394 yards	Par 4
	Medal	391	Par 4
	Ladies'	349	Par 4

14	152 yards	Par 3
	152	Par 3
	145	Par 3

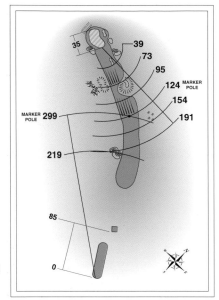

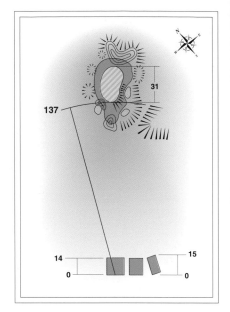

15	Championship	467 yards	Par 4
	Medal	421	Par 4
	Ladies'	386	Par 5

16	434 yards	Par 4
	420	Par 4
	391	Par 4

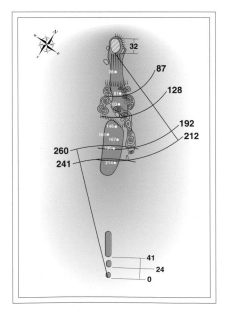

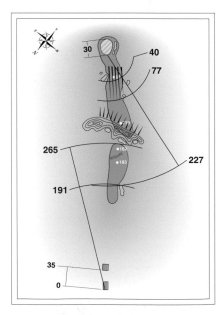

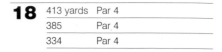

17	Championship	508 yards	Par 5
	Medal	489	Par 5
	Ladies'	450	Par 5

18	413 yards	Par 4
	385	Par 4
	334	Par 4

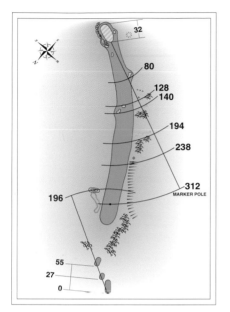

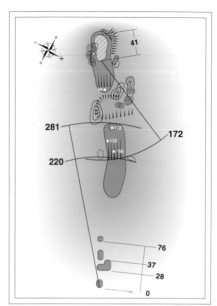

253

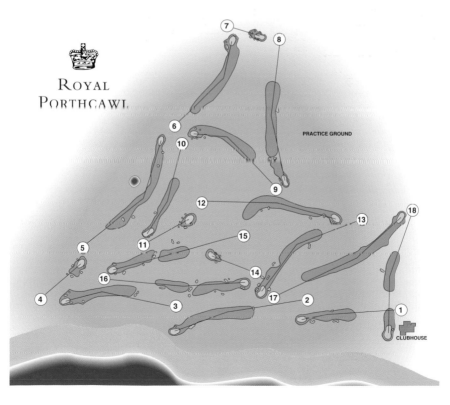

ROYAL
PORTHCAWL

however, because both the drive and the approach demand the utmost concentration. The hole dog-legs left and has a stone wall out of bounds running all the way up the left of the fairway and literally bordering the green; if you wander too far to the right with your drive, a pair of bunkers lie in wait, and the view of what is an extremely narrow and sloping green becomes restricted. With the second shot you must choose between laying up – and leaving yourself a tricky uphill pitch – or going for glory and risking the wall on the left and a sea of gorse on the right. If your attempt to find the green falls 30 yards short, you could find yourself visiting the deepest and nastiest bunker in Wales. Hit the best two shots of your life and you have nothing to fear!

The 6th, 7th and 8th are carved out of gorse and broom and comprise the least 'linksy', and possibly least memorable, sequence of holes. But they are not weak holes: the 6th has a very subtle green complex; the 7th is extremely short, measuring little more than 100 yards, yet boasts some very bold bunkering, while the par five 8th features a second stone wall boundary and an impressive cross bunker to carry with the approach.

The 9th may be the best par four on the course. In addition to being very scenic, at just 371 yards it provides classic proof that a two-shot hole needn't have great length to be extremely challenging. It is a sharp dog-leg left, although an elevated tee enables you to see the entire hole. The drive is downhill to an undulating fairway that tilts from right to left; disaster awaits the player who tries to bite off too much of the dog-leg as there is a steep fall-away and a mass of gorse and scrub immediately left of the fairway. The second shot is played uphill to a green which slopes from back to front and is surrounded by cavernous bunkers. The penal 9th at Royal Porthcawl would grace Pine Valley.

The 10th invites you to charge downhill, only for the 12th to order you back up; sandwiched between these two holes is the splendid par three 11th, a very testing short hole where the green tends to gather the ball, but only after you have successfully negotiated a bunker-

In a similar fashion to the 5th at Royal Portrush, the 18th at Royal Porthcawl runs downhill to a green overlooking the ocean.

strewn ridge that runs diagonally across the entrance to the green.

A good long drive is required at the 13th – anything less and your second shot may be fully or semi-blind. Take your time as you saunter along this hole, as it provides the best views on the course: seascape, landscape and golfscape. The 14th is the last of the short holes and the final opportunity to visit a really deep pot bunker. The green is table-shaped and not dissimilar to the 'Postage Stamp' at Troon. Miss it at your peril!

Now for a cavalier finish. Like the 2nd and 3rd, the 15th and 16th are very much a pair. In a sense they mirror those early holes, for each is a fairly formidable two-shotter, but rather than driving over sand and hitting down to a green snug to the shore, the 15th and 16th call for spectacular downhill drives and searching second shots played uphill over sand-dunes to an exposed green. The other major difference is that the 15th and 16th run in opposite directions; thus, depending on the wind direction, one of the holes may be significantly tougher.

The 17th is not the best par five at Porthcawl (the 5th is surely that), but it features a double dog-leg, another stone wall and, I am reliably informed, a ghost! On cool misty November days, the ghost of the Maid of Sker makes her appearance near the 17th green. Short putts are often missed in a hurry.

The 18th at Porthcawl is one of the most exhilarating closing holes in British golf. There are echoes of the famous 5th at Portrush, with the green backing on to the sea, but whereas the drive is the dramatic shot at Portrush, it is the approach at Porthcawl. Even if this thrilling shot is successfully executed – and judgment of distance is key – the green is very large and full of slopes.

A three at the final hole is richly prized and worthy of special celebration at the 19th hole. A celebration is a very likely event in the clubhouse at Royal Porthcawl, for it has a very relaxed, jovial atmosphere. From roaming cattle to restless spirits, golf never was, and never will be dull at Wales's premier links.

Hole	Championship	Medal	Par	Stroke Index	Ladies'	Par	Stroke Index
1	326	326	4	15	328	4	15
2	447	416	4	3	370	5	11
3	420	377	4	7	332	4	5
4	197	193	3	11	143	3	13
5	513	476	5	13	425	5	7
6	394	391	4	5	349	4	3
7	116	116	3	17	113	3	17
8	490	476	5	9	418	5	9
9	371	368	4	1	311	4	1
Out	3274	3139	36		2789	37	
10	337	327	4	16	296	4	6
11	187	187	3	8	143	3	18
12	476	476	5	12	427	5	10
13	443	413	4	4	353	4	2
14	152	152	3	18	145	3	16
15	467	421	4	2	386	5	8
16	434	420	4	6	391	5	12
17	508	489	5	14	450	5	4
18	413	385	4	10	334	4	14
In	3417	3270	36		2925	38	
Out	3274	3139	36		2789	37	
Total	6691	6409	72		5714	75	

strokesaver.
GOLF'S No1 DISTANCE GUIDE

The most accurate and informative Distance Guide available.
Full colour illustrations of each hole.
All relevant distances shown to prominent reference points.
Used by many of the world's top golfers.
Laser measurement, accurate to 1mm.
Key promotional aid for sponsored events.
Can be personalised with a company's name, logo or message.
Each guide adds to collectors library.
Variation of layout to suit competitive or commercial requirement.
Certified course measurement service.
Ideal resale item.

For information contact Strokesport, Abbey Mill Business Centre, Paisley PA1 1TJ.
Telephone: 0141 848 1199   Fax: 0141 887 1642